PRINCETON ILLUS

 G000166151

BIRDS

OF EUROPE, RUSSIA,
CHINA, AND JAPAN

NON-PASSERINES:
LOONS TO WOODPECKERS

PRINCETON ILLUSTRATED CHECKLISTS

Birds of Eastern Africa, by Ber van Perlo

Birds of Southern Africa, by Ber van Perlo

Birds of Southern South America and Antarctica,
by Martín R. de la Peña and Maurice Rumboll

Birds of Western and Central Africa, by Ber van Perlo

Birds of Mexico and Central America, by Ber van Perlo

Birds of South America: Non-Passerines: Rheas to Woodpeckers,
by Francisco Erize, Jorge R. Rodriguez Mata, and Maurice Rumboll

Birds of Europe, Russia, China, and Japan: Passerines: Tyrant Flycatchers to Buntings,
by Norman Arlott

Birds of Europe, Russia, China, and Japan: Non-Passerines: Loons to Woodpeckers,
by Norman Arlott

PRINCETON ILLUSTRATED CHECKLISTS

BIRDS

OF EUROPE, RUSSIA, CHINA, AND JAPAN

NON-PASSERINES: LOONS TO WOODPECKERS

Written and illustrated by
NORMAN ARLOTT

Princeton University Press
Princeton and Oxford

I would like to dedicate this book
to my wife Marie.

Published in the United States, Canada, and the Philippine Islands by
Princeton University Press, 41 William Street, Princeton, New Jersey 08540

Originally published in English by HarperCollins Publishers Ltd. under the title:
FIELD GUIDE TO THE BIRDS OF THE PALEARCTIC: NON-PASSERINES

Library of Congress Control Number 2008938700

ISBN 978-0-691-13685-1

nathist.press.princeton.edu

Edited and designed by Fluke Art, Cornwall
Printed and bound in Hong Kong by Printing Express Ltd.

10 9 8 7 6 5 4 3 2 1

CONTENTS

ACKNOWLEDGEMENTS

Bird books take a relatively short time to paint and write, but the knowledge that enables them to be completed is gained over many, many years. I can remember my passion started when I was a very young boy bird-nesting (now, quite rightly, frowned upon) with my father. That passion has since been enhanced by being fortunate enough to be in the field with, and to be inspired by, some well-known and not so well-known 'birders'. In particular, I must mention the following, who have encouraged me and allowed me to pick their brains over the years: the late John G. Williams, the late Eric Hosking, the late Crispin Fisher, Robert Gillmor, the late Basil Parsons, Brian Leflay and Moss Taylor. I was also given special help by Richard and Nathan Sale who took on the task of preparing the distribution maps. Julie Dando deserves special praise for her skill and patience in putting together the various component parts of this book. This book could not have gone ahead without the help of the staff at the British Museum at Tring, especially Mark Adams and Robert Prys-Jones. Without publishers there would not be a book, so it gives me great pleasure to thank everyone at HarperCollins, particularly Myles Archibald and Julia Koppitz. Last, but definitely not least, I must thank friends and family who have had to put up with my various mood changes whilst trying to sort out some of the more difficult aspects of putting this book together, of whom my wife Marie probably endured more than most.

White-backed Woodpecker (*Dendrocopus leucotos*)

INTRODUCTION

When originally encouraged to take on this project I knew that I wanted it to do two things: to be a reminder of birds already seen and to be a helpful nudge towards what to look for when searching for new birds. I did not want to produce just a coloured checklist or the ultimate field guide – size alone meant that the latter, with the restriction on the amount of text and number of plates, was not possible anyway. I decided that most of the text in this book would be based on the type of notes I make before embarking on a field trip to a new area; hopefully they will, along with the illustrations, help to identify most birds that will be encountered. Obviously, the use of more in-depth tomes will be required for some of the trickier species (*see* Further Reading).

Hopefully within these pages, added to my previous Passerine volume, I have been able to add to the pleasure of anticipation or memory, and perhaps even add some extra piece of knowledge about the birds of this vast region.

Cormorant (*Phalacrocorax carbo*)

AREA AND SPECIES COVERED

When deciding on the species to include in this guide, the biggest problem came when trying to define the Palearctic area. Having looked at various compilations I could find no reason not to follow the excellently argued and put together checklist by Mark Beaman. I have used his area of delineation (there is not room here to duplicate his explanations for where the Palearctic boundaries should be placed; *see* map) and his species list, only adding species that have appeared in the area since his book was published. I hope that any new additions, from early 2008 on, will be incorporated into expected future updates. I have also had to tweak the established order a little to aid plate composition – hopefully this will not cause too much aggravation.

The area of the
Palearctic

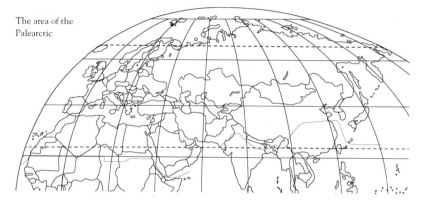

Every species of the region, and most major subspecies, have been depicted in breeding plumage, and in non-breeding plumage when it differs significantly. To keep the book to a manageable size, no juvenile plumages have been illustrated, although, when necessary, a short passage in 'Field Notes' has been included.

PLATES

The abbreviations and symbols used on the plates are as follows:

♂	=	Male
♀	=	Female
br	=	Breeding
n-br	=	Non-breeding
Nom	=	Nominate race

NOMENCLATURE

I have headlined the English names that I believe are those used by most birders in the field, which means I have, in many cases reverted to 'old school' names rather than some of the more modern interpretations, e.g. Oystercatcher rather than the long-winded Eurasian Oystercatcher. Most of these 'new' names, along with others that are well-known, are included in parenthesis.

IDENTIFICATION

It is hoped that the illustrations will be all that is needed to identify a specific bird, but quite obviously with some of the trickier species more information is needed, hence the need for Field Notes, Song/Call and Habitat.

FIELD NOTES: Because of the need to keep text to a minimum, this section rarely mentions those aspects of a bird that should be obvious from the illustrations, e.g. wingbars, bill shape etc. It is used mainly to point to a bird's habits or to mention facets of identification that are hidden in a standing or perched bird.

SONG/CALL: Probably the first sign of a bird's presence. The descriptions are shown in *italics*. Where space has allowed I have included different interpretations of the same song. Although difficult to produce an accurate reproduction of a bird song/call in the written word this section is worth studying in order to get a feel for what is often the most important area of bird identification.

HABITAT: The distribution maps should be consulted in conjunction with this section. The main habitat preferences mentioned are those in which a species breeds, also included are wintering habitats if appropriate.

RACES: Included to show distinct variations, it will be seen that many of the depicted races have been or are about to be considered full species. General areas of occurrence are given.

Question marks occur where no definitive answers have been found to date, usually relating to the 'splitting' of species and whether a bird is definitely extinct.

Bee-eater (*Merops apiaster*)

11

BIRD TOPOGRAPHY

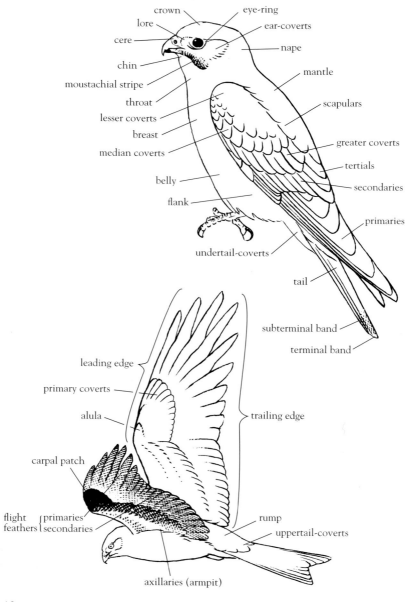

crown

eye-ring

lore

ear-coverts

cere

nape

chin

mantle

moustachial stripe

scapulars

throat

lesser coverts

greater coverts

breast

tertials

median coverts

secondaries

belly

flank

primaries

undertail-coverts

tail

subterminal band

terminal band

leading edge

primary coverts

alula

trailing edge

carpal patch

flight feathers { primaries secondaries

rump

uppertail-coverts

axillaries (armpit)

SPECIES DESCRIPTIONS
AND COLOUR PLATES

1 OSTRICH

1 OSTRICH *Struthio camelus* Male 210–275cm, Female 175–190cm FIELD NOTES:
Unmistakable, even at some distance. Flightless. Immature very similar to adult female.
SONG/CALL: During breeding season males give a far-carrying booming *ooom ooom booo-ooooo*.
At other times usually silent, apart from various hissing and snorting utterances. HABITAT:
Dry open grassland, semi-desert with sparse vegetation.

1

♀

♂

2 DIVERS AND GREBES

1 RED-THROATED DIVER (RED-THROATED LOON) *Gavia stellata* 53–69cm FIELD
NOTES: Juvenile as winter adult but with greyish face and neck. SONG/CALL: Male utters a rolling,
growling *oorroo-uh oorroo-uh*, the female a slightly longer, higher-pitched *aarroo aarroo aarroo*.
Also a barking and mewing. In flight gives a goose-like *kah kah kah kah kah*. HABITAT: By lakes
and pools or marine inlets, winters on shallow coastal waters and sometimes on inland lakes.

2 BLACK-THROATED DIVER (BLACK-THROATED or ARCTIC LOON) *Gavia
arctica* 58–73cm FIELD NOTES: Often winters in small groups. Juvenile very similar to winter
adult but with slight scaling on back. SONG/CALL: A loud, mournful *clowee-cok-clowee-cok-
clowee*, a snoring *knarr-knorr-knarr-knorr* and a gull-like *aaah-owww*. HABITAT: By large, deep
lakes, winters in coastal waters.

3 PACIFIC DIVER (PACIFIC LOON) *Gavia pacifica* 56–66cm FIELD NOTES: Recently
split from the similar Black-throated Diver. SONG/CALL: A loud, mournful *ooalee-koo ooalee-
koo ooalee-koo* also a yodelling *o-lo-lee* and various growls and croaks. HABITAT: By freshwater
tundra lakes, winters in coastal waters.

4 GREAT NORTHERN DIVER (GREAT NORTHERN or COMMON LOON)
Gavia immer 69–91cm FIELD NOTES: Juvenile as winter adult but with pale scaly fringes on
back. SONG/CALL: A wailing *a-a-whoo-kwee-wheeooo-kwee-wheeooo*, a manic-laughing *ho-
yeyeyeyeyeye*, a drawn-out howl and a low moan. HABITAT: By large lakes, winters off coasts
and less so on inland lakes.

5 YELLOW-BILLED DIVER (YELLOW-BILLED LOON, WHITE-BILLED DIVER)
Gavia adamsii 76–91cm FIELD NOTES: Juvenile as winter adult but with pale scaly fringes on
back. SONG/CALL: Very similar to Great Northern Diver but louder and harsher. HABITAT: By
lakes, winters at sea.

6 PIED-BILLED GREBE *Podilymbus podiceps* 31–38cm (Vagrant) FIELD NOTES: When
alarmed often swims with body mostly or partially submerged. SONG/CALL: Silent in non-breeding
season. HABITAT: In native N America: freshwater lakes, wintering on open lakes and estuaries.

7 LITTLE GREBE (DABCHICK) *Tachybaptus ruficollis* 25–29cm FIELD NOTES: Juvenile
as winter adult but with black streaks on face. SONG/CALL: A high-pitched whinnying trill
and various twitterings, also a *beeh-ibto go on* contact call and, when alarmed, a metallic
whit whit. HABITAT: Vegetated lakes, ponds and rivers, also on more open waters, including
sheltered coastal bays, in winter.

8 GREAT CRESTED GREBE *Podiceps cristatus* 46–51cm FIELD NOTES: In flight upperwing
shows large white patches on secondaries and forewing. SONG/CALL: A barking *rah-rah-rah*
also various croaks, growls and slow nasal moaning. HABITAT: Lakes and rivers with fringing
vegetation, also on large reservoirs, estuaries and sheltered coastal waters in winter.

9 RED-NECKED GREBE *Podiceps grisegena* 40–50cm FIELD NOTES: In flight similar to
Great Crested Grebe but neck darker and shorter. SONG/CALL: Wailing, braying and squeaking
noises, also a grating *cherk-cherk-cherk*. HABITAT: Lakes with surrounding vegetation, winters
on more open waters including estuaries and sheltered coastal waters.

10 SLAVONIAN GREBE (HORNED GREBE) *Podiceps auritus* 31–38cm FIELD NOTES:
Winter birds much like miniature Great Crested Grebe when in flight. SONG/CALL: A far-
carrying, rattling *joarrh* also an accelerating trill, similar to that of Little Grebe. HABITAT:
Vegetated lakes and ponds, more open waters in north. Winters on sheltered coastal waters,
less so on inland waters.

11 BLACK-NECKED GREBE (EARED GREBE) *Podiceps nigricollis* 28–34cm FIELD
NOTES: Often gregarious in winter quarters. In flight upperwing shows a large white secondary
patch. SONG/CALL: A flute-like *poo-eeet* and a vibrant, trilled *tssrrrroooooeep*. HABITAT: Shallow
lakes and ponds with fringing vegetation, winters on more open waters, including sheltered
coastal waters.

3 ALBATROSSES, FULMAR, PETRELS AND SHEARWATERS

1 BLACK-BROWED ALBATROSS (BLACK-BROWED MOLLYMAWK) *Thalassarche melanophris* 80–95cm (Vagrant) FIELD NOTES: Juvenile shows greyish bill with dark tip, greyish breast band and dark underwing with only a hint of pale central strip. Occurs around trawlers and follows ships. SONG/CALL: Usually silent. HABITAT: Maritime.

2 YELLOW-NOSED ALBATROSS (YELLOW-NOSED MOLLYMAWK) *Thalassarche chlororhynchos* 71–81cm (Vagrant) FIELD NOTES: Juvenile has head white and all-black bill. Occurs around trawlers and sometimes follows ships. SONG/CALL: Usually silent. HABITAT: Maritime.

3 SHY ALBATROSS (SHY MOLLYMAWK or WHITE-CAPPED ALBATROSS) *Thalassarche cauta* 96–100cm (Vagrant) FIELD NOTES: Juvenile has greyish bill with dark tip, pale head with dusky breast band and similar diagnostic underwing pattern as adult. Found around trawlers and following ships. SONG/CALL: Usually silent. HABITAT: Maritime.

4 BLACK-FOOTED ALBATROSS *Phoebastria nigripes* 68–74cm FIELD NOTES: Some adults show pale greyish head and underparts. Juvenile sooty-brown with a whitish area at base of bill. Often around trawlers and ships. SONG/CALL: Usually silent away from breeding sites. HABITAT: Breeds on island beaches or slopes with little vegetation, otherwise maritime.

5 LAYSAN ALBATROSS *Phoebastria immutabilis* 79–81cm FIELD NOTES: Juvenile as adult although bill probably greyer. No other dark-backed albatross with white head and underparts occurs in N Pacific. Occasionally follows ships. SONG/CALL: Generally silent. HABITAT: Breeds on islands with little or no vegetation, otherwise maritime.

6 SHORT-TAILED ALBATROSS (STELLER'S ALBATROSS) *Phoebastria albatrus* 84–94cm FIELD NOTES: Juvenile generally dark brown with pink bill, goes through various intermediate stages before adult plumage attained. SONG/CALL: Generally silent. HABITAT: Breeds on islands with steep volcanic slopes, otherwise maritime.

7 WANDERING ALBATROSS (SNOWY or WHITE-WINGED ALBATROSS) *Diomedea exulans* 107–135cm (Vagrant) FIELD NOTES: Juvenile chocolate-brown with white face, underwing much as adult. Many adults have upperwing mainly black, only very old birds attain plumage shown. SONG/CALL: Usually silent. HABITAT: Maritime.

8 FULMAR (NORTHERN FULMAR) *Fulmarus glacialis* 45–50cm FIELD NOTES: Intermediate forms occur. Much stiffer-winged in flight than gulls. SONG/CALL: Guttural cackling, varying in speed. HABITAT: Breeds mainly on sea cliffs. Winters at sea.

9 CAPE PETREL (PINTADO PETREL, CAPE PIGEON) *Daption capense* 38–40cm (Vagrant) FIELD NOTES: Flight Fulmar-like. Usually in large flocks. Follows ships and trawlers. SONG/CALL: Generally silent. HABITAT: Maritime away from southern breeding sites.

10 BULWER'S PETREL *Bulweria bulwerii* 26–28cm FIELD NOTES: Usually flies low over water in erratic buoyant manner. Tail wedge-shaped when fanned. SONG/CALL: At colonies utters a hoarse *hroo-hroo-hroo…* HABITAT: Breeds in holes on rocky slopes or cliffs. Winters at sea.

11 JOUANIN'S PETREL *Bulweria fallax* 30–32cm FIELD NOTES: Faster more swooping and towering flight than Bulwer's Petrel. SONG/CALL: Silent. HABITAT: Maritime.

12 CORY'S SHEARWATER (MEDITERRANEAN SHEARWATER) *Calonectris diomedea* 46–53cm FIELD NOTES: Flight can appear lazy although is actually quite fast. Often follows ships and trawlers. SONG/CALL: At breeding sites utters a harsh wailing *keeoowwrrah*, otherwise silent. HABITAT: Crevices in cliffs and rocky slopes on barren islands. Winters at sea. RACES: *C. d. edwardsii* (Cape Verde Shearwater) (fig 12b) Cape Verde Islands.

13 STREAKED SHEARWATER (WHITE-FACED SHEARWATER) *Calonectris leucomelas* 48cm FIELD NOTES: Often in large flocks. Sometimes shows pale crescent at base of tail. Flight action similar to Cory's Shearwater. Follows fishing boats. SONG/CALL: Generally silent. HABITAT: Breeds on forested offshore islands. Winters at sea.

4 PETRELS

1 KERMADEC PETREL *Pterodroma neglecta* 38cm (Vagrant) FIELD NOTES: White flash at base of primaries diagnostic. 'Gadfly' flight typical of genus – beating wings to gain height followed by long glides and wide banking arcs. SONG/CALL: Generally silent? HABITAT: Maritime.

2 HERALD PETREL (TRINIDADE PETREL) *Pterodroma arminjoniana* 35–39cm (Vagrant) FIELD NOTES: Much individual variation in the three main colour morphs. Flight typical of genus. Occasionally follows ships. SONG/CALL: Generally silent. HABITAT: Maritime.

3 FEA'S PETREL (CAPE VERDE PETREL, GON-GON) *Pterodroma feae* 36–37cm FIELD NOTES: Recently split from Soft-plumaged Petrel. Flight typical of the genus. Occasionally follows ships. SONG/CALL: At breeding sites utters a cackling *gon-gon* also a mournful wail ending with a hiccup. Silent at sea. HABITAT: Breeds on cliffs, otherwise maritime.

4 ZINO'S PETREL (MADEIRA PETREL, FREIRA) *Pterodroma madeira* 32–33cm FIELD NOTES: Recently split from Soft-plumaged Petrel. Probably not possible to separate from Fea's Petrel in the field. SONG/CALL: Much like Fea's Petrel. Silent at sea. HABITAT: Breeds on cliffs, otherwise maritime.

5 SOFT-PLUMAGED PETREL *Pterodroma mollis* 33–36cm (Vagrant) FIELD NOTES: In the field very similar to Fea's and Zino's Petrel and unless breast-band complete probably not separable. SONG/CALL: Generally silent. HABITAT: Maritime.

6 MOTTLED PETREL (SCALED or PEALE'S PETREL) *Pterodroma inexpectata* 33–35cm FIELD NOTES: Non-breeding visitor. Flight wild with high bounding arcs. SONG/CALL: Generally silent at sea. HABITAT: Maritime.

7 PROVIDENCE PETREL (SOLANDER'S PETREL) *Pterodroma solandri* 40cm FIELD NOTES: Non-breeding visitor. Flight typical of genus. SONG/CALL: Silent at sea? HABITAT: Maritime.

8 ATLANTIC PETREL (SCHLEGEL'S or HOODED PETREL) *Pterodroma incerta* 43cm (Vagrant) FIELD NOTES: Non-breeding visitor. In worn plumage chin and throat paler, greyer faced with a pale collar on nape. Flight typical of genus. Often follows ships. SONG/CALL: Silent at sea. HABITAT: Maritime.

9 BLACK-CAPPED PETREL (DIABLOTIN, CAPPED PETREL) *Pterodroma hasitata* 35–46cm (Vagrant) FIELD NOTES: Some individuals show a much reduced white collar. Flight typical of the genus. SONG/CALL: Silent at sea. HABITAT: Maritime.

10 BONIN PETREL *Pterodroma hypoleuca* 30cm FIELD NOTES: Typical fast, bounding 'gadfly' flight. Does not follow ships. SONG/CALL: Generally silent. HABITAT: Breeds among vegetation in sandy areas or high slopes on oceanic islands, otherwise maritime.

11 BLACK-WINGED PETREL *Pterodroma nigripennis* 28–30cm FIELD NOTES: Non-breeding visitor. Occasionally soars at a great height hanging in the wind. SONG/CALL: In display-flight utters a shrill *weet-weet-weet* or similar, unlikely to be heard while in Palearctic. HABITAT: Maritime.

12 DARK-RUMPED PETREL (HAWAIIN PETREL) *Pterodroma phaepygia* 43cm (Vagrant) FIELD NOTES: White on side of rump variable. Typical 'gadfly' flight. SONG/CALL: Generally silent. HABITAT: Maritime.

13 WHITE-NECKED PETREL (WHITE-NAPED PETREL) *Pterodroma cervicalis* 43cm (Vagrant) FIELD NOTES: Strong, 'gadfly' flight, less vigorous than smaller *Pterodroma* species. SONG/CALL: Generally silent. HABITAT: Maritime.

14 STEJNEGER'S PETREL *Pterodroma longirostris* 26cm FIELD NOTES: Non-breeding visitor. Flight rapid, weaving and banking with jerky, bat-like wingbeats. SONG/CALL: Generally silent. HABITAT: Maritime.

light   intermediate   intermediate

light

dark   dark

1

2

3

4

5

6

7

8

9

10

11

12

13

14

5 SHEARWATERS

1 FLESH-FOOTED SHEARWATER (PALE-FOOTED SHEARWATER) *Puffinus carneipes* 40–45cm FIELD NOTES: Non-breeding visitor. Lazy flaps followed by long glides on stiff wings. Gregarious. SONG/CALL: Generally silent. HABITAT: Maritime.

2 GREAT SHEARWATER (GREATER SHEARWATER) *Puffinus gravis* 43–51cm FIELD NOTES: Non-breeding visitor. Fast, strong wingbeats followed by long glides on stiff, straight wings. SONG/CALL: Noisy, sounding like fighting cats when feeding around trawlers, otherwise generally silent. HABITAT: Maritime.

3 WEDGE-TAILED SHEARWATER *Puffinus pacificus* 41–46cm FIELD NOTES: Slow wing flaps followed by short glides. More bounding flight in strong winds. Often around fishing boats. SONG/CALL: Generally silent. HABITAT: Breeds on flat ground on offshore islands, otherwise maritime.

4 BULLER'S SHEARWATER (NEW ZEALAND or GREY-BACKED SHEARWATER) *Puffinus bulleri* 46cm (Vagrant) FIELD NOTES: Gregarious. Flight similar to Wedge-tailed Shearwater. SONG/CALL: Generally silent. HABITAT: Maritime in Palearctic.

5 SOOTY SHEARWATER *Puffinus griseus* 40–46cm FIELD NOTES: Non-breeding visitor. Quick wing flaps followed by a long glide. Often scavenges around trawlers. SONG/CALL: Generally silent. HABITAT: Maritime.

6 SHORT-TAILED SHEARWATER (SLENDER-BILLED SHEARWATER) *Puffinus tenuirostris* 41–43cm FIELD NOTES: Non-breeding visitor. Similar in habits to Sooty Shearwater. Gregarious. SONG/CALL: Generally silent. HABITAT: Maritime.

7 CHRISTMAS SHEARWATER *Puffinus nativitatis* 35–38cm (Vagrant) FIELD NOTES: Buoyant flight with quick wingbeats followed by low level glides. SONG/CALL: Generally silent. HABITAT: Maritime.

8 MANX SHEARWATER *Puffinus puffinus* 30–38cm FIELD NOTES: Rapid wingbeats followed by a low, swinging (side to side) glide. Scavenges around fishing boats. Gregarious. SONG/CALL: At breeding grounds emits raucous cackles and screams. At sea generally silent. HABITAT: Breeds in burrows on offshore islands and coastal cliffs, otherwise maritime.

9 MEDITERRANEAN SHEARWATER (YELKOUAN or LEVANTINE SHEARWATER) *Puffinus yelkouan* 30–38cm FIELD NOTES: Habits and flight action much as Manx Shearwater, although said to be more 'fluttering'. SONG/CALL: Said to be similar to Manx Shearwater. Generally silent away from breeding ground. HABITAT: Breeds in burrows on offshore islands, otherwise maritime.

10 BALEARIC SHEARWATER *Puffinus mauretanicus* 35–40cm FIELD NOTES: Habits and flight actions similar to Manx Shearwater although can appear more 'fluttering'. SONG/CALL: As Manx Shearwater? HABITAT: Breeds in burrows and crevices, otherwise maritime.

11 NORTH ATLANTIC LITTLE SHEARWATER (MACRONESIAN SHEARWATER) *Puffinus baroli* 25–30cm FIELD NOTES: Fast, shallow wingbeats followed by a short, low glide, also fluttering flight close to sea surface. SONG/CALL: At breeding grounds utters a high-pitched crowing, otherwise silent. HABITAT: Breeds in crevices and burrows on islands, otherwise maritime. RACES: *P. b. boydi* (fig 11b) Cape Verde Islands.

12 AUDUBON'S SHEARWATER *Puffinus lherminieri* 27–33cm FIELD NOTES: Fluttering wingbeats followed by short, low glides. Often gregarious. This race is a non-breeding visitor. SONG/CALL: Generally silent at sea. HABITAT: Maritime. RACES: *P. l. persicus* (Persian Shearwater) (fig 12b) Arabian Sea; *P. l. bannermani* (Bannerman's Shearwater) Bonin and Volcano Islands, not illustrated.

6 STORM-PETRELS

1 WILSON'S STORM-PETREL *Oceanites oceanicus* 15–19cm FIELD NOTES: Yellow webs between toes only noticeable at close range. Often dangles feet and dances on sea surface when feeding. Attracted to fishing vessels. SONG/CALL: A rapid 'chattering' occasionally uttered while feeding. HABITAT: Maritime.

2 WHITE-FACED STORM-PETREL (WHITE-FACED or FRIGATE PETREL) *Pelagodroma marina* 20–21cm FIELD NOTES: Yellow webs between toes only noticeable at close range. Feeds in a series of swinging bounces, dangling feet at each bounce, often looks as though walking on water. SONG/CALL: At breeding sites utters a slow *koo-koo-koo-koo....* HABITAT: Breeds in burrows on islands, otherwise maritime.

3 WHITE-BELLIED STORM-PETREL *Fregetta grallaria* 20cm (Vagrant) FIELD NOTES: Feeds by hugging waves, legs often dangling and body swinging from side to side, bouncing from trough to trough. SONG/CALL: Generally silent at sea. HABITAT: Maritime.

4 BLACK-BELLIED STORM-PETREL *Fregetta tropica* 20cm FIELD NOTES: Feeding actions very similar to White-bellied Storm-petrel. SONG/CALL: Generally silent at sea. HABITAT: Maritime.

5 STORM-PETREL (EUROPEAN or BRITISH STORM-PETREL) *Hydrobates pelagicus* 14–17cm FIELD NOTES: Feeds excitedly, repeatedly hovering or fluttering before dipping to seize food. Follows ships and fishing boats. SONG/CALL: At breeding site utters a harsh purring *arrr-r-r-r-r-r-r-r...* ending with a grunt or hiccup-like sound. Generally silent at sea. HABITAT: Breeds in crevices or burrows on rocky coasts and islands. Maritime after breeding.

6 FORK-TAILED STORM-PETREL (GREY STORM-PETREL) *Oceanodroma furcata* 20–23cm FIELD NOTES: Feeds by snatching food from sea surface when flying or sitting on water. Follows ships. SONG/CALL: Generally silent away from breeding sites. HABITAT: Breeds on offshore islands, among trees or in grassy areas on rocky hillsides, otherwise maritime.

7 LEACH'S STORM-PETREL (LEACH'S PETREL) *Oceanodroma leucorhoa* 19–22cm FIELD NOTES: Feeds erratically with bounding flight then hovers, with shallow wingbeats, often with foot pattering, to seize food from sea surface. SONG/CALL: At breeding sites utters a slow purring, ending in a high *whee-chaa*, also a screaming *par-kiki-kar-koo whuk-kuk-kuk-kuh-kuh*. Generally silent at sea. HABITAT: Breeds in a wide variety of crevices or burrows on rocky coasts and offshore islands, otherwise maritime.

8 SWINHOE'S STORM-PETREL (SWINHOE'S PETREL) *Oceanodroma monorhis* 19–20cm FIELD NOTES: Flight and feeding actions much as Leach's Petrel, although some reports say it does not use foot pattering. SONG/CALL: A trilling chatter at breeding sites, usually silent at sea. HABITAT: Breeds on offshore islands, otherwise maritime.

9 MADEIRAN STORM-PETREL (HARCOURT'S or BAND-RUMPED STORM-PETREL) *Oceanodroma castro* 19–21cm FIELD NOTES: Methodical search for food, even flight with glides, hovers usually without foot pattering to take prey. SONG/CALL: At breeding sites makes a low, prolonged purring *urr-rrr-rrr-rrr-rrr-rrr-rrr* ending with a sharp *wika*, also a high-pitched *klair chuch-a chuk chuk chuk*, usually silent at sea. HABITAT: Breeds in rock crevices or burrows on islands, otherwise maritime.

10 MATSUDAIRA'S STORM-PETREL (SOOTY STORM-PETREL) *Oceanodroma matsudairae* 24–25cm FIELD NOTES: Feeds on the wing, holding wings in a shallow V while dipping down to pick food from sea surface. Follows ships. SONG/CALL: Away from breeding site generally silent. HABITAT: Breeds on Islands off S Japan, otherwise maritime.

11 TRISTRAM'S STORM-PETREL (SOOTY or STEJNEGER'S STORM-PETREL) *Oceanodroma tristrami* 24–25cm FIELD NOTES: Feeds in flight using foot pattering as prey is snatched from sea surface. SONG/CALL: Away from breeding colonies usually silent. HABITAT: Breeds in recesses in scree or burrows on islands off SE Japan, otherwise maritime.

7 FRIGATEBIRDS, TROPICBIRDS, BOOBIES AND GANNETS

All young frigatebird species undergo a complicated series of plumage changes before full adult plumage gained; see *Seabirds: an identification guide*, by P. Harrison for details.

1 GREAT FRIGATEBIRD *Fregata minor* 86–100cm (Vagrant) FIELD NOTES: Scavenges around boats and aggressively pursues other seabirds to force regurgitation. SONG/CALL: Generally silent at sea. HABITAT: Mainly maritime.

2 MAGNIFICENT FRIGATEBIRD *Fregata magnificens* 95–110cm FIELD NOTES: Scavenging actions similar to Great Frigatebird. Colonial breeder. Inflates gular pouch when displaying. SONG/CALL: At breeding sites rattling and drumming sounds made by vibrating and snapping bill. Generally silent at sea. HABITAT: Breeds on rocky islets, usually in trees. Maritime.

3 LESSER FRIGATEBIRD *Fregata ariel* 71–81cm (Vagrant) FIELD NOTES: Actions and habits as Great Frigatebird. SONG/CALL: Generally silent at sea. HABITAT: Maritime.

4 ASCENSION FRIGATEBIRD *Fregata aquila* 89–96cm (Vagrant) FIELD NOTES: Actions and habits similar to Great Frigatebird. SONG/CALL: Generally silent at sea. HABITAT: Maritime.

5 RED-BILLED TROPICBIRD *Phaethon aethereus* 90–105cm FIELD NOTES: Flight pigeon-like, fluttering wingbeats followed by long glides. Catches fish by hovering then plunge-diving on half-closed wings. Juvenile has yellowish bill, black nape collar and lacks elongated tail streamers. SONG/CALL: Shrill, rasping *kee-arrr*. HABITAT: Breeds on offshore Islands. Maritime after breeding.

6 RED-TAILED TROPICBIRD *Phaethon rubricauda* 78–81cm FIELD NOTES: Feeding and flight actions similar to Red-billed Tropicbird. Juvenile similar to Red-billed Tropicbird juvenile but with less black on primaries, blackish bill and no black nape collar. SONG/CALL: A harsh, rapid *keek-keek-keek-keek….* HABITAT: Breeds on small oceanic islands, maritime after breeding.

7 WHITE-TAILED TROPICBIRD *Phaethon lepturus* 70–82cm (Vagrant) FIELD NOTES: Feeding and flight actions similar to Red-billed Tropicbird. Juvenile similar to Red-billed Tropicbird juvenile but lacks black nape collar. SONG/CALL: A squeaky *chip-chip-chip….* HABITAT: Maritime.

8 BROWN BOOBY *Sula leucogaster* 64–74cm FIELD NOTES: Feeds by plunge-diving, usually at an angle and not vertical like Gannet. Often gregarious. Attracted to ships. Juvenile has white parts tinged brown, bill greyish. SONG/CALL: At breeding sites females utters grunts and honks while male gives high-pitched whistles. HABITAT: Breeds on offshore islands otherwise maritime.

9 RED-FOOTED BOOBY *Sula sula* 66–77cm FIELD NOTES: Actions similar to Brown Booby. Variations on the brown morph include a white-tailed form and a white-headed, white-tailed form. SONG/CALL: Generally silent at sea. HABITAT: Maritime.

10 MASKED BOOBY (WHITE or BLUE-FACED BOOBY) *Sula dactylatra* 81–92cm FIELD NOTES: Plunge-dives usually more vertical than other boobies. Juvenile very similar to adult Brown Booby but paler mantle with white collar on hindneck, brown of head not extending to upper breast. SONG/CALL: Generally silent at sea. HABITAT: Maritime.

11 CAPE GANNET *Morus capensis* 84–94cm (Vagrant) FIELD NOTES: Actions as Gannet, which is often thought to be conspecific. Juvenile probably inseparable from Gannet. SONG/CALL: Generally silent at sea. HABITAT: Maritime.

12 GANNET (NORTHERN GANNET) *Morus bassanus* 87–100cm FIELD NOTES: Feeds by vertical plunge-dive, from as high as 30m. Young birds go through various stages before attaining adult plumage, starting generally brown sprinkled with white spots to mainly white with brown blotches on back and wings. Sub-adult resembles Cape Gannet, being white with black primaries and secondaries with a black shaft streak on central tail feathers. SONG/CALL: At breeding sites, and when communal feeding, utters a harsh grating *urrah*. HABITAT: Breeds mainly on rocky islets, otherwise maritime.

8 CORMORANTS, SHAG AND DARTER

1 CORMORANT (GREAT CORMORANT) *Phalacrocorax carbo* 80–100cm FIELD NOTES: In flight outstretched neck shows slight kink. Often perches holding wings 'out to dry'. Juvenile dark brown above, dirty white below, greyer on breast. SONG/CALL: At breeding colonies utters various deep, guttural calls, otherwise generally silent. HABITAT: Coastal cliffs, estuaries, inland lakes, reservoirs and rivers. RACES: *P. c. lucidus* (White-breasted Cormorant) (fig 1b) Africa, sometimes treated as a full species; *P. c.sinensis* (fig 1c) C Europe to China.

2 JAPANESE CORMORANT (TEMMINCK'S CORMORANT) *Phalacrocorax filamentosus* 92cm FIELD NOTES: In flight similar to Cormorant. Juvenile dark brown above whitish below. SONG/CALL: Away from breeding colonies usually silent. HABITAT: Rocky coasts, rarely inland.

3 PELAGIC CORMORANT *Phalacrocorax pelagicus* 63–73cm FIELD NOTES: Flies with neck held straight. Juvenile dark brown. SONG/CALL: Silent away from breeding sites. HABITAT: On rocky coasts, feeds and winters in coastal inlets, bays and open sea.

4 RED-FACED CORMORANT *Phalacrocorax urile* 79–89cm FIELD NOTES: Flies with neck held straight. Juvenile brown above, slightly paler below, facial skin brownish. SONG/CALL: Generally silent away from breeding colonies. HABITAT: Exclusively marine. Breeds on rocky coasts.

5 DOUBLE-CRESTED CORMORANT *Phalacrocorax auritus* 74–91cm (Vagrant) FIELD NOTES: In flight outstretched neck has a distinct kink. Juvenile dark brownish above, underparts dull brown apart from greyish-white throat, foreneck and upper breast. SONG/CALL: Away from breeding colonies usually silent. HABITAT: In native N America: coastal areas, lakes, reservoirs and rivers.

6 SHAG (EUROPEAN SHAG) *Phalacrocorax aristotelis* 65–80cm FIELD NOTES: Flies with neck held straight. Juvenile brown above scaled paler, below greyish-brown with whiter throat, foreneck and upper breast variably mottled greyish. SONG/CALL: At breeding colonies utters various clicks and grunts, otherwise silent. HABITAT: Breeds on rocky coasts, wanders to other coastal areas, exceptionally to inland freshwater sites, during non-breeding season.

7 SOCOTRA CORMORANT *Phalacrocorax nigrogularis* 77–84cm FIELD NOTES: Flies with neck held straight. Invariably found in large flocks. Juvenile greyish-brown above whitish below, facial skin pinkish. SONG/CALL: Away from breeding colonies generally silent. HABITAT: Coastal locations such as rocky islands, sandbanks and cliffs.

8 PYGMY CORMORANT *Phalacrocorax pygmeus* 45–55cm FIELD NOTES: Sociable, breeds colonially often mixed with herons and egrets. Juvenile upperparts brown, underparts greyish-brown on breast, whitish on belly, chin and throat. SONG/CALL: Grunts and croaks uttered at breeding colonies otherwise mainly silent. HABITAT: Breeds on lakes, marshes and rivers with dense vegetation, may visit brackish waters in winter.

9 LONG-TAILED CORMORANT (REED CORMORANT) *Phalacrocorax africanus* 50–55cm FIELD NOTES: Sociable. Juvenile similar to Pygmy Cormorant but whiter on breast and belly. SONG/CALL: Hissing and cackling uttered at breeding colonies otherwise silent. HABITAT: Coastal islands, mangroves.

10 DARTER (AFRICAN DARTER) *Anhinga rufa* 85–97cm FIELD NOTES: In flight holds neck with a distinct kink. Juvenile dull version of non-breeding adult. SONG/CALL: Usually silent. Various rattles and grunts given during nesting. HABITAT: Lakes, rivers, marshes etc, where trees and stumps provide perches.

9 BITTERNS, NIGHT HERONS AND GREEN HERONS

1 BITTERN (EURASIAN or GREAT BITTERN) *Botaurus stellaris* 70–80cm FIELD NOTES: Secretive. SONG/CALL: A deep, far-carrying booming preceded by a short muffled *up-RUMBH*. HABITAT: Freshwater and brackish reedbeds.

2 AMERICAN BITTERN *Botaurus lentiginosus* 60–85cm (Vagrant) FIELD NOTES: Juvenile lacks black neck streak. SONG/CALL: Unlikely to be heard calling in the Palearctic. HABITAT: In native America: freshwater and brackish marshes and bogs.

3 LEAST BITTERN *Ixobrychus exilis* 28–36cm (Vagrant) FIELD NOTES: Skulking. SONG/CALL: A hard *kok* when alarmed. HABITAT: In native America: vegetation around marshes, lakes, rivers.

4 LITTLE BITTERN *Ixobrychus minutus* 33–38cm FIELD NOTES: Skulking. SONG/CALL: A low, repeated *hoogh* or similar. When flushed utters a low *ker-ak* or *ker*. HABITAT: Freshwater marshes, lakes, pools and rivers, with adjoining vegetation.

5 YELLOW BITTERN (CHINESE LITTLE or LONG-NOSED BITTERN) *Ixobrychus sinensis* 30–40cm FIELD NOTES: Skulking. SONG/CALL: In flight utters a sharp *kakak kakak*. HABITAT: Vegetation surrounding marshes, lakes, paddyfields etc.

6 SCHRENCK'S BITTERN (VON SCHRENCK'S BITTERN) *Ixobrychus eurhythmus* 33–39cm FIELD NOTES: Skulking. Juvenile similar to adult female. SONG/CALL: A low, repeated *gup*. In flight utters a low squawk. HABITAT: Marshes, pools and paddyfields.

7 CINNAMON BITTERN (CHESTNUT BITTERN) *Ixobrychus cinnamomeus* 40–41cm FIELD NOTES: Juvenile heavily streaked above and below. SONG/CALL: A low *kwok-kwok-kwok…* sometimes ending with two or three quieter notes. In flight utters a croak. HABITAT: Flooded paddyfields and grassy areas, swamps, reedbeds and overgrown ditches.

8 DWARF BITTERN (AFRICAN DWARF BITTERN) *Ixobrychus sturmii* 30cm (Vagrant) FIELD NOTES: Secretive. Juvenile more rufous below with pale fringes to back and wing feathers. SONG/CALL: A loud croak when alarmed. HABITAT: In native Africa: swamps with dense cover.

9 BLACK BITTERN (YELLOW-NECKED or MANGROVE BITTERN) *Dupetor flavicollis* 54–66cm (Vagrant) FIELD NOTES: Secretive. Female browner and paler below. Juvenile has pale rufous fringes to back and wing feathers. SONG/CALL: Utters a hoarse croak in flight. HABITAT: In native India, S China: forest streams, dense reedy swamps.

10 MALAYAN NIGHT HERON (TIGER BITTERN) *Gorsachius melanolophus* 49cm FIELD NOTES: Shy. Primaries white-tipped. Juvenile greyish-brown densely spotted with white. SONG/CALL: A deep *oo oo oo oo…*, also croaks and a rasping *arh-arh-arh*. HABITAT: Subtropical jungle, paddyfields, reedbeds and marshes.

11 JAPANESE NIGHT HERON (JAPANESE BITTERN) *Gorsachius goisagi* 49cm FIELD NOTES: Skulks. Primaries with extensive rufous tips. Juvenile has dark crown with spotted and streaked neck. SONG/CALL: A deep *buo-buo* usually uttered at night. Emits a croak while feeding. HABITAT: Dense undergrowth in mountain forests.

12 NIGHT HERON (BLACK-CROWNED NIGHT HERON) *Nycticorax nycticorax* 58–65cm FIELD NOTES: Juvenile has back and wings dark brown spotted buff-white. Head, neck and underparts pale streaked brown. SONG/CALL: Various croaks given at breeding colonies. In flight utters a frog-like croak. HABITAT: Marshes, lakes and rivers with extensive border vegetation.

13 GREEN-BACKED HERON (STRIATED or LITTLE HERON) *Butorides striata amurensis* 40–48cm FIELD NOTES: Juvenile browner with pale spots on wings and dark streaking on neck and underparts. SONG/CALL: When alarmed utters a harsh *kyah*. HABITAT: Mangroves, paddyfields, ponds and rivers with thick cover.

14 GREEN HERON *Butorides virescens* 40–48cm (Vagrant) FIELD NOTES: Actions as Green-backed Heron. SONG/CALL: When alarmed gives a harsh *kyowk*. HABITAT: In native America: marshes, lakes, rivers, mudflats and reefs.

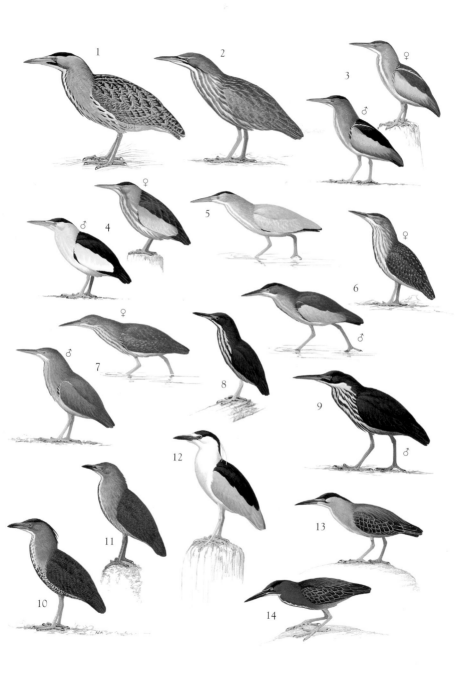

10 EGRETS, SQUACCO HERON AND POND HERONS

1 CATTLE EGRET *Bubulcus ibis* 48–53cm FIELD NOTES: Sociable. Often feeds on insects disturbed by grazing animals. SONG/CALL: Usually fairly silent. HABITAT: Colonial nester, often near water, feeds in dry grassland, arable fields and marshes. RACES: *B. i. coromandus* (Eastern Cattle Egret) (fig 1b) SE China to S Japan.

2 SQUACCO HERON *Ardeola ralloides* 44–47cm FIELD NOTES: In flight appears largely white. Often skulking. SONG/CALL: Utters a harsh *kaahk*. HABITAT: Well-vegetated marshes, lakes, ponds, rivers and coastal lagoons. Outside of breeding season also rice fields, flooded fields etc.

3 INDIAN POND HERON (PADDYBIRD) *Ardeola grayii* 42–45cm FIELD NOTES: In flight appears largely white. Regularly feeds in the open. SONG/CALL: A harsh squawk, similar to Squacco Heron. HABITAT: Various wetlands such as marshes, ponds, paddyfields, lagoons etc.

4 CHINESE POND HERON *Ardeola bacchus* 42–45cm FIELD NOTES: In flight appears largely white. Roosts and breeds in colonies, often with other heron species. SONG/CALL: When alarmed utters a harsh croak. HABITAT: Marshes, paddyfields, ponds, lagoons etc.

5 SNOWY EGRET *Egretta thula* 55–65cm (Vagrant) FIELD NOTES: Habits much as Little Egret although often feeds in a more dashing manner. More extensive yellow on rear of tarsus. In non-breeding dress loses back plumes and most of the head plumes. SONG/CALL: Away from breeding colonies usually silent. HABITAT: In native Americas: favours salt, brackish and freshwater areas, feeds in dry grassland, usually near water.

6 CHINESE EGRET (SWINHOE'S EGRET) *Egretta eulophotes* 65–68cm FIELD NOTES: In non-breeding dress the facial skin and legs are yellowish-green and the head and back plumes are lost. Often feeds by dashing to and fro with wings held half open and flapped. SONG/CALL: Other than low croaks usually silent. HABITAT: Tidal mudflats, coastal bays and occasionally ponds and paddyfields.

7 PACIFIC REEF EGRET (EASTERN REEF EGRET or HERON) *Egretta sacra* 58–66cm FIELD NOTES: Usual feeding action is lethargic with a more rapid pursuit when potential prey is spotted. SONG/CALL: A hoarse croak and, when alarmed, a harsh *arrk*. HABITAT: Rocky coasts, visits mudflats and various freshwater areas close to coasts.

8 WESTERN REEF EGRET (WESTERN REEF HERON) *Egretta gularis* 55–67cm FIELD NOTES: Intermediates with varying amounts of darkish feathers also occur. Habits much as Little Egret. Loses head, back and breast plumes in non-breeding plumage. SONG/CALL: Utters a guttural croak when feeding or alarmed, otherwise usually silent. HABITAT: Rocky and sandy coasts, tidal mudflats, coastal lagoons and estuaries, less so inland. RACES: *E. g. schistacea* (fig 8b) Red Sea and Persian Gulf, yellow bill and facial skin.

9 LITTLE EGRET *Egretta garzetta* 55–65cm FIELD NOTES: Has yellow or yellowish-orange facial skin and feet for a short period at the onset of breeding. Loses head, back and breast plumes in non-breeding plumage. SONG/CALL: Gives a hoarse *aaah* or *kgarrk* when disturbed. HABITAT: Lakes, rivers, marshland and coastal estuaries also saltpans and rice fields and occasionally on dry grassland.

10 INTERMEDIATE EGRET (YELLOW-BILLED or PLUMED EGRET) *Egretta intermedia* 65–72cm FIELD NOTES: At onset of breeding facial skin becomes green and bill and tibia turn pinkish-red. In non-breeding dress loses back and breast plumes. SONG/CALL: Utters a *kwark* or *kuwark* when disturbed. HABITAT: Freshwater lakes, rivers and marshes, less so in brackish or saltwater areas.

11 GREAT WHITE EGRET (GREAT EGRET) *Ardea alba* 85–102cm FIELD NOTES: At the onset of breeding bill becomes black with yellowish base and facial skin turns greenish. In non-breeding dress loses long back plumes. SONG/CALL: A dry, rattling *krr-rr-rr-rra*. HABITAT: Breeds on well-vegetated freshwater lakes and marshes, also visits other wetland areas including coastal locations in non-breeding season.

11 HERONS

1 LITTLE BLUE HERON *Egretta caerulea* 61–64cm (Vagrant) FIELD NOTES: Juvenile white, very similar to 'white egrets' but most have darkish tips to primaries and yellowish-green legs and feet. First-winter birds have wings and back blotched with dusky feathers. SONG/CALL: A harsh *gerr* usually given when disturbed. HABITAT: In native N and S America: lakes, marshes and estuaries, also coastal pools and inlets.

2 TRICOLORED HERON (LOUISIANA HERON) *Egretta tricolor* 63–68cm (Vagrant) FIELD NOTES: Juvenile has rufous neck with white foreneck stripe and rufous tinge to back and wings. SONG/CALL: A harsh croak, usually given when disturbed. HABITAT: In native N and S America: coastal marshes and mangroves, less so on freshwater lakes, rivers and marshes.

3 BLACK HERON (BLACK EGRET) *Egretta ardesiaca* 52–55cm (Vagrant) FIELD NOTES: Often arches wings, umbrella-like, while feeding. SONG/CALL: Generally silent. HABITAT: In native Africa: various fresh and saltwater areas i.e. lakes, marshes, mangroves, coastal mudflats etc.

4 HERON (GREY HERON) *Ardea cinerea* 90–98cm FIELD NOTES: In flight has arched wings. Often stands motionless at waters edge, in trees or in pastures. Juvenile has crown dull black. SONG/CALL: At breeding colonies harsh croaks as well as non-vocal bill-snapping. Usual flight utterance is a harsh *frannk*. HABITAT: Various wetlands including marshes, lakes, rivers, estuaries etc. RACES: *A. c. monicae* (Mauritanian Heron) (fig 4b) Mauritania, sometimes treated as a full species.

5 GREAT BLUE HERON *Ardea herodias* 110–125cm (Vagrant) FIELD NOTES: Actions very similar to Heron. Juvenile browner than juvenile Heron. SONG/CALL: A harsh *kraak*. HABITAT: In native N and C America: marshes, lakes, coastal mudflats etc.

6 BLACK-HEADED HERON *Ardea melanocephala* 90–95cm (Vagrant) FIELD NOTES: In flight below shows prominent white wing lining. Often feeds in grasslands far from water. SONG/CALL: A harsh *kuark*. HABITAT: In native Africa: lakes, rivers, marshes, coastal areas and pastures.

7 PURPLE HERON *Ardea purpurea* 78–90cm FIELD NOTES: In flight shows deeper, angular neck bulge, and is darker winged, than Heron. Juvenile browner overall than adult and shows less dark stripes on neck. SONG/CALL: At breeding colonies various harsh utterances. In flight gives a similar call to Heron, although higher pitched. HABITAT: Breeds in marshes and lakes with dense reedbeds, during non-breeding season often visits more open wetlands. RACES: *A. p. bournei* (Bourne's Heron) (fig 7b) Cape Verde Island, sometimes considered a full species.

8 GOLIATH HERON *Ardea goliath* 135–150cm FIELD NOTES: Large, man-sized, make it virtually unmistakable. Juvenile a dull version of adult. SONG/CALL: In flight gives a deep, loud *kowoorrk-kowoorrk-woorrk-work-worrk*. HABITAT: Lakes, rivers, marshes and coastal mudflats etc.

12 HAMERKOP AND STORKS

1 HAMERKOP *Scopus umbretta* 48–56cm FIELD NOTES: Unmistakable. Builds massive domed nest in trees or on cliffs. SONG/CALL: A loud, yelping *yik-purrr yik-yik-yik-purr-purr-yik-yik*. In flight utters a nasal *yip* or *kek*. HABITAT: Wadis that have running water and are well vegetated.

2 PAINTED STORK *Mycteria leucocephala* 93–100cm (Vagrant) FIELD NOTES: In flight shows dark underwing. Colonial breeder. Juvenile greyer, face brownish and bill paler. SONG/CALL: Generally silent. During breeding display gives a weak 'fizzing' call along with bill-clapping. HABITAT: In native India, S Asia: lakes, ponds and rivers.

3 YELLOW-BILLED STORK *Mycteria ibis* 95–105cm (Vagrant) FIELD NOTES: Lacks pink tinge in non-breeding plumage. In flight underwing has black primaries and secondaries with white coverts, tail black. Juvenile dull version of adult. SONG/CALL: Generally silent away from breeding sites. HABITAT: In native Africa: lakes, marshes, rivers and coastal lagoons.

4 WOOLLY-NECKED STORK *Ciconia episcopus* 75–92cm (Vagrant) FIELD NOTES: Underwing black. Juvenile dull version of adult, forehead white with dark streaks. SONG/CALL: Generally silent. HABITAT: In native Africa and India: wet or dry grasslands near water, also coastal mudflats.

5 ABDIM'S STORK (WHITE-BELLIED STORK) *Ciconia abdimii* 69–81cm FIELD NOTES: In flight from above shows white rump and back. Below like Black Stork but with larger white patch on wing. Juvenile browner version of adult. SONG/CALL: A high-pitched *peep peep peep*. HABITAT: Dry plains and semi-deserts.

6 BLACK STORK *Ciconia nigra* 95–105cm FIELD NOTES: In flight underwing is black with white triangle on axillaries. Juvenile a browner version of adult, bill and legs greyish-green. SONG/CALL: Generally silent. At nest site gives a rasping *shi-luu shi-luu shi-luu*. HABITAT: Breeds in forested area with marshes, rivers and wet pastures. At other times may be found by lakes, rivers, estuaries or dry grassland.

7 ORIENTAL STORK *Ciconia boyciana* 110–150cm FIELD NOTES: In flight below similar to White Stork, from above shows white edges to secondaries. SONG/CALL: Generally silent. Communication during display is mainly made by bill-clapping. HABITAT: Islands of trees or scattered trees in river valleys, marshes and wet meadows, otherwise occurs at lakes, marshes and coastal intertidal areas.

8 WHITE STORK *Ciconia ciconia* 100–115cm FIELD NOTES: In flight underwing has black primaries and secondaries with white coverts, tail white. Juvenile like adult but bill with extensive black tip. Often breeds on buildings. SONG/CALL: Generally silent. At nest site communicates mostly by bill-clapping. HABITAT: Breeds in trees or on buildings in towns and villages, feeds adjacent wet pastures, marshes etc.

9 MARABOU STORK (MARABOU) *Leptoptilos crumeniferus* 115–130cm (Vagrant) FIELD NOTES: Unmistakable on the ground. In flight can look like Black Stork but lacks black neck and is much larger. In non-breeding and juvenile plumage throat pouch smaller. SONG/CALL: Generally silent. HABITAT: In native Africa: open savannas with lakes, pools, marshes, rivers etc. Also found around rubbish dumps.

13 IBISES, SPOONBILLS AND FLAMINGOES

1 GLOSSY IBIS *Plegadis falcinellus* 55–65cm FIELD NOTES: Often encountered feeding alongside herons and spoonbills. Flies with neck extended and legs protruding beyond tail. Juvenile a dull version of non-breeding adult. SONG/CALL: A grunting *grru* or *graa*. Various grunting and croaking notes uttered at breeding sites. HABITAT: Breeds in freshwater marshes, by lakes and rivers with surrounding vegetation. During migration also occurs on wet meadows, paddyfields and coastal lagoons.

2 BALD IBIS (WALDRAPP, NORTHERN BALD or HERMIT IBIS) *Geronticus eremite* 70–80cm FIELD NOTES: Very rare. Legs do not protrude beyond tail in flight. Juvenile has black feathering on head and face replacing bare reddish skin of adult. SONG/CALL: At breeding sites a guttural *hrump* and a hoarse *hyoh*, otherwise generally silent. HABITAT: Breeds on cliffs in semi-arid hill country, feeding in nearby dry fields and along streams and rivers.

3 CRESTED IBIS (JAPANESE or ORIENTAL CRESTED IBIS) *Nipponia nippon* 60cm FIELD NOTES: Endangered (Extinct?). In flight from below, tail and wings show strong pink tinge. Juvenile generally dirty cream with dark primaries. Legs are light brown. SONG/CALL: Mostly silent. Utters a *gak-gak-gak* when disturbed and, in flight, a single *gak*. HABITAT: Breeds in forest patches in mountain valleys, feeding in nearby lakes, streams, ponds and paddyfields. Moves to lowland wetlands in non-breeding season.

4 SACRED IBIS *Threskiornis aethiopicus* 65–75cm FIELD NOTES: Gregarious. In flight shows black tips to primaries and secondaries. Bare pink-red 'arms' on underwing. Juvenile has black head flecked with white feathers. SONG/CALL: Utters squealing yelps and short barks at breeding sites, otherwise generally silent. HABITAT: Freshwater marshes, rivers, coastal marshes and cultivated areas.

5 BLACK-HEADED IBIS (ORIENTAL or BLACK-NECKED IBIS) *Threskiornis melanocephalus* 65–75cm FIELD NOTES: Usually in small flocks. Eastern counterpart of Sacred Ibis. Juvenile has bare skin restricted to face, rest of neck feathered white with dark flecks. SONG/CALL: Generally silent, apart from strange grunts at breeding sites. HABITAT: Reed swamps, flooded grassland, reservoirs and coastal lagoons.

6 SPOONBILL (EURASIAN or WHITE SPOONBILL) *Platalea leucorodia* 80–90cm FIELD NOTES: Sociable, often mixes with herons and egrets. In non-breeding plumage loses yellow tinge to crest and breast. Juvenile similar to adult non-breeding but with pinkish bill and legs, and darkish tips to primaries. SONG/CALL: Usually silent. HABITAT: Brackish and freshwater lakes, reed swamps, also coastal mudflats and lagoons.

7 BLACK-FACED SPOONBILL (LESSER SPOONBILL) *Platalea minor* 60–84cm FIELD NOTES: Habits similar to Spoonbill. In non-breeding season loses yellow tinge on crest and breast. Juvenile has dark tips to primary feathers. SONG/CALL: Generally silent away from breeding sites. HABITAT: Tidal mudflats, saltmarshes, estuaries and inland lakes.

8 AFRICAN SPOONBILL *Platalea alba* 91cm (Vagrant) FIELD NOTES: Habits much as Spoonbill. Juvenile lacks red facial skin, bill dusky yellow, legs blackish. SONG/CALL: Generally silent away from breeding sites. HABITAT: In native Africa: brackish and freshwater wetlands also coastal lagoons.

9 GREATER FLAMINGO *Phoenicopterus roseus* 120–145cm FIELD NOTES: Unmistakable. The similar-sized, bright pink Caribbean Flamingo (*P. rubra*), which has often been recorded, is an escapee from collections. Juvenile dirty grey-brown. SONG/CALL: In flight utters a honking *kla-ha*. Feeding flocks emit a constant, low, goose-like growling. HABITAT: Salt lakes, sea bays and less often on freshwater lakes.

10 LESSER FLAMINGO *Phoenicopterus minor* 80–90cm (Vagrant) FIELD NOTES: Note shorter neck as well as small size. Juvenile dirty grey-brown with black bill. SONG/CALL: In flight utters a high-pitched *kwirrik*. Feeding flocks give a constant low murmuring. HABITAT: In native Africa: alkaline lakes, coastal lagoons.

14 PELICANS AND SWANS

1 DALMATION PELICAN *Pelecanus crispus* 160–180cm FIELD NOTES: In non-breeding plumage crest smaller and bill pouch dull yellow. Juvenile brownish-grey, especially on wings. SONG/CALL: Various barking, hissing and grunting noises given at breeding colonies, otherwise fairly silent. HABITAT: Breeds by shallow lakes and marshes with bordering vegetation. After breeding also on larger open lakes and sheltered coastal waters.

2 WHITE PELICAN (GREAT WHITE PELICAN) *Pelecanus onocrotalus* 140–175cm FIELD NOTES: Bill pouch yellow in non-breeding plumage. Juvenile brown on wings and neck. SONG/CALL: In flight utters a deep croak and various grunts and growls at breeding colonies, otherwise mainly silent. HABITAT: Breeds on lakes and lagoons usually with extensive fringing vegetation. After breeding also occurs on small lakes, pools, rivers and sheltered coastal waters.

3 PINK-BACKED PELICAN *Pelecanus rufescens* 125–132cm FIELD NOTES: In non-breeding plumage duller, crest smaller and bill pouch pale yellow. Black loral spot diagnostic at all ages. Juvenile browner on wings. SONG/CALL: Gives various guttural calls at breeding colonies otherwise generally silent. HABITAT: Freshwater and saltwater lakes, mangroves and sheltered coastal waters.

4 MUTE SWAN *Cygnus olor* 125–155cm FIELD NOTES: Juvenile dull brownish-grey, bill lacking frontal knob is pinkish-grey with black areas as adult. In flight wings make a distinctive musical throbbing noise. SONG/CALL: Utters various hisses, grunts and snorts. HABITAT: Rivers, lakes, reservoirs, large ponds, estuaries and sheltered coastal waters.

5 BEWICK'S SWAN (TUNDRA SWAN) *Cygnus columbianus bewickii* 115–140cm FIELD NOTES: Juvenile greyish-brown, paler than juvenile Whooper Swan, base of bill pink. SONG/CALL: Various honking and yapping call. In flight gives a low *hoo-hoo*. HABITAT: Breeds on Arctic tundra with nearby pools, lakes and rivers. In winter on pastures, flooded grassland and cereal fields, uses lakes and sheltered coastal waters on migration. RACES: *C. c. columbianus* (Whistling Swan) (fig 5b) N America.

6 WHOOPER SWAN *Cygnus cygnus* 140–165cm FIELD NOTES: Juvenile greyish-brown, slightly darker than juvenile Bewick's Swan, base of bill pink. SONG/CALL: Various honking and bugling calls. In flight gives a deep *hoop-hoop-hoop*. HABITAT: Breeds by pools, lakes and rivers in northern taiga. In winter on farmland, flooded pastures and occasionally on coastal inlets and bays.

7 TRUMPETER SWAN *Cygnus buccinator* 150–180cm (Vagrant) FIELD NOTES: Habits and juvenile similar to Whooper Swan, which is often considered to be conspecific. SONG/CALL: A deep, bugling *ko-hoh*. HABITAT: In native N America: lakes, ponds and marshes, on estuaries in winter.

8 BLACK SWAN *Cygnus altratus* 115–140cm FIELD NOTES: Introduced from Australia. Unmistakable. In flight shows white primaries and outer secondaries. Juvenile duller with grey bill. SONG/CALL: A high-pitched musical, bugling. HABITAT: Introductions favour park lakes and secluded wooded lakes, but may turn up on lakes, flooded fields and coastal bays.

15 TREE DUCKS, SHELDUCKS, KNOB-BILLED DUCK AND GEESE

1 FULVOUS TREE DUCK (FULVOUS WHISTLING DUCK) *Dendrocygna bicolour* 45–53 cm (Vagrant) FIELD NOTES: Usually in small parties. SONG/CALL: A whistling *k-weeoo* also a harsh *kee*. HABITAT: In native tropical America, Africa and India: lowland freshwater lakes and marshes with fringing vegetation.

2 LESSER TREE DUCK (LESSER WHISTLING DUCK) *Dendrocygna javanica* 38–42cm (Vagrant) FIELD NOTES: Usually in flocks of 20–50. SONG/CALL: In flight utters a constant thin, whistled *whi-whee*. HABITAT: In native tropical Asia: freshwater pools, lakes and swamps.

3 WHITE-FACED TREE DUCK (WHITE-FACED WHISTLING DUCK) *Dendrocygna viduata* 45–53cm (Vagrant) FIELD NOTES: Often in very large flocks. SONG/CALL: A whistled *tsri-tsri-trseeo*. HABITAT: In native S America and Africa: freshwater marshes, lakes and rivers.

4 EGYPTIAN GOOSE *Alopochen aegyptiaca* 63–73cm FIELD NOTES: Often perches on trees or buildings. Some individuals greyer than shown. In flight shows extensive white forewing, above and below. SONG/CALL: Male utters a harsh, wheezy hiss. Female has a noisy, braying *honk-haah-haah-haah*. HABITAT: Freshwater lakes and rivers also nearby pastures or parkland.

5 RUDDY SHELDUCK *Tadorna ferruginea* 61–67cm FIELD NOTES: In flight shows extensive white forewing, above and below. SONG/CALL: Utters a honking *aakh* or *ah-onk* also a repeated, trumpet-like *pok-pok-pok-pok*. HABITAT: Lakes and rivers in open country, sometimes found far from water on upland plateaux. Winters by lowland lakes and rivers.

6 CRESTED SHELDUCK *Tadorna cristata* 60–63cm FIELD NOTES: Extinct? In flight shows extensive white forewing, above and below. SONG/CALL: Unrecorded. HABITAT: Thought to have bred by rivers in montane forests and wintered in coastal districts.

7 SHELDUCK (COMMON SHELDUCK) *Tadorna tadorna* 58–67cm FIELD NOTES: Extensive white forewing, above and below, which tends to make it appear black and white in flight. SONG/CALL: Male utters a thin whistling *sliss-sliss-sliss-sliss*, female gives a rapid, nasal *gag-ag-ag-ag-ag-ak*. HABITAT: Breeds on estuaries, sandy or muddy seashores, also by lakes and rivers.

8 SPUR-WINGED GOOSE *Plectropterus gambensis* 75–100cm (Vagrant) FIELD NOTES: In flight shows white forewing and extensive white on underwing. Female lacks forehead knob. SONG/CALL: Mainly silent. HABITAT: In native Africa: marshes, lakes and rivers in open grassland.

9 KNOB-BILLED DUCK (COMB DUCK) *Sarkidiornis melanotos* 56–76cm (Vagrant) FIELD NOTES: Usually in small groups. SONG/CALL: Mainly silent. HABITAT: In native tropical Asia and Africa: lakes, swamps and rivers in open, lightly wooded areas.

10 CANADA GOOSE *Branta canadensis* 90–100cm FIELD NOTES: Gregarious. SONG/CALL: A varied, musical honk. HABITAT: Lakes, ponds and various types of grassland.

11 LESSER CANADA GOOSE (CACKLING GOOSE) *Branta hutchinsii* 55cm (Vagrant) FIELD NOTES: Recently split from Canada Goose. Very small. SONG/CALL: High-pitched cackling *yelk yelk a'lick a-lick*. HABITAT: In native Canada: Arctic coastal tundra.

12 BARNACLE GOOSE *Branta leucopsis* 58–71cm FIELD NOTES: Forms large winter flocks. SONG/CALL: Flight notes likened to the yelping of a pack of dogs. HABITAT: Breeds in high-Arctic coastal areas. Winters on coastal grasslands.

13 BRENT GOOSE (BRANT) *Branta bernicla* 55–66cm FIELD NOTES: Juveniles lack white neck marks. SONG/CALL: A rolling, gargling *raunk raunk raunk*. HABITAT: Breeds in high-Arctic coastal tundra with pools and inlets. Winters on coastal mudflats and grassland. RACES: *B. b. nigricans* (Black Brant) (fig 13b) NE Siberia winters E Asia.

14 RED-BREASTED GOOSE *Branta ruficollis* 53–55cm FIELD NOTES: Forms large winter flocks. SONG/CALL: A high-pitched *kik-yoik kik-yik*. HABITAT: Breeds on tundra or open wooded tundra near rivers. Winters on salt-steppe, lowland pasture, crop and stubble fields.

16 GEESE

1 SWAN GOOSE (CHINESE GOOSE) *Anser cygnoides* 81–94cm FIELD NOTES: Juvenile slightly duller and lacking white at base of bill. SONG/CALL: Various honking and cackling calls uttered mainly in flight. All calls similar to those of the domestic goose. HABITAT: Breeds on steppe and wooded steppe marshes, lakesides, river valleys and deltas. Winters on lowland marshes and wet cultivation.

2 BEAN GOOSE *Anser fabalis* 66–84cm FIELD NOTES: Wary. Usually in smaller flocks than other grey geese. Juvenile more scaly on back, otherwise much as adult. SONG/CALL: A *wink-wink* and a deep, nasal *hank-hank*, also typical goose cackling. HABITAT: Breeds on damp tundra, coastal areas, islands, birch and coniferous forests. Winters in open country, including damp steppe and agricultural land. RACES: *A. f. rossicus* (fig 2b) N Russia, NW Siberia.

3 PINK-FOOTED GOOSE *Anser brachyrhynchus* 60–75cm FIELD NOTES: In flight shows light grey forewing (not as pale as Greylag Goose). Juvenile duller with scaly back. SONG/CALL: A *wink-wink* and a high-pitched *ahng-ahng-ahng*, also a constant cackling from flocks in flight. HABITAT: Breeds on tundra in mountain areas. Winters on saltmarsh and lowland farmland.

4 GREYLAG GOOSE *Anser anser* 75–90cm FIELD NOTES: In flight has a distinctive pale grey forewing. SONG/CALL: In flight gives a deep, honking *aahng-ahng-ung*. All calls similar to those of the domesticated farmland goose. HABITAT: Breeds in open country wetland with nearby damp grassland. Winters on farmland, estuaries, lakes and reservoirs. RACES: *A. a. rubrirostris* (fig 4b) E Europe, Asia.

5 WHITE-FRONTED GOOSE (GREATER WHITE-FRONTED GOOSE) *Anser albifrons* 64–78cm FIELD NOTES: Juvenile lacks white at base of bill and has unmarked belly. SONG/CALL: In flight has a musical *lyo-lyok*, also typical goose cackling. HABITAT: Breeds on lowland tundra often by rivers and lakes. Winters on open steppe, grassland, stubble fields and saltmarsh. RACES: *A. a. flavirostris* (Greenland White-fronted Goose) (fig 5b) W Greenland.

6 LESSER WHITE-FRONTED GOOSE *Anser erythropus* 53–66cm FIELD NOTES: Juvenile lacks white at base of bill and has unmarked belly. In west of region odd individuals sometimes found in flocks of other grey geese. SONG/CALL: In flight repeats a squeaky *kyu-yu-yu*. HABITAT: Breeds on damp, bushy tundra, forest edge and mountain foothills. Winters in open areas including salt steppe, meadows and arable farmland.

7 BAR-HEADED GOOSE *Anser indicus* 71–76cm FIELD NOTES: Juvenile lacks nape bars, has crown and hind neck dark grey. SONG/CALL: In flight utters a nasal honking. HABITAT: Breeds on high-altitude lakes and marshes.

8 EMPEROR GOOSE *Anser canagicus* 66–89cm FIELD NOTES: Juvenile has head and neck dark grey flecked paler. SONG/CALL: In flight gives a hoarse, high-pitched *kla-ha kla-ha* or a shrill *yang-yang*. HABITAT: Breeds by coastal tundra lakes, also by pools on inland tundra. Winters on rocky seashores and estuaries.

9 ROSS'S GOOSE *Anser rossii* 53–66cm (Vagrant) FIELD NOTES: Juvenile white phase has pale greyish hind crown, nape and scapulars. SONG/CALL: In flight gives a grunt-like *kug* and a weak cackling *kek ke-gak*. HABITAT: In native Arctic Canada and N America: breeds on Arctic tundra, winters mainly on farmland.

10 SNOW GOOSE (BLUE GOOSE) *Anser caerulescens* 65–84cm FIELD NOTES: Juvenile white phase has crown, hind neck, back and wings grey, the latter with feathers edged white. Juvenile blue phase all over dark slaty-brown. SONG/CALL: In flight utters a nasal, cackling *la-luk*, said to resemble the barking of a small dog. HABITAT: Breeds in low tundra in close proximity to water. Winters on pastures, stubble fields usually in lowland coastal areas.

blue phase

blue phase

white phase

white phase

17 DUCKS

1 WIGEON (EURASIAN WIGEON) *Anas penelope* 45–50cm FIELD NOTES: In flight male shows a large white patch on upperwing. Very gregarious outside of breeding season. Grazes more than most other ducks. SONG/CALL: Male gives a clear, whistling *wheeooo* and the female a growling *krrr*. HABITAT: Breeds near lakes and marshes in open or light wooded country. Winters mainly on estuaries, flooded water meadows and to lesser extent on internal freshwater lakes.

2 AMERICAN WIGEON (BALDPATE) *Anas americana* 45–50cm (Vagrant) FIELD NOTES: In flight, upperwing pattern similar to Wigeon. Centre of underwing white, Wigeon usually greyer. SONG/CALL: Similar to Wigeon but weaker and throatier. HABITAT: In native N America: breeds in similar situations to Wigeon, prefers freshwater marshes in winter.

3 FALCATED DUCK (FALCATED TEAL) *Anas falcate* 48–54cm FIELD NOTES: Sociable, large winter flocks which often include Wigeon and Pintail. SONG/CALL: Male gives a low whistle followed by a wavering *uit-trr*. Females utter a throaty quack. HABITAT: Breeds around lowland water meadows and lakes. Winters in similar habitats as well as rivers, and to a lesser extent estuaries.

4 GADWALL *Anas strepera* 46–55cm FIELD NOTES: In flight both male and female show white secondary patch on upperwing. Usually found in small groups. Can be quite wary. SONG/CALL: Usually fairly silent. Male gives a sharp *ahrk* also a low whistle. Female has a mechanical Mallard-like quack. HABITAT: Breeds and winters in lowland, open country freshwater areas with fringing vegetation, less often on estuaries.

5 BAIKAL TEAL (FORMOSA TEAL) *Anas formosa* 39–43cm FIELD NOTES: Eclipse male shows 'shadow' of distinctive adult facial pattern. Forms large winter flocks often mixed with other duck species. SONG/CALL: Male utters a *wot-wot-wot* often persistently. Females utter a low quack. HABITAT: Breeds by pools in taiga swamps and marshes at the edge of tundra. Winters in various fresh and brackish-water areas.

6 TEAL (COMMON TEAL) *Anas crecca* 34–38cm FIELD NOTES: Forms very large winter flocks. Flight is rapid with much twisting and turning. SONG/CALL: Males utter a soft, high-pitched *preep-preep*. Females rather silent although often gives a nasal *quack* when alarmed. HABITAT: Breeds on freshwater lakes and pools with fringing vegetation. Winters in similar locations as well as saltmarshes, estuaries and sheltered coastal bays.

7 GREEN-WINGED TEAL *Anas carolinensis* 34–38cm (Vagrant) FIELD NOTES: Recently split from Teal. Female inseparable from Teal. SONG/CALL: As Teal. HABITAT: In native N America: as Teal.

8 CAPE TEAL (CAPE WIGEON) *Anas capensis* 44–48cm (Vagrant) FIELD NOTES: Sexes similar. SONG/CALL: Male utters a nasal squeak, although in our area would be mostly silent. HABITAT: In native Africa: freshwater, brackish or saline lakes, flooded wetlands, marshes and, less often, coastal areas.

9 MALLARD *Anas platyrhynchos* 50–65cm FIELD NOTES: Many of the 'odd' ducks on ornamental ponds are descendants of this species. SONG/CALL: The male utters a rasped *kreep*. The females *quack-quack-quack* is probably the one of best known of bird calls. HABITAT: Virtually any river, lake, pond or estuary.

10 AMERICAN BLACK DUCK (BLACK DUCK) *Anas ruripes* 53–61cm (Vagrant) FIELD NOTES: In flight shows striking white underwing. Beware, melanistic Mallards can look similar. SONG/CALL: Similar to Mallard. HABITAT: In native N America: similar to Mallard.

18 DUCKS

1 SPOT-BILLED DUCK (SPOTBILL) *Anas poecilorhyncha* 58–63cm FIELD NOTES: In flight, from above, shows large white patch on tertials, from below has dark primaries and secondaries contrasting with white coverts. Occurs in small parties, may form larger flocks after breeding. SONG/CALL: Almost indistinguishable from Mallard. Generally silent. HABITAT: Well-vegetated, shallow freshwater lakes and marshes, less often on rivers. RACES: *A. p. zonorhyncha* (Chinese Spotbill) E and NE China. In flight shows less of a white patch on tertials. Much the commonest race in the Palearctic.

2 PHILIPPINE DUCK *Anas luzonica* 48–58cm (Vagrant) FIELD NOTES: Unmistakeable. In flight from below shows whitish coverts and dark greyish primaries and secondaries. Juvenile similar but duller. SONG/CALL: Much like Mallard but slightly more harsh. HABITAT: In native Philippine Islands: lakes, ponds, rivers, marshes and tidal creeks.

3 PINTAIL (NORTHERN PINTAIL) *Anas acuta* 51–56cm (male with tail 61–66cm) FIELD NOTES: Long neck and tail make for an elongated look in flight. Very gregarious, forms very large flocks in non-breeding season. SONG/CALL: Male has a mellow, Teal-like *proop-proop*. Female utters a series of repeated, weak, quacks and a low croak when flushed. HABITAT: Breeds in wet meadows, marshy lakes and by slow rivers. Winters on lakes, estuary mudflats, marshes and coastal lagoons.

4 RED-BILLED TEAL (RED-BILLED DUCK or RED-BILLED PINTAIL) *Anas erythrorhyncha* 43–48cm (Vagrant) FIELD NOTES: In flight shows distinctive buff-white secondaries on upperwing. Underwing dark. Very similar White-cheeked Pintail, often escapee from collections, is generally more buff with a pale 'pintail' and has red of bill restricted to the base. SONG/CALL: Mainly silent. Display call unlikely to be heard in Palearctic. HABITAT: In native Africa: shallow freshwater lakes and marshes.

5 GARGANEY *Anas querquedula* 37–41cm FIELD NOTES: In flight from above male shows pale grey forewing, separated from green secondaries, which have wide white trailing edge, by a white wingbar. At distance can look white winged. Usually in pairs or small parties. After breeding forms into large flocks. SONG/CALL: Males utter a rattling *knerek*. Female has a high, nasal quack. HABITAT: Freshwater lakes and marshes with extensive vegetation. On migration often on inshore waters. Winters on open freshwater lakes.

6 BLUE-WINGED TEAL *Anas discors* 37–41cm (Vagrant) FIELD NOTES: Male unmistakeable. Female has distinctive pale oval area at base of bill. In flight both sexes show a pale, bright blue forewing. No white trailing edge to secondaries. SONG/CALL: Males utter a thin *tsee-tsee*. Female has a high-pitched quack. HABITAT: In native N America: open country and grasslands with shallow lakes and pools.

7 CAPE SHOVELER *Anas smithii* 51–53cm (Vagrant) FIELD NOTES: Usually in pairs. In flight female very similar to female Shoveler but generally darker bodied, male wing pattern very like that of male Shoveler. Legs yellow, orange on Shoveler. SONG/CALL: Male utters a soft, hollow *took-took-took*. Female has a weak, husky quack. HABITAT: In native Africa: shallow freshwater and brackish-water lakes, marshes and tidal estuaries.

8 SHOVELER (NORTHERN or EUROPEAN SHOVELER) *Anas clypeata* 44–52cm FIELD NOTES: Male unmistakeable. Usually in pairs or small parties. In flight large bill, and wings that appear placed nearer tail, make bird look 'front heavy'. Upperwing of male shows pale blue forewing separated from green secondaries by white wingbar, female wing duller with smaller wingbar. SONG/CALL: During display male gives a hollow *sluk-uk* or *g-dunk*. Female has a quacking *gak-gak-gak-ga-ga*. HABITAT: Freshwater lakes and marshes with surrounding and emergent vegetation. In non-breeding season also occurs on more open waters including estuaries and coastal lagoons.

19 DUCKS

1 MARBLED DUCK (MARBLED TEAL) *Marmaronetta angustirostris* 39–42cm FIELD NOTES: Gregarious. Often difficult to see when in lakeside vegetation. Upperwing shows pale grey-buff secondaries and primaries the latter having dark tips. SONG/CALL: Generally silent. HABITAT: Shallow freshwater and brackish lakes with developing and border vegetation.

2 RED-CRESTED POCHARD *Netta rufina* 53–57cm FIELD NOTES: Male in eclipse plumage has red bill otherwise similar to female. Upperwing of both sexes show white flight-feathers with a black trailing edge. SONG/CALL: Generally silent. HABITAT: Freshwater lakes with fringing vegetation, also rivers, river deltas and coastal waters.

3 SOUTHERN POCHARD (AFRICAN POCHARD) *Netta erythrophthalma brunnea* 48–51cm (Vagrant) FIELD NOTES: Usually in small groups with larger concentrations after breeding. Upperwing of both sexes show distinctive white flight-feathers with a black trailing edge. SONG/CALL: Generally silent. HABITAT: In native Africa: large freshwater and brackish lakes.

4 CANVASBACK *Aythya valisineria* 48–61cm (Vagrant) FIELD NOTES: Gregarious. In flight shows uniform grey upperwing. SONG/CALL: Generally silent away from breeding sites. HABITAT: In native N America: breeds in marshes with areas of open water. Winters on open lakes, estuaries and sheltered coastal waters.

5 POCHARD (COMMON or EUROPEAN POCHARD) *Aythya farina* 42–49cm FIELD NOTES: Gregarious. From above, both sexes show pale grey flight-feathers contrasting with darker grey forewing. SONG/CALL: Generally silent. HABITAT: Lakes with surrounding vegetation. In non-breeding season also on open lakes, reservoirs and occasionally on coastal waters.

6 REDHEAD *Aythya americana* 45–56cm (Vagrant) FIELD NOTES: Gregarious. In flight upperwing of both sexes shows pale secondaries contrasting with rest of wing. SONG/CALL: Generally silent away from breeding sites. HABITAT: In native N America: breeds on freshwater lakes and marshes, also on tidal bays and brackish lagoons in winter.

7 RING-NECKED DUCK *Aythya collaris* 37–46cm (Vagrant) FIELD NOTES: Occurs in small groups with larger flocks in winter. In flight both sexes show pale grey secondaries contrasting with darker primaries and black forewing. SONG/CALL: Generally silent. HABITAT: In native N America: freshwater lakes and pools. Winters on large lakes, brackish lagoons and tidal bays.

8 BAER'S POCHARD (BAER'S or SIBERIAN WHITE-EYE) *Aythya baeri* 41–46cm FIELD NOTES: Occurs in pairs or small parties. In flight upperwing of both sexes have white secondaries and inner primaries, contrasting with dark outer primaries, trailing edge and forewing. SONG/CALL: Generally silent. HABITAT: Freshwater lakes and pools with developing and fringing vegetation.

9 FERRUGINOUS DUCK (COMMON WHITE-EYE, WHITE-EYED POCHARD) *Aythya nyroca* 38–42cm FIELD NOTES: Occurs in pairs or small flocks. In flight upperwing of both sexes has distinct wide white bar on secondaries and primaries. SONG/CALL: Generally silent. HABITAT: Freshwater lakes with surrounding and developing vegetation. Winters on open water and coastal lagoons.

10 TUFTED DUCK *Aythya fuligula* 40–47cm FIELD NOTES: Gregarious. In flight upperwing of both sexes show distinct wide white bar on secondaries and primaries. SONG/CALL: Usually silent. HABITAT: Breeds on freshwater lakes, ponds and rivers with fringing vegetation.

11 SCAUP (GREATER SCAUP) *Aythya marila* 40–51cm FIELD NOTES: Gregarious. In flight upperwing of both sexes like Tufted Duck but with paler forewing. SONG/CALL: Mostly silent. HABITAT: Breeds on freshwater pools and lakes in tundra fringe areas. Winters on coastal waters and locally on freshwater lakes and reservoirs.

12 LESSER SCAUP *Aythya affinis* 38–46cm (Vagrant) FIELD NOTES: Gregarious. In flight upperwing of both sexes have wide white bar restricted to the secondaries, inner primaries are grey. SONG/CALL: Generally silent. HABITAT: In native N America: breeds on freshwater lakes and pools. Winters on lakes, estuaries and sheltered coastal waters.

white undetail
variety

white faced variety

20 DUCKS

1 EIDER (COMMON EIDER) *Somateria mollissima* 50–71cm FIELD NOTES: In flight male has black flight-feathers, rest of wing white. Female general colour varies from rufous to greyish-brown. SONG/CALL: Male utters a crooning *ahOOoo*, female a grating *krrr*. HABITAT: Breeds on coastal shores including small islands. Winters mainly on coastal waters. RACES: *S. m. borealis* (fig 1b) Iceland.

2 KING EIDER *Somateria spectabilis* 47–63cm FIELD NOTES: In flight male upperwing is black with a white forewing patch. SONG/CALL: Similar to Eider. In flight utters a low croak. HABITAT: Breeds on high-Arctic tundra, winters on open sea.

3 SPECTACLED EIDER (FISCHER'S EIDER) *Somateria fischeri* 52–57cm FIELD NOTES: In flight male wing pattern similar to Eider. SONG/CALL: Male utters a weak crooning note, female has a harsh croak. HABITAT: Breeds on coastal tundra, locally inland. Winters at sea.

4 STELLER'S EIDER *Polysticta stelleri* 43–47cm FIELD NOTES: Secondaries on female upperwing shows a white bar and trailing edge. Male upperwing dark with large white forewing patch. SONG/CALL: Male relatively silent. Female utters barks, growls and whistles. HABITAT: Breeds on Arctic tundra. Winters on inshore coastal waters.

5 COMMON SCOTER *Melanitta nigra* 44–54cm FIELD NOTES: Gregarious all year, usually in very large winter flocks. Often seen flying low over sea in long undulating lines. SONG/CALL: Male gives a soft *pju*, female utters a grating *karr*. HABITAT: Breeds by tundra lakes and pools. Winters mainly on coastal waters.

6 BLACK SCOTER *Melanitta americana* 44–54cm FIELD NOTES: Recently split from Common Scoter, habits similar. Female inseparable from Common Scoter although bill tends to be more swollen at base. SONG/CALL: As Common Scoter. HABITAT: As Common Scoter.

7 SURF SCOTER *Melanitta perspicillata* 45–66cm (Vagrant) FIELD NOTES: Gregarious, from small parties to large winter flocks. In Palearctic stragglers found among Common Scoters. SONG/CALL: Generally silent. HABITAT: In native America: winters on coastal waters.

8 VELVET SCOTER *Melanitta fusca* 51–58cm FIELD NOTES: Forms large flocks throughout the year. In flight both sexes show white secondaries. SONG/CALL: Male utters a loud piping and female a hoarse *braa-ah-braa-ah….* HABITAT: Breeds by freshwater lakes. Winters on coastal waters.

9 WHITE-WINGED SCOTER *Melanitta deglandi stejnegeri* 51–58cm FIELD NOTES: Recently split from Velvet Scoter, habits similar. In flight both species show white secondaries. SONG/CALL: Little-studied, said to differ from Velvet Scoter? HABITAT: As Velvet Scoter.

10 BUFFLEHEAD *Bucephala albeola* 32–39cm (Vagrant) FIELD NOTES: Unmistakable. Diagnostic white head patch shows well in flight. Wing pattern similar to respective sexes of Goldeneye. SONG/CALL: Generally silent apart from an occasional growl given by male. Female utters a series of guttural notes. HABITAT: In native N America: lakes, pools and rivers in wooded country. Winters on large lakes, rivers and coastal waters.

11 BARROW'S GOLDENEYE *Bucephala islandica* 42–53cm FIELD NOTES: Male upperwing similar to male Goldeneye with the addition of a black bar dividing secondary and median coverts. Female upperwing similar to female Goldeneye but with less white on coverts, which is split by one black bar. SONG/CALL: During display male utters a soft *ka-KAA*. Female has several low growling notes. HABITAT: Breeds on lakes, pools and rivers. Often on inshore coastal waters in winter.

12 GOLDENEYE (COMMON GOLDENEYE) *Bucephala clangula* 42–50cm FIELD NOTES: Male upperwing has large white patch on secondaries and coverts, female has same patch but split by two black bars on coverts. SONG/CALL: During display male gives strange whistles and dry notes. Female gives a purring *brra bra….* HABITAT: Breeds in woodland close to rivers and lakes. Winters on lakes, reservoirs and coastal waters.

21 DUCKS AND PYGMY-GOOSE

1 COTTON PYGMY-GOOSE (COTTON TEAL) *Nettapus coromandelianus* 30–37cm (Vagrant) FIELD NOTES: Male upperwing shows white primaries, with black tips, and white trailing edge to secondaries. Female upperwing lacks white primaries. SONG/CALL: Male utters a sharp *car-car-carawak*. Female gives a weak quack. HABITAT: In native tropical Asia: vegetated lakes and pools.

2 WOOD DUCK (CAROLINA WOOD DUCK) *Aix sponsa* 43–51cm (Vagrant) FIELD NOTES: Eclipse male has pink bill otherwise similar to female. SONG/CALL: Male utters a thin, rising *jeeeeee*. Female has a sharp *cr-r-ek cr-r-ek* and squealed *oo-eek* when flushed. HABITAT: In native N America: lakes, ponds and rivers in wooded country.

3 MANDARIN (MANDARIN DUCK) *Aix galericulata* 41–49cm FIELD NOTES: Eclipse male has pink-red bill otherwise similar to female. SONG/CALL: Generally silent, during display male utters a whistle and a sharp *hwick* in flight. Female sometimes gives short clucking notes. HABITAT: Lakes and rivers with surrounding trees and bush.

4 HARLEQUIN DUCK *Histrionicus histrionicus* 38–45cm FIELD NOTES: Eclipse male as breeding female but with pale stripe on side of breast and white-edged scapulars. SONG/CALL: Male utters a high-pitched whistle during display. Female has various harsh calls. HABITAT: Breeds by fast-flowing mountain rivers. Winters on coastal waters, especially rocky bays.

5 LONG-TAILED DUCK (OLDSQUAW) *Clangula hyemalis* 36–47cm (male with tail 48–60cm) FIELD NOTES: Often forms large, often sexually segregated, winter flocks. SONG/CALL: Male gives a yodelling *ow-ow-owlee..caloocaloo*. Female has various weak quacks. HABITAT: Breeds on Arctic tundra, lakes and pools, also by rivers and coastal inlets. Winters on coastal waters.

6 SMEW *Mergellus albellus* 38–44cm FIELD NOTES: In winter often in sexually segregated flocks. Upperwing of both sexes shows white wing patch. SONG/CALL: During display male gives low croaks and whistles, otherwise fairly silent. Female gives a low growling. HABITAT: Breeds by lakes, pools and rivers in forest areas. Winters on lakes, estuaries and coastal bays.

7 HOODED MERGANSER *Lophodytes cucullatus* 42–50cm (Vagrant) FIELD NOTES: Male in eclipse has pale eye, otherwise as breeding female. SONG/CALL: Generally silent. HABITAT: In native N America: lakes and rivers in forest areas, in winter also on large lakes and coastal lagoons.

8 RED-BREASTED MERGANSER *Mergus serrator* 52–58cm FIELD NOTES: Both sexes show much white on upperwing. SONG/CALL: In display male gives a cat-like mewing and various soft notes, otherwise generally silent. Female utters various harsh and grating calls. HABITAT: Breeds on estuaries, lakes and rivers in wooded areas. Winters on inshore coastal waters.

9 SCALY-SIDED MERGANSER (CHINESE MERGANSER) *Mergus squamatus* 52–62cm FIELD NOTES: Little-recorded. Both sexes show much white on upperwing. SONG/CALL: As Red-breasted Merganser. HABITAT: Breeds by rivers in mountain forest areas. Winters on rivers and lakes.

10 GOOSANDER (COMMON MERGANSER) *Mergus merganser* 58–72cm FIELD NOTES: Upperwing of male shows large white patch, female patch less extensive. SONG/CALL: During display male gives a twanging *uig-a*. Female has various harsh notes. HABITAT: Breeds by lakes and rivers in forest areas. Winters mainly on large lakes.

11 RUDDY DUCK *Oxyura jamaicensis* 35–43cm FIELD NOTES: Sociable. SONG/CALL: Usually silent. During display most sounds made by tapping bill against inflated chest, this producing a bubbling of water around breast. HABITAT: Lakes with bordering vegetation.

12 WHITE-HEADED DUCK (WHITE-HEADED STIFFTAIL) *Oxyura leucocephala* 43–48cm FIELD NOTES: Usually in small parties, larger flocks in winter. SONG/CALL: Males emit rattling and piping calls during display. Female utters low, harsh notes. HABITAT: Breeds and winters on small lakes with developing and fringing vegetation, also found on larger lakes and coastal lagoons after breeding.

22 LAMMERGEIER AND VULTURES

1 LAMMERGEIER (BEARDED VULTURE) *Gypaetus barbatus* 100–115cm FIELD NOTES: Juvenile generally dark brownish-black with whitish patch on mantle, below ash-grey from breast to undertail-coverts. SONG/CALL: Generally silent apart from a shrill *feeeeee* uttered during aerial display. HABITAT: Breeds in mountains with sheer crags, during winter resorts to lower areas.

2 EGYPTIAN VULTURE *Neophron percnopterus* 60–70cm FIELD NOTES: Juvenile generally dark brownish-black, some show pale fringes to wing feathers. SONG/CALL: Usually silent. HABITAT: Breeds in mountain areas, after breeding more open areas, also encountered near human habitation and rubbish dumps.

3 HOODED VULTURE *Necrosyrtes monachus* 62–72cm (Vagrant) FIELD NOTES: Juvenile has dark down on hind neck and crown, greyer facial skin. SONG/CALL: Usually silent. HABITAT: In native Africa: savanna, woodlands, towns and villages, also often around rubbish dumps.

4 INDIAN WHITE-BACKED VULTURE (WHITE-RUMPED VULTURE) *Gyps bengalensis* 75–85cm FIELD NOTES: In flight from above shows white rump and lower back. Juvenile generally dark with pale streaking on underparts and upperwing-coverts. SONG/CALL: When joining other birds at roost, or carcasses, gives a strident, creaky *kakakaka*. HABITAT: Open country, towns and villages.

5 GRIFFON VULTURE (EURASIAN GRIFFON or EURASIAN GRIFFON VULTURE) *Gyps fulvus* 95–105cm FIELD NOTES: In flight juvenile shows uniform pale sandy underwing-coverts. SONG/CALL: At roosts, or carcasses, gives various hisses and grunts. HABITAT: Mountains and neighbouring grasslands.

6 HIMALAYAN GRIFFON VULTURE (HIMALAYAN GRIFFON) *Gyps himalayensis* 120cm FIELD NOTES: Juvenile generally dark with whitish head and neck, and pale shaft streaks above and below. Underwing shows pale lines on coverts. SONG/CALL: Occasionally utters whistling and clucking noises. HABITAT: High-altitude mountain areas.

7 RÜPPELL'S GRIFFON VULTURE (RÜPPELL'S VULTURE or RÜPPELL'S GRIFFON) *Gyps rueppellii* 85–95cm (Vagrant) FIELD NOTES: Juvenile generally plain dark brown, bill grey, in flight underwing shows dull whitish bar on lesser coverts. SONG/CALL: Various hisses, grunts, groans and guttural rattles, usually given during disputes over carcasses. HABITAT: In native Africa: mountains, rocky outcrops, hills, savannas and grasslands.

8 RED-HEADED VULTURE (KING VULTURE) *Sarcogyps calvus* 85cm FIELD NOTES: Juvenile generally dull brown with white down on head, in flight shows dull grey-white belly and white undertail feathers. SONG/CALL: Hoarse croaks and screams usually given during disputes over carcasses. HABITAT: Open country with nearby habitation and wooded hills.

9 LAPPET-FACED VULTURE (NUBIAN VULTURE) *Torgus tracheliotus* 95–105cm FIELD NOTES: Juvenile is all-dark below, including underwing. SONG/CALL: Usually silent although may utter a growling *churr* and various metallic notes. HABITAT: Semi-desert, savannas, grasslands with scattered acacias. RACES: *T. t. negevensis* (fig 9b) S Israel.

10 BLACK VULTURE (EURASIAN, CINEROUS or MONK VULTURE) *Aegypius monachus* 100–110cm FIELD NOTES: Juvenile generally dark brown-black. SONG/CALL: Usually silent. HABITAT: Forest areas on hills and mountains, semi-arid alpine meadows and grassland.

23 FISH EAGLES, SEA EAGLE, BATELEUR, HAWK EAGLE AND EAGLES

1 AFRICAN FISH EAGLE *Haliaeetus vocifer* 74–84cm (Vagrant) FIELD NOTES: Juvenile underwing pattern shows large white patches at base of primaries and white line on coverts. Underparts brown scalloped pale with white breast band, head grey-white streaked brown, tail white with wide black tip. SONG/CALL: A ringing or yelping *kyow-kow-kow*. HABITAT: In native Africa: lakes, rivers, estuaries and lagoons.

2 PALLAS'S FISH EAGLE (PALLAS'S SEA EAGLE) *Haliaeetus leucoryphus* 76–84cm FIELD NOTES: In flight juvenile underwing shows wide whitish bar on greater coverts and large white patch on base inner primaries. Tail wholly black. SONG/CALL: A hoarse, barking *kvok kvok kvok*. HABITAT: Lakes, rivers and extensive marshes.

3 WHITE-TAILED EAGLE (WHITE-TAILED SEA EAGLE) *Haliaeetus albicilla* 69–92cm FIELD NOTES: Juvenile generally dark brown, tail feathers dark with pale centres, bill grey, underwing shows pale axillaries. SONG/CALL: A shrill *klee klee klee klee*, in alarm utters a lower *klek klek klek*. HABITAT: Rocky islands, lakes, marshes and large rivers from desert to Arctic areas.

4 BALD EAGLE *Haliaeetus leucocephalus* 79–84cm (Vagrant) FIELD NOTES: Juvenile generally dark brown, in flight from below shows pale band on median coverts and pale axillaries, tail whitish with wide black tip. SONG/CALL: A loud, cackling *kweek-kik-ik-ik-ik-ik-ik* and a lower *kak-kak-kak-kak*. HABITAT: In native N America: rock coasts, islands, coastal lagoons, freshwater lakes and rivers.

5 STELLER'S SEA EAGLE (WHITE-SHOULDERED SEA EAGLE) *Haliaeetus pelagicus* 85–94cm FIELD NOTES: Juvenile lacks white shoulders, in flight from below wing shows whitish patch at base of primaries, white bands on median coverts and white axillaries, tail mainly white. SONG/CALL: A barking *kyow-kyow-kyow* and a stronger *kra kra kra kra* when involved in disputes. HABITAT: River valleys, river mouths and rocky coasts.

6 BATELEUR (BATELEUR EAGLE) *Terathopius ecaudatus* 60cm FIELD NOTES: Juvenile generally medium to dark brown, owl-like, brown tail a little longer than adult. SONG/CALL: A loud *yaaaow*, also a downslurred *wee weeye weeye weeye….* HABITAT: Open savanna, thornbush grassland and open woodland.

7 MOUNTAIN HAWK-EAGLE (HODGSON'S HAWK-EAGLE) *Spizaetus nipalensis orientalis* 67–86cm FIELD NOTES: Juvenile has plain buff underparts and underwing-coverts. SONG/CALL: A shrill whistle and a sharp, repeated *kee-kikik*. HABITAT: Mountain forests. RACES: *S. n. nipalensis* (fig 7b) Himalayas.

8 BOOTED EAGLE *Hieraaetus pennatus* 50–57cm FIELD NOTES: Some variation occurs in both morphs especially in colour of underwing-coverts which can be more rufous tinged. Juveniles much as respective adult morphs. SONG/CALL: A shrill, chattering *ki-ki-ki…*, also a buzzard-like *hiyaah*. HABITAT: Forests mixed with open areas such as scrub, grassland etc.

9 BONELLI'S EAGLE *Hieraaetus fasciatus* 65–72cm FIELD NOTES: Juvenile pale rufous, or whitish, below, underwing shows pale primaries, tipped black, also primary coverts tipped black, all coverts plain pale rufous or buff-white. SONG/CALL: Usually silent apart from a shrill *iuh* and a whistled *eeeoo* given during display. HABITAT: Dry hills and mountains with rocky gorges either open or sparse scrub or forest, after breeding visits open lowlands.

pale
phase

dark
phase

pale
phase

dark
phase

24 EAGLES

1 BLACK EAGLE (INDIAN or ASIAN BLACK EAGLE) *Ictinaetus malayensis* 69–81cm
FIELD NOTES: Often seen soaring low over forests. Juvenile has buff head, underparts and
underwing-coverts all streaked dark brown. SONG/CALL: A plaintive *kleeee-kee* or *hee-lee-leeuw*.
HABITAT: Mountain and hill forests.

2 LESSER SPOTTED EAGLE *Aquila pomarina* 57–64cm FIELD NOTES: Has a very rare
pale morph, similar to pale Spotted Eagle morph. Juvenile shows a small rufous nape patch
and extensive white tips to secondaries and secondary coverts, other coverts faintly tipped
white. In flight from above wings have a white trailing edge, a small white patch at base of
primaries and a white lower rump. SONG/CALL: A high-pitched, yelping *k-yeep* and during
display utters a whistled *wiiiik*. HABITAT: Lowland, moist, woods near meadows also dry
mountain forests.

3 SPOTTED EAGLE (GREATER SPOTTED EAGLE) *Aquila clanga* 59–69cm FIELD
NOTES: Pale morph very rare. Juvenile similar to Lesser Spotted Eagle, differs mainly by being
generally darker on head, underwing-coverts and upperwing-coverts, many individuals
have more distinct spotting on head, mantle and wing-coverts. SONG/CALL: A yelping *kyak*,
lower pitched than Lesser Spotted Eagle. HABITAT: Woodland with nearby wetlands, in non-
breeding season wetlands with or without trees.

4 STEPPE EAGLE *Aquila nipalensis* 67–87cm FIELD NOTES: Gape extends to rear of eye.
Juvenile underwing has a wide white band formed by white tips to all coverts. SONG/CALL: In
breeding season utters a barking *ow*, otherwise mainly silent. HABITAT: Breeds in steppe and
semi-desert in mountain or hill and lowland areas.

5 TAWNY EAGLE *Aquila rapax* 65–75cm FIELD NOTES: Gape extends to middle of eye.
General colour very variable, often appears scruffy, pale morphs usually show pale uppertail-
coverts. Juvenile similar to adult but usually paler and on upperwing has pale tips to coverts
and white trailing edge. SONG/CALL: In breeding season utters a repeated, barking *kowk*,
otherwise normally silent. HABITAT: Mountain forest and neighbouring plains and valleys.
RACES: *A. r. vindhiana* (Asian Tawny Eagle) (fig 5b) Himalayas.

6 IMPERIAL EAGLE (EASTERN IMPERIAL EAGLE) *Aquila heliaca* 72–84cm FIELD
NOTES: Juvenile greyer, with pale spots or streaks on head, mantle and wing-coverts,
underparts grey-buff streaked darker on breast. In flight wing pattern similar to juvenile
Tawny Eagle. SONG/CALL: A deep, barking *owk*. HABITAT: Upland and steppe forests, feeding
on open plains or cultivated areas.

7 SPANISH IMPERIAL EAGLE (ADALBERT'S EAGLE) *Aquila adalberti* 72–85cm
FIELD NOTES: Often considered conspecific with Imperial Eagle. Juvenile rufous-brown on
head, mantle, upperwing-coverts, underwing-coverts and underparts, all virtually unspotted.
SONG/CALL: As Imperial Eagle. HABITAT: Forests with undergrowth brush, away from areas of
human disturbance.

8 GOLDEN EAGLE *Aquila chrysaetos* 76–93cm FIELD NOTES: In flight juvenile shows
large white patches at base of primaries and white tail with black terminal band. SONG/CALL:
Generally silent, sometimes gives a fluty whistle in flight. HABITAT: Mountains, steppe and
locally marshes, preferring areas with sparse vegetation.

9 VERREAUX'S EAGLE (BLACK EAGLE) *Aquila verreauxii* 80–90cm FIELD NOTES: In
flight all ages show diagnostic 'pinched-in' effect at wing base. Juvenile, in flight from below,
has large pale patch at base of primaries and whitish belly and vent, above has rufous nape
and mantle and pale fringes to wing-coverts. SONG/CALL: Usually silent although various
calls described such as a *chorr-chorr-chorr* an upslurred *iiy-iii* and a melodious *keee-uup*.
HABITAT: Desert mountains, especially those inhabited by hyraxes, sometimes frequents more
vegetated mountains.

25 SERPENT EAGLE, SHORT-TOED EAGLE AND HARRIERS

1 CRESTED SERPENT EAGLE *Spilornis cheela* 50cm FIELD NOTES: Soars above forest canopy. Juvenile has wings and body white below, the latter with fine dark streaks the former with fine barring. Above, feathers fringed pale. SONG/CALL: In flight utters a shrill *kwee-kwee kwee-kwee kwee-kwee-kwee.* HABITAT: Open hill forests and plantations. RACES: *S. c. perplexus* (Ryukyu Serpent Eagle) (fig 1b) S Ryukyu Islands.

2 SHORT-TOED EAGLE (SHORT-TOED SNAKE EAGLE) *Cicaetus gallicus* 62–67cm FIELD NOTES: Variable, can lack hood or have hood more pronounced. Often hovers when searching for prey. SONG/CALL: A plaintive *weeo* or *weeooo*, also a gull-like *woh-woh-woh.* HABITAT: Varied, including open woodland, heathland, damp grassland and semi-desert.

3 MARSH HARRIER (WESTERN or EURASIAN MARSH HARRIER) *Circus aeruginosus* 48–56cm FIELD NOTES: Soars with wings held in shallow V. Juvenile similar to female but often lacks pale forewing, and more rarely lacks pale crown. SONG/CALL: In display gives a strident *whee-ah*, also a *chek-ek-ek-ek-ek* when alarmed. HABITAT: Breeds in reedbeds, also feeds over pastures, grasslands and saltmarsh, especially on passage or in winter quarters.

4 EASTERN MARSH HARRIER (SPOTTED MARSH HARRIER) *Circus spilonotus* 47–55cm FIELD NOTES: Actions and habits similar to Marsh Harrier. Juvenile similar to male Marsh Harrier but with darker secondaries and darker face. SONG/CALL: As Marsh Harrier? HABITAT: Similar to Marsh Harrier.

5 HEN HARRIER (NORTHERN HARRIER) *Circus cyaneus* 44–52cm FIELD NOTES: Soars with wings level or in a shallow V. Juvenile similar to adult female but with rufous tinged underparts, including underwing-coverts and a distinct dark crescent on ear-coverts. SONG/CALL: During display utters a *chuk-uk-uk-uk-uk*, when alarmed female gives a twittering *chit-it-it-it-it-et-it-et-it-et* and male a *chek-ek-ek-ek.* HABITAT: Breeds on moorland, heathland, grassland and young conifer plantations, also occurs on marshes, saltmarsh and open country.

6 PALLID HARRIER *Circus macrourus* 40–48cm FIELD NOTES: Soars with wings held in a shallow V. Juvenile has underparts, including underwing-coverts, plain rufous, and a pale collar between dark neck and ear-coverts. Upperparts much as adult female. SONG/CALL: In display gives a high-pitched *kik-kik-kik.* HABITAT: Open country and grasslands.

7 MONTAGU'S HARRIER *Circus pygargus* 43–47cm FIELD NOTES: Soars with wings held in a shallow V. Juvenile has underparts, including underwing-coverts, plain rufous. Upperparts similar to adult female. SONG/CALL: During display utters a rapid *kyeh-kyeh-kyeh*, in alarm gives a shrill *chekk-ekk-ekk-ekk.* HABITAT: Open grasslands, cereal crops, heathland, moorland, marshes and young conifer plantations.

8 PIED HARRIER *Circus melanoleucos* 41–49cm FIELD NOTES: Soars with wings held in a shallow V. Juvenile dark brown above with white uppertail-coverts. Underparts, including underwing-coverts, rufous streaked darker, face pattern much as adult female. SONG/CALL: Generally silent. Female recorded as uttering a *chak-chak-chak-chak-chack-chack* when alarmed. HABITAT: Open grasslands, marshes, paddyfields and stubble fields.

26 GOSHAWKS AND SPARROWHAWKS

1 DARK CHANTING GOSHAWK (CHANTING GOSHAWK) *Melierax metabates*
38–48cm FIELD NOTES: Juvenile generally earth-brown with pale barring from lower breast
to undertail-coverts and pale streaks on throat and upper breast. Tail greyish barred brown,
rump pale barred dark. Cere yellowish, legs yellowish-orange. SONG/CALL: In display gives a
fluting *wheeu-wheeu-wheeu…* or a *kleeee-yeu*. HABITAT: Open woodland, olive groves.

2 GABAR GOSHAWK *Micronisus gabar* 30–36cm (Vagrant) FIELD NOTES: There is a rare
dark morph, generally black with pale bars on underside of tail and flight-feathers. Juvenile
generally brown above, below whitish, throat and breast streaked, lower breast and flanks
barred, rufous-brown. Tail barred light and dark brown. SONG/CALL: In display utters a rapid
kik-kik-kik-kik. HABITAT: In native Africa: open woodland, thorn-scrub and acacia savanna.

3 GOSHAWK (NORTHERN GOSHAWK) *Accipiter gentilis* 48–62cm FIELD NOTES:
Female larger and browner-grey. Juvenile generally brown above, pale buff-white below with
dark streaking. SONG/CALL: Usually silent, when alarmed utters a loud *kyee-kyee-kyee*. HABITAT:
Forests and neighbouring countryside. RACES: *A. g. albidus* (fig 3b) NE Siberia to Kamchatka.

4 BESRA *Accipiter virgatus* 29–36cm FIELD NOTES: Typical sparrowhawk, perching
inconspicuously before giving chase to avian prey. Juvenile lacks rufous flanks otherwise
much as adult female. SONG/CALL: A rapid *tchew-tchew-tchew*. HABITAT: Forested hills and
mountains.

5 JAPANESE SPARROWHAWK (JAPANESE LESSER or ASIATIC SPARROWHAWK)
Accipiter gularis 29–34cm FIELD NOTES: Feeding habits as Besra. Juvenile has breast streaked,
not barred, otherwise much as adult female. SONG/CALL: Harsh cries. HABITAT: Mixed,
deciduous and coniferous forests.

6 SPARROWHAWK (EURASIAN or NORTHERN SPARROWHAWK) *Accipiter nisus*
28–38cm FIELD NOTES: Hunting technique as Besra. Juvenile very similar to adult female.
SONG/CALL: When alarmed gives a rapid *kew-kew-kew-kew-kew*. HABITAT: Various woodlands,
open areas with hedgerows also copses, orchards and large gardens.

**7 CHINESE SPARROWHAWK (HORSFIELD'S SPARROWHAWK, GREY FROG
HAWK)** *Accipiter soloensis* 27–35cm FIELD NOTES: Mainly catches prey on ground, e.g. frogs.
Female a little bigger, with breast showing indication of barring. Juvenile superficially like
juvenile Besra, but in flight shows plain underwing-coverts. SONG/CALL: A rapid, accelerating
piping that descends in pitch. HABITAT: Woodland, often near wetlands.

8 SHIKRA (LITTLE BANDED GOSHAWK) *Accipiter badius* 30–36cm FIELD NOTES:
Hunts from hidden perch, taking prey, mainly lizards or birds from trees or ground. Rarely
indulges in aerial chases. Juvenile generally brown above, pale buff below with dark streaking
and dark line down centre of throat. SONG/CALL: A piping *keeu-keeu-keeu* also a shrill *kewik*.
HABITAT: Forest edge, open woodland, orchards and gardens.

9 LEVANT SPARROWHAWK *Accipiter brevipes* 33–38cm FIELD NOTES: During migration
often seen in large flocks. Juvenile generally brown above, pale buff below blotched and
streaked dark with dark line down centre of throat. SONG/CALL: A shrill *kee-wik kee-wik kee-
wik*. HABITAT: Deciduous forests, wooded plains, copses and orchards.

27 BUZZARDS

1 WHITE-EYED BUZZARD (WHITE-EYED BUZZARD-EAGLE) *Butastur teesa* 36–43cm
FIELD NOTES: Sits for long periods on prominent perch from which it drops onto ground based
prey. Juvenile similar to adult but less strongly marked below, head paler with facial and
throat stripes narrower or lacking. SONG/CALL: A melancholic *pit-weer pit-weer*. HABITAT: Dry
open country with scattered trees and scrub.

2 GREY-FACED BUZZARD (FROG HAWK) *Butastur indicus* 46cm FIELD NOTES: Hunts
frogs, lizards and rodents, usually using dead tree as lookout site. Juvenile paler, breast has
dark streaking. SONG/CALL: A tremulous *chit-kwee*. HABITAT: Wooded areas with nearby open
country.

3 SWAINSON'S HAWK *Buteo swainsoni* 48–56cm (Vagrant) FIELD NOTES: Variable.
There is a dark morph in which underparts are generally dark brown, with dark rufous
underwing-coverts. Usually hunts from a perch, although recorded hawking insects in flight.
SONG/CALL: A whistling *kieeer*. HABITAT: In native America: prairies, woodland, steppe and
desert.

4 BUZZARD (COMMON BUZZARD) *Buteo buteo* 51–57cm FIELD NOTES: Variable.
Regularly perches in the open on telegraph poles, posts or trees, also spends long periods
soaring. Juvenile lacks broad dark band at tip of tail and is streaked below. SONG/CALL: A
mewing *peeeooo*. HABITAT: Woodland and woodland edge with adjacent open land, also
mountains. During winter often occurs in more open country. RACES: *B. b. vulpinus* (Steppe
Buzzard) (fig 4b) N and E Europe, C Asia. Socotra Buzzard, recorded as vagrant in the
Middle East, has not been allocated to any race but is regarded by some authorities as a full
species, it most resembles *B. b. vulpinus*. Not illustrated.

5 LONG-LEGGED BUZZARD *Buteo rufinus* 50–65cm FIELD NOTES: Variable. Three
main colour morphs, medium morph is generally rufous. Juvenile has tail finely barred. Often
sits on prominent perch for prolonged periods. SONG/CALL: A mellow *aaah*. HABITAT: Steppe,
semi-desert, open woodland of plains, hills and mountains.

6 UPLAND BUZZARD (MONGOLIAN BUZZARD) *Buteo hemilasius* 66–71cm FIELD
NOTES: Variable. Typical buzzard actions and habits, recorded as taking quite large prey i.e.
hares and snowcocks. SONG/CALL: A prolonged, nasal mewing. HABITAT: Open grassy areas,
mountain slopes and plateaux.

7 ROUGH-LEGGED BUZZARD (ROUH-LEGGED HAWK) *Buteo lagopus* 50–60cm
FIELD NOTES: Variable, some have pale belly, there is also a rare dark morph with black body
and underwing-coverts which is very similar to dark morph of Long-legged Buzzard. Juvenile
paler below with single, broad greyish tail tip. Actions and habits much as other buzzards.
SONG/CALL: A low-pitched, cat-like *peeeooo*. HABITAT: Tundra, mainly treeless but also wooded
areas in years of lemming and vole abundance. Winters in open country.

8 HONEY BUZZARD (EUROPEAN, EURASIAN or WESTERN HONEY BUZZARD)
Pernis apivorus 52–60cm FIELD NOTES: Very variable. Juvenile equally variable but underwing
and tail usually more evenly barred. Follows wasps to their nests in order to remove larvae
and wax. Often in large numbers on migration, especially around the Straits of Gibraltar and
the Bosporus. SONG/CALL: A clear, melancholy *whee-oo* or *whi-whee-oo*. HABITAT: Forests with
open areas, uses more open areas during migration.

9 CRESTED HONEY BUZZARD (ORIENTAL or EASTERN HONEY BUZZARD)
Pernis ptilorhyncus 52–68cm FIELD NOTES: Actions and habits very similar to Honey Buzzard.
Juvenile paler below with flight-feathers more barred, tail has fainter and thinner large bars.
SONG/CALL: A high-pitched *wee-wey-uho* or *weehey-weehey*. HABITAT: Forests, open woodland
on migration in more open areas.

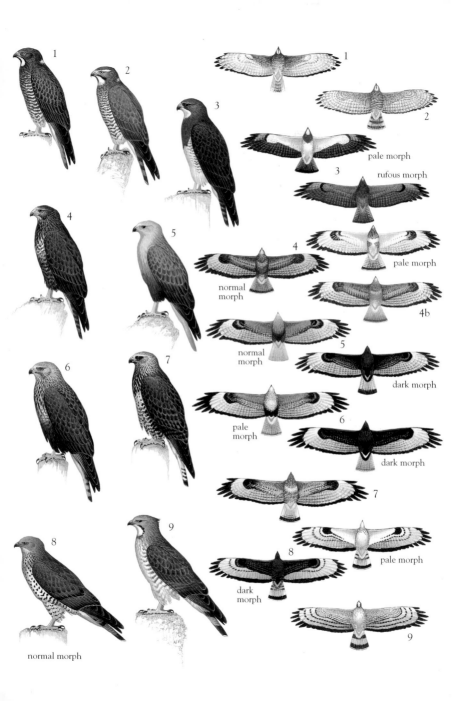

normal morph

pale morph

rufous morph

normal
morph

normal
morph

pale
morph

dark morph

dark morph

pale morph

dark
morph

pale morph

28 KITES AND OSPREY

1 BLACK-SHOULDERED KITE (BLACK-WINGED KITE) *Elanus caeruleus* 31–35cm
FIELD NOTES: Often hovers. In flight shows large black patch on upperwing-coverts. Grey upperparts of juvenile tinged brownish with pale fringes, breast and crown washed rusty.
SONG/CALL: Various interpretations noted, including a harsh *w-eeyah*, a sharp *kree-ak* and a piping *pii-uu*. HABITAT: Grasslands, semi-desert, open plains with scattered trees, also forest fringes.

2 AFRICAN SWALLOW-TAILED KITE (SCISSOR-TAILED or FORK-TAILED KITE)
Chelictinia riocourii 35cm (Vagrant) FIELD NOTES: Tern-like in flight, often hovers. Juvenile washed brown above with paler fringes, tail forked but lacking elongated outer feathers.
SONG/CALL: A high-pitched whinnying. HABITAT: In native Africa: arid and semi-arid savanna.

3 AMERICAN SWALLOW-TAILED KITE *Elanoides forficatus* 56–66cm (Vagrant)
FIELD NOTES: Agile in flight. Juvenile as adult but streaked on head and breast. SONG/CALL:
A *peat-peat-peat*, *klee-klee-klee* or soft whistling notes. HABITAT: In native N and S America:
tropical forests often in swampy and marsh areas.

4 BLACK KITE *Milvus migrans* 55–60cm FIELD NOTES: Flight action often appears 'loose'
with constant twisting of tail. Fork in tail often disappears when tail spread. Juvenile grey-
buff below streaked dark, pale fringes to mantle and wings and dark eye surround. SONG/CALL:
A whinnying *pee-errrr*. HABITAT: Open country, often near wet areas, with or without
woodland, also around human habitations. RACES: M. m. lineatus (Black-eared Kite) (fig 4b)
Siberia, Japan; M. m. aegyptius (Yellow-billed Kite) (fig 4c) Egypt, SW Arabia. Both races
often considered to be full species.

5 RED KITE *Milvus milvus* 60–66cm FIELD NOTES: Flight action much like Black Kite.
Juvenile very similar to adult although underparts paler. SONG/CALL: A mewing *peee-ooo*
followed by a drawn out *peee-oooo-eee-ooo-eee-ooo-eee-ooo....* HABITAT: Forests or scattered
woodlands with nearby grasslands or wetlands. RACES: M. m. fasciicauda (Cape Verde Kite)
(fig 5b) Cape Verde Islands. Often considered a full species.

6 BRAHMINY KITE (RED-BACKED KITE) *Haliastur indus* 45–51cm (Vagrant) FIELD
NOTES: Juvenile generally rusty-brown streaked paler, in flight from below can appear much
like adult Long-legged Buzzard but without dark carpal patches and dark trailing edge to
wing. SONG/CALL: A wheezy squeal. HABITAT: In native India and SE Asia: mainly wet areas,
inland and coastal.

7 OSPREY *Pandion haliatus* 55–63cm FIELD NOTES: Feeds on fish, hovering over water
before plunging feet first onto prey. Juvenile as adult but feathers of mantle and upperwing
fringed pale. SONG/CALL: In display gives a series of mournful whistles *yeelp-yeelp-yeelp....*
When alarmed utters a hoarse, sharp *kew-kew-kew-kew*. HABITAT: Freshwater lakes, rivers,
coastal lagoons and estuaries.

29 FALCONS

1 LESSER KESTREL *Falco naumanni* 29–32cm FIELD NOTES: A social bird, breeds in colonies and migrates and winters in flocks. White claws are diagnostic. Typically hovers less than Kestrel and in level flight wingbeats appear faster and more shallow. SONG/CALL: A rasping *chay-chay-chay* given at breeding colonies or roosts, also a Kestrel-like *keerrrl* and a *kikikik* when disturbed. HABITAT: Buildings, ruins and cliffs in dry, usually open, areas also in and around towns.

2 KESTREL (COMMON or EURASIAN KESTREL) *Falco tinnunclus* 31–37cm FIELD NOTES: Frequently hovers or uses prominent perches, such as telegraph poles when seeking prey. Claws black. SONG/CALL: A shrill *kee-kee-kee-kee* and a trilling *vriii*. HABITAT: Almost any type of open country with scattered trees, also inland and coastal cliffs, villages, towns and cities. Has adapted to motorways, major roads and railways, hunting on embankments and verges, using bridges for breeding.

3 AMERICAN KESTREL *Falco sparverius* 21–31cm (Vagrant) FIELD NOTES: Head pattern diagnostic. Behaviour much as Kestrel although flight more rapid. SONG/CALL: A shrill *killy-killy-killy*. HABITAT: In native N and S America: wide variety, much as Kestrel.

4 RED-NECKED FALCON (RED-HEADED MERLIN or FALCON) *Falco chicquera* 30–36cm FIELD NOTES: Often hunts in pairs with a dashing, low flight. SONG/CALL: Shrill, querulous screaming, used to warn off intruders from breeding site. HABITAT: Open country with scattered trees.

5 RED-FOOTED FALCON (WESTERN RED-FOOTED FALCON) *Falco vespertinus* 28–31cm FIELD NOTES: Highly manoeuvrable flight in pursuit of flying insects. Sometimes hovers. Colonial breeder. Juvenile looks quite similar to female Amur Falcon, but underparts buff streaked dark, undertail white and fringes of upperparts rufous, crown pale brown streaked dark. SONG/CALL: A chattering *kekekekeke…* female gives a lower, slower *kwee-kwee-kwee….* HABITAT: Open country with patches of trees including orchards, also in villages and towns.

6 AMUR FALCON (EASTERN or MANCHURIAN RED-FOOTED FALCON) *Falco amurensis* 28–30cm FIELD NOTES: Habits similar to Red-footed Falcon. Juvenile similar to juvenile Red-footed Falcon but crown darker. SONG/CALL: Shrill Kestrel-like cries. HABITAT: Open wooded areas and woodland margins.

7 MERLIN *Falco columbarius aesalon* 25–30cm FIELD NOTES: When pursuing prey flight is often dashing and slightly undulating with twists and turns. SONG/CALL: Around breeding site male utters a chattering *kikikikiki…* female call similar but lower and slower. HABITAT: Various, such as moorland, tundra, shrubby steppe and taiga bog even more varied in winter including coastal areas. RACES: *F. c. pallidus* (fig 7b) S Urals, N and E Kazakhstan.

8 SOOTY FALCON *Falco concolor* 33–36cm FIELD NOTES: Hunting flight energetic with fast glides and sudden stoops. Juvenile like pale morph Eleonora's Falcon (plate 30) but face buff and underparts paler. SONG/CALL: At nest site gives a loud *keee-keee-keee…* otherwise generally silent. HABITAT: Low mountains and hills in desert areas and small unvegetated islands.

30 FALCONS

1 HOBBY (EURASIAN or NORTHERN HOBBY) *Falco subbuteo* 30–36cm FIELD NOTES: Fast acrobatic flier, catches prey, mainly insects and small birds, in flight. Juvenile much as adult but background colour of underparts, including thighs and undertail-coverts, buff. SONG/CALL: A rapid *kew-kew-kew-kew…*. HABITAT: Wooded steppe, open areas with stands of trees, also woodland edge.

2 ELEONORA'S FALCON *Falco eleonorae* 36–40cm FIELD NOTES: Fast acrobatic flier. Colonial nester. Juvenile has underwing-coverts contrasting to the flight-feathers unlike those of the very similarly plumaged juvenile Hobby. SONG/CALL: In flight gives a nasal *kyeh-kyeh-kyeh-kyah*. HABITAT: Islands and coastal cliffs.

3 LANNER (LANNER FALCON) *Falco biarmicus* 40–50cm FIELD NOTES: Hunts mainly by high-speed aerial chase, attacks often carried out by a pair of birds. Juvenile has bold dark streaking on breast, belly and flanks. SONG/CALL: A rapid *kre-kre-kre…* and a plaintive *ueeh*. HABITAT: Variable, forested mountains to dry open desert. RACES: *F. b. tanypterus* Middle East and NE Africa, paler on back and crown. Not illustrated.

4 SAKER (SAKER FALCON) *Falco cherrug* 45–55cm FIELD NOTES: Usually hunts at low level, most prey taken on the ground, predominantly rodents. Occasionally hovers. Juvenile is darker above and has heavier spotting below. SONG/CALL: A harsh *kek-kek-kek…*. HABITAT: Steppe, wooded steppe, open woodland and cliffs. RACES: Form '*altaicus*' (Altai Falcon) (fig 4b) Altai Mountains, more scientific evidence is needed before it is decided if this is a sub-species of Saker or a 'true' species.

5 LAGGER FALCON *Falco jugger* 43–46cm FIELD NOTES: Prey caught in mid-air and on ground. Juvenile generally dark brown above with heavy dark streaking below, throat pale. SONG/CALL: A shrill *whi-ee-ee*. HABITAT: Arid or semi-arid open country, cultivated areas and towns and villages.

6 GYR FALCON (GYRFALCON) *Falco rusticolus* 48–60cm FIELD NOTES: Mainly hunts at low level, prey usually taken on the ground. All morphs tend to intergrade with each other. Juveniles generally darker above and more strongly streaked below. SONG/CALL: A harsh *kak-kak-kak…*. HABITAT: Breeds in tundra and taiga, also occurs in cultivated and coastal areas during non-breeding season.

7 PEREGRINE (PEREGRINE FALCON) *Falco peregrinus* 36–48cm FIELD NOTES: Prey usually captured and killed in mid-air following high-speed pursuit and stoop. Juvenile brown above with dark streaking below, head pattern as adult but browner. SONG/CALL: A loud *ka-yak ka-yak ka-yak…* or when alarmed a shrill *kek-kek-kek…*. HABITAT: Coastal, mountain and lowland cliffs, city buildings, also on ground in taiga bogs. In winter occurs in open country, wetlands and estuaries.

8 BARBARY FALCON *Falco peregrinoides* 35–42cm FIELD NOTES: Actions and habits much as Peregrine, which is often regarded as conspecific. Juvenile has browner upperparts and is dark streaked below. SONG/CALL: A scolding *kek-kek-kek…*. HABITAT: Semi-desert mountains, hills and sea cliffs, also found in adjacent plains or valleys.

1

2
pale morph
dark morph

1

pale morph

2

dark morph

3

4

4b

3

4

5

5

dark morph

6

medium morph

6
dark morph

medium morph

7

8

pale morph

6
pale morph

7

8

31 TRAGOPANS, MONALS AND PHEASANTS

1 BLOOD PHEASANT *Ithaginis cruentus* Male 44–48cm, Female 39–42cm FIELD NOTES: Usually encountered in small parties. Often tame, rarely flies. SONG/CALL: A repeated *chuck* or *chic* a high-pitched, repetitive *see* and when maintaining contact gives a loud *sree-cheeu-cheeu-cheeu* or a high trill. HABITAT: High-altitude rhododendron scrub, also in pine, bamboo and juniper forests. Resorts to lower forests during bad winters. RACES: *I. c. geoffroyi* (fig 1b) SE Tibet; *I. c. kuseri* (fig 1c) SE Tibet.

2 WESTERN TRAGOPAN (BLACK-HEADED TRAGOPAN) *Tragopan melanocephala* Male 68–73cm, Female 60cm FIELD NOTES: Wary and skulking. During display inflates bare throat and horns. SONG/CALL: A bleating, repeated *khuwah*, said to sound like a lost goat, lamb or child. In alarm gives a similar sounding *waa waa waa*. HABITAT: Mid-altitude, oak dominated forests, descends to lower altitudes in winter.

3 SATYR TRAGOPAN (CRIMSON TRAGOPAN) *Tragopan satyr* Male 67–72cm, Female 58cm FIELD NOTES: Very wary and skulking. Often disappears into tree branches when alarmed. During display inflates bare throat and horns. SONG/CALL: A wailing *wah waah oo-ah oo-aaaaa* repeated a dozen or so times. In alarm gives a *wak wak wak*. HABITAT: High-altitude oak forests with dense bamboo and rhododendron understorey.

4 BLYTH'S TRAGOPAN (GREY-BELLIED TRAGOPAN) *Tragopan blythii* Male 65–70cm, Female 58cm FIELD NOTES: Little-known, actions and habits probably much as other of the genus. SONG/CALL: During display gives a *gock gock gock* and a loud repeated moaning *ohh-ohhah-ohaah ohaaah ohaaaha ohaaaha ohaaaha*. HABITAT: Densely wooded valleys and hillsides, up to 3300m.

5 TEMMINCK'S TRAGOPAN (CRIMSON-BELLIED TRAGOPAN) *Tragopan temminckii* Male 64cm, Female 58cm FIELD NOTES: Wary. Often feeds in trees. During spectacular display inflates bare throat, showing off dark blue oval, spotted pale blue, surrounded by pale blue rim with red patches. SONG/CALL: During breeding season gives an eerie *woh – woah – woah – woah - waah - waah - waah - waah - griiiik*. HABITAT: Rhododendron and bamboo in evergreen and mixed forests, up to 3600m.

6 KOKLASS PHEASANT (KOKLAS) *Pucrasia macrolopha xanthospila* Male 56–64cm, Female 52–56cm FIELD NOTES: Wary. Feeds early or late. Roosts in trees. SONG/CALL: A loud *kok-kok-kok ko-kras* or similar. When alarmed male gives a harsh *kwak kwak kwak* and female a musical *qui-quik qui-quik qui-quik*. HABITAT: Coniferous and mixed forests, with thick understorey, up to 4000m. RACES: *P. m. nipalensis* (fig 6b) W Himalayas.

7 HIMALAYAN MONAL (IMPEYAN PHEASANT, IMPERIAN MONAL) *Lophophorus impejanus* 64–72cm FIELD NOTES: Terrestrial feeder, singly or in small parties. SONG/CALL: A *kur-lieu* or *kleeh-wick*, alarm note very similar. HABITAT: Coniferous and mixed forest with thick understorey, up to 4350m.

8 SCLATER'S MONAL (CRESTLESS MONAL) *Lophophorus sclateri* 64–68cm FIELD NOTES: Little-recorded, probably similar to Himalayan Monal. SONG/CALL: A loud *go-li*, also a plaintive cry when alarmed. HABITAT: Coniferous forest with bamboo understorey also subalpine rhododendron scrub, up to 4200m.

9 CHINESE MONAL *Lophophorus lhuysii* 75–80cm FIELD NOTES: Action and habits as others of the genus. SONG/CALL: A repeated *guli* and a whistled *guo-guo-guo* uttered every few minutes, starting high then dropping before fading to an end. When alarmed gives a series of low *gee* notes. HABITAT: Alpine and subalpine rocky meadows, from 3000–4900m.

10 KALIJ PHEASANT (KALIJ) *Lophura leucomelanos* Male 63–74cm, Female 50–60cm FIELD NOTES: Wary. Usually in small groups feeding early and late. Roosts in trees. SONG/CALL: During breeding gives a loud chuckle and drums wings against body. Uses a *kurr-kurr-kurrchi-kurr* to keep contact, and in alarm gives a *koorchi koorchi* or *whoop-keet-keet*. HABITAT: Temperate forests from 2100–3200m.

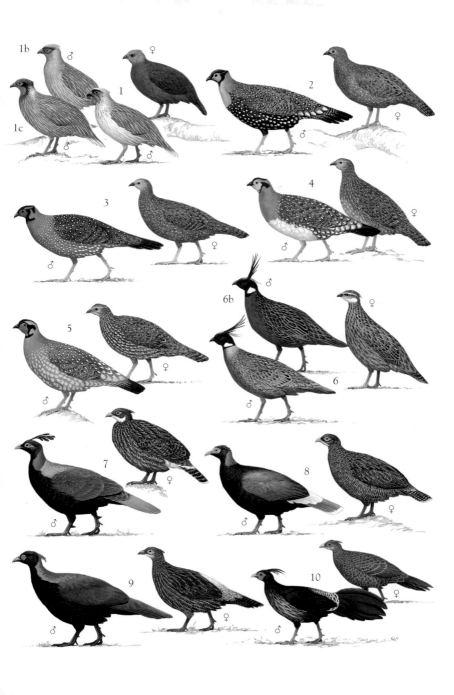

32 PARTRIDGES

1 CHUKAR (CHUKAR PARTRIDGE) *Alectoris chukar* 32–34cm FIELD NOTES: Usually in small parties, in cold winters has been encountered in vast flocks. When disturbed generally runs away. Some southern races have upperparts paler and greyer. SONG/CALL: Typically a *chuck chuck chuck* or *chuck chuck chuck chuckARR chuckARR chuckARR*, when flushed often gives a repeated *wit-too-wittoo-wittoo*. HABITAT: Mountain slopes with sparse cover, semi-arid hills, desert plains, sand dunes and forest clearings.

2 PRZEVALSKI'S PARTRIDGE (RUSTY-NECKLACED PARTRIDGE) *Alectoris magna* 36–38cm FIELD NOTES: Non-breeding season flocks average about 30, small summer parties are made up of unmated males. Sometimes considered to be a race of Chukar. SONG/CALL: A repeated *ga ga ga gela gela gela*. When flushed gives *fei-ji fei-ji fei-ji* or *ja ja ja*. When alarmed at the nest utters a whistling *dirdir dirdir dirdir*. HABITAT: Sparsely vegetated ravines and canyons of rocky mountain slopes and rugged plateaux.

3 ROCK PARTRIDGE *Alectoris graeca* 32–35cm FIELD NOTES: Parties usually number no more than 15 birds, sometimes larger during severe winter weather. Some hybridisation takes place in NE Greece with Chukar and SE France with Red-legged Partridge. SONG/CALL: A rapidly repeated, grating *chitti-ti-tok chitti-ti-tok chitti-ti-tok*. When flushed gives a *wittoo-wittoo-witoo*. HABITAT: Subalpine zone of mountains, rocky and grassy hillsides.

4 RED-LEGGED PARTRIDGE (FRENCH PARTRIDGE) *Alectoris rufa* 32–34cm FIELD NOTES: Usually occurs in small parties of 6–10 birds, larger groups have been recorded in winter. Tends to run away when disturbed. SONG/CALL: A harsh, grating *go-CHAK-CHAK go-CHAK-CHAK go-CHAK-CHAK* and a *chuk-chuk-chukAR-CHUKAR*. When disturbed gives a squeaky *cheeragh cheeragh cheeragh*. HABITAT: Dry open country, farmland, grassy hillsides and locally in mountains in south of range.

5 BARBARY PARTRIDGE *Alectoris barbara* 32–34cm FIELD NOTES: Usually occurs in pairs or small groups. Loath to fly, generally runs rapidly away when disturbed. SONG/CALL: A repeated *kutchuk kutchuk* with the odd *chukor* added. When flushed gives a squealing *kree-ah kree-ah* or a loud *chuckachew chew-chew*. HABITAT: Bushy cover of desert wadis, hillsides and mountain sides, also orchards, coastal dunes and woodland clearings.

6 PHILBY'S PARTRIDGE (PHILBY'S ROCK PARTRIDGE) *Alectoris philbyi* 34cm FIELD NOTES: Occurs in pairs or small parties. Little-studied. SONG/CALL: A repeated *chuk chuk-a-chuk-kar* or *chuk chuk chuk kar*. When disturbed gives a *chork chork chork* also a squealing *chuk-a-chuk-a-chuk* and a babbling *chuk-a-chuk-oo*. HABITAT: Mountain plateaux and barren rocky slopes.

7 ARABIAN PARTRIDGE (ARABIAN RED-LEGGED PARTRIDGE) *Alectoris melanocephala* 39cm FIELD NOTES: Generally keeps to cover, in pairs or parties of up to 15. Mostly active in early morning and evening when venturing to drinking sources. SONG/CALL: An accelerating *kok kok kok kok kok chok-chok-chok-chok*, also a rapid *chuck-chuck-chuck-chuck-chuk*. When disturbed gives a *kerkow-kerkow-kerkow*. HABITAT: Variable, including mountain slopes, rocky hillsides, sandy or stony plains with scattered bushes or trees.

8 SEE-SEE PARTRIDGE *Ammoperdix griseogularis* 24cm FIELD NOTES: Occurs in small parties, although larger parties gather at drinking sites. When approached tends to run rather than fly. SONG/CALL: A far-carrying, repeated *wheet-div* or *hoe-it*. When alarmed rapid, piping *bwuit-bwuit-bwuit*. HABITAT: Barren stony hillsides, open stony land in semi-desert, also wadis.

9 SAND PARTRIDGE *Ammoperdix heyi* 22–25cm FIELD NOTES: Generally in parties of up to 10, although larger parties occur at drinking sites. When approached crouches before running, rather than flying, away. SONG/CALL: A yelping *kew-kew-kew* or *watcha-watcha-watcha*, also a loud *quip* or *qu-ip*. When flushed utters an explosive *wuit-wuit-wuit*. HABITAT: Rocky hillsides, ravines and wadis generally with nearby water. RACES: *A. h. intermedia* (fig 9b) W Saudi Arabia, Yemen and Oman.

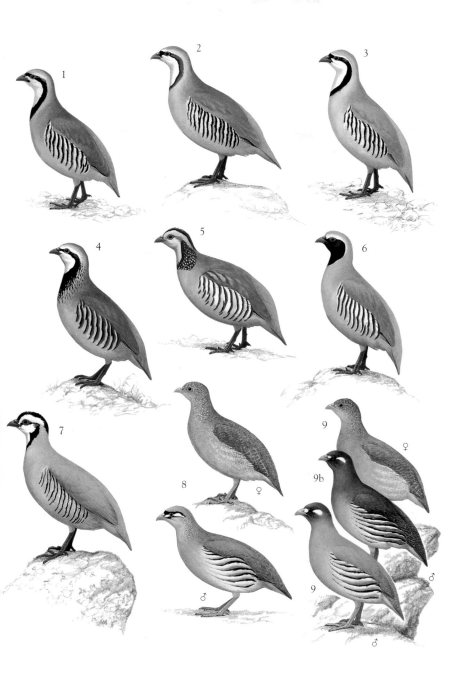

33 PARTRIDGES, HILL PARTRIDGE, BAMBOO PARTRIDGE AND FRANCOLINS

1 BLACK FRANCOLIN *Francolinus francolinus* 33–36cm FIELD NOTES: Usually in pairs or family parties. Very shy, keeps to cover except when 'singing'. Reluctant to fly. Juvenile like dull version of female, underparts weakly streaked and barred on flanks. SONG/CALL: Generally silent apart from a strident, grating *clip gek-ge-gek gek-ge-gek* advertising call. HABITAT: Lowland cultivated areas and grassland with bushy cover, lake edges with scrub and reeds. RACES: *F. f. bogdanovi* (fig 1b) S Iran and Afghanistan.

2 GREY FRANCOLIN *Francolinus pondicerianus mecranensis* 30–32cm FIELD NOTES: Usually in small parties. When approached tends to run rapidly for cover rather than fly. Occasionally perches in bushes mainly to 'sing' and roost. Juvenile duller, lacks dark throat border. SONG/CALL: A loud *kat-ee-la kat-ee-la kat-ee-la* usually preceded by up four sharp, rising notes. When alarmed utters a high *kirr-kirr*. HABITAT: Thorn scrub, dry plains, semi-desert and scrubby cultivation.

3 DOUBLE-SPURRED FRANCOLIN *Francolinus bicalcaratus ayesha* 30–33cm FIELD NOTES: Generally in pairs or small parties. Difficult to flush, preferring to run into deep cover rather than fly. Roosts in trees. Juvenile duller with black barring on flanks. SONG/CALL: A deep, grating *krrak krrak krrak krrak krrak....* HABITAT: Open country with scrub and bush cover also scrubby woodland, cultivation and streamsides.

4 TIBETAN PARTRIDGE *Perdix hodgsoniae* 28–31cm FIELD NOTES: In non-breeding season occurs in groups of 10–15. Usually runs for cover rather than fly. Juvenile is dull grey above with dark vermiculations, below dull buff with dark barring and white shaft streaks, head shows a dull shadow of adult head pattern. SONG/CALL: A rattling *scherrrrreck-scherrrrreck*. When flushed utters a shrill *chee chee chee chee chee*. HABITAT: Rocky mountain slopes and alpine meadows with scrub, descends to lower levels in winter.

5 PARTRIDGE (GREY PARTRIDGE) *Perdix perdix* 29–31cm FIELD NOTES: Apart from breeding season usually occurs in parties of 5–15. Juvenile lacks adult patterning, drab brown above with dark mottling and white shaft streaks, below dull buff with white shaft streaks. SONG/CALL: A harsh, metallic *kiERRR R-R-R-ik* often likened to the squeak when opening a rusty gate. When flushed gives a rapid *skip skip kip kip kip-ip-ip-ip*. HABITAT: Farmland, open grassland, semi-desert with scrub and locally in montane meadows.

6 DAURIAN PARTRIDGE (MONGOLIAN or BEARDED PARTRIDGE) *Perdix dauurica* 28–30cm FIELD NOTES: During non-breeding season occurs in parties of 15–30 with much larger numbers recorded in winter. Habits little-recorded, presumed as Partridge. SONG/CALL: As Partridge. HABITAT: Very varied including lightly wooded areas adjoining grassland, wooded steppe, shrubby meadows, riverine scrub and farmsteads.

7 HILL PARTRIDGE (COMMON or NECKLACED HILL-PARTRIDGE) *Arborophila torqueola* 28-30cm FIELD NOTES: Feeds in forest leaf litter in groups of 5–10. Juvenile like dull version of adult but lacks rufous underpart markings. SONG/CALL: A mournful, repeated *pooo* or *pheaw* followed by a rising 3–6 double whistles *do-eat do-eat do-eat do-eat*. Also duets, female utters a *kwikwikwikwikwik* while male joins with a series of *do-eat* calls. HABITAT: Montane oak forest mixed with laurel and rhododendron.

8 CHINESE BAMBOO PARTRIDGE *Bambusicola thoracica* 30–32cm FIELD NOTES: Occurs in pairs or groups of up to 20 with larger groups recorded in winter. Juvenile brown backed with pale shaft streaks, underparts dull ochre with pale shaft streaks, head lacks bright colours of adult, face and crown brown, supercilium pale greyish-buff. SONG/CALL: A loud *gi-gi-gi-gi-gi- gigeroi-gigeroi* also a dueted *killl-killy e-put-kwai*, in non-breeding season utters a *sih-mo-kuai sih-mo-kuai* often written as *people pray people pray*. HABITAT: Dense bushes, not necessarily bamboo, dry bush areas and parks. RACES: *B. t. sonorivox* (fig 8b) introduced in Japan.

34 GROUSE, PTARMIGAN AND CAPERCAILLIE

1 SIBERIAN GROUSE (SIBERIAN SPRUCE or SHARP-WINGED GROUSE) *Falcipennis falcipennis* 38–43cm FIELD NOTES: Can be very tame. Feeds on ground and in trees. In display male cocks and fans tail while stretching neck upwards. SONG/CALL: Displaying male gives a cooing-whistle, followed by a clicking before leaping into the air. HABITAT: Coniferous forests also mixed forests with dense understorey.

2 HAZEL GROUSE (HAZELHEN) *Bonasa bonasia* 35–40cm FIELD NOTES: Feeds on the ground but often perches in trees. Some birds can be more brown tinged. In flight shows black band at end of tail. SONG/CALL: A repeated, high, penetrating *seeeeeeee-seee-see....* When alarmed gives a *plit plit* or *pitt pitt pitt.* HABITAT: Mixed conifer and deciduous forest.

3 SEVERTSOV'S GROUSE (SEVERTSOV'S or BLACK-BRESTED HAZEL GROUSE, CHINESE GROUSE) *Bonasa sewerzowi* 34cm FIELD NOTES: Feeds on the ground and in trees. In flight shows black bands on tail. SONG/CALL: Little-known. A hoarse *en er en er en er...* given by male during a confrontation with another male, and a *ze ze ze-dackdack* uttered by an alarmed female are the only records. HABITAT: Montane conifer forests with thickets of birch or willow.

4 WILLOW GROUSE (WILLOW PTARMIGAN) *Lagopus lagopus* 37–42cm FIELD NOTES: In flight has striking white wings. During spring both sexes have patches of white on mantle. SONG/CALL: A nasal, guttural *go-bak go-back go-back ak-ak-ak* and an accelerating *ko-ko-ko-ko-ko-kokokokokokrrr.* During display-flight gives an *aa* followed by a *ka-ka-ka-ka-ka...* and on landing a *kohWA-kohWA-kohWA.* HABITAT: Open tundra, moorland and heathland. RACES: *L. l. scoticus* (Red Grouse) (fig 4b) British Isles.

5 PTARMIGAN (ROCK PTARMIGAN) *Lagopus muta* 34–36cm FIELD NOTES: In flight has striking white wings. During spring both sexes show white patches on mantle. SONG/CALL: A dry *ARR-arr-kakarr* a grating *kar-r-rk* and during display-flight utters a *AA-ka-ka* followed by *ka-ka-ka* with a *kwa-kwa* on landing. HABITAT: Rocky areas on mountains and tundra.

6 BLACK GROUSE (BLACKCOCK: male GREYHEN: female) *Tetrao tetrix* Male 60cm, Female 45cm FIELD NOTES: In normal stance tail long with outer feathers curved outwards, lyre-shaped. In flight shows whitish underwing-coverts. Groups of males perform display in a 'lek'. SONG/CALL: During display gives a low bubbling crooning interspersed with sneezed *choo-EESH.* Various warning sounds recorded such as a *guck guck* and a *tuett-tuett-tuett....* HABITAT: Forest edge, open woodland with clearings, moorland and heathland with tree cover.

7 CAUCASIAN BLACK GROUSE (CAUCASIAN GROUSE or BLACKCOCK) *Tetrao mlokosiewiczi* Male 50–55cm, Female 37–42cm FIELD NOTES: In flight shows white underwing-coverts. Groups of males perform display in a 'lek'. SONG/CALL: Generally silent. Sounds from 'lekking' birds are made by wingbeats and bill snapping. HABITAT: Low scrub on alpine meadows and slopes, above tree-line.

8 BLACK-BILLED CAPERCAILLIE (SMALL-BILLED, SPOTTED, ROCK or SIBERIAN CAPERCAILLIE) *Tetrao parvirostri* Male 90–97cm, Female 69–75cm FIELD NOTES: Actions and habits similar to Capercaillie. SONG/CALL: A *tack-tack-tack* rolling into a climatic *tr-r-rack.* HABITAT: Mainly larch woods in mountains and plains.

9 CAPERCAILLIE (WESTERN or EURASIAN CAPERCAILLIE) *Tetrao urogallus* Male 74–90cm, Female 54–63cm FIELD NOTES: Wary. During display male raises and fans tail while stretching neck upwards. SONG/CALL: When agitated utters a harsh *koor KRERK koroor.* During display male makes various knocking sounds which lead into a short 'drum-roll' followed by a loud 'pop' and harsh wheezes, female gives a chuckling *kok-kok.* HABITAT: Mature coniferous and mixed forests with peaty clearings. RACES: *T. u. taczanowskii* (fig 9b) C Siberia, south to the Altai range and NW Mongolia.

35 GUINEAFOWL, TURKEY, SNOW PARTRIDGE, MONAL PARTRIDGES AND SNOWCOCKS

1 HELMETED GUINEAFOWL *Numida meleagris sabyi* 60–65cm FIELD NOTES: Very sociable, often recorded in massive numbers at waterholes. Roosts in trees. SONG/CALL: A loud, raucous *kek-kek-kek-kek-kek-kek-kek*. Female utters a far-carrying *ka-bak*. Flocks give a *chenk-chenk-chenk* contact call, also a plaintive *CHER-cheeng CHER-cheeng*. HABITAT: Scrubby grassland. Found on partly wooded hillsides in Cape Verde Islands.

2 WILD TURKEY *Meleagris gallopavo* Male 100–125cm, Female 76–95cm FIELD NOTES: Unmistakable. Introduced, but probably not fully established, in Austria and Germany. SONG/CALL: Well-known 'gobbling' also a liquid *cluk-cluck*, a yelping *keeow keeow keeow* and a *putt* or *perk* when alarmed. HABITAT: Deciduous and mixed woodland with extensive clearings.

3 SNOW PARTRIDGE *Lerwa lerwa* 38–40cm FIELD NOTES: Approachable. Occurs in pairs or small groups, with larger groups of 20–30 in winter. SONG/CALL: A clear *jiju jiju jiju* that gradually quickens and rises in pitch, also a *huei huei* when flushed. HABITAT: Grassy mountain slopes, above tree-line, with scattered shrub interspersed with scree and snow patches, 3000–5500m.

4 VERREAUX'S MONAL PARTRIDGE (CHESTNUT-THROATED PARTRIDGE) *Tetraophasis obscurus* 48cm FIELD NOTES: Walks off with tail cocked when disturbed. Little else recorded. SONG/CALL: Gives a 'loud cry' when flushed otherwise calls reported to be similar to Szechenyi's Monal Partridge. HABITAT: Mountains, on rocky slopes and in juniper and rhododendron scrub, meadows and ravines, 3000–4100m.

5 SZECHENYI'S MONAL PARTRIDGE (BUFF-THROATED PARTRIDGE) *Tetraophasis szechenyii* 50cm FIELD NOTES: In non-breeding season usually encountered in family parties of 4–12, although larger groups are recorded. When disturbed tends to 'freeze' or fly into forest cover, hiding in a tree until danger has passed. SONG/CALL: Loud, far-carrying 2–3 note cackling interspersed with monosyllabic grating notes. HABITAT: In coniferous, mixed coniferous, oak and rhododendron forest, also on rocky slopes with grass and scrub above the tree-line, 3200–4875m.

6 CASPIAN SNOWCOCK *Tetraogallus caspius* 58–62cm FIELD NOTES: Behaviour as Caucasian Snowcock. SONG/CALL: A rising *oou-wee-eee-eee-et* the last note very high-pitched. When alarmed gives a *chok-chok-chok*. HABITAT: Above tree-line on mountain slopes with crags, ravines and open grassy areas, above 1800m.

7 CAUCASIAN SNOWCOCK *Tetraogallus caucasicus* 52–56cm FIELD NOTES: Shy and wary. Occurs in pairs or small parties of 3–9. Often walks with tail raised and undertail-coverts fluffed-out. SONG/CALL: A mellow, curlew-like *ooolee-oooweeyuh*, also a low-pitched *pok-pok-pok-pok-pok* uttered by feeding parties or when flushed. HABITAT: Grassy slopes with snow patches, rocky outcrops with ravines on mountains above the tree-line, 1800–4000m.

8 ALTAI SNOWCOCK *Tetraogallus altaicus* 58cm FIELD NOTES: Habits similar to Caucasian Snowcock. Very large groups have been recorded during harsh winters. SONG/CALL: Not well documented, said to be like others of the group although perhaps more raucous than Himalayan Snowcock. HABITAT: Open montane areas above the tree-line including semi-desert, steppe and alpine meadows, 2000–3600m.

9 TIBETAN SNOWCOCK *Tetraogallus tibetanus* 50–56cm FIELD NOTES: Habits much as Caucasian Snowcock. SONG/CALL: Main breeding season call is a croaking *gu-gu-gu-gu*. Also recorded is a chuckling *chuck-aa-chuck-aa-chuck-chuck-chee-da da-da*. HABITAT: High alpine pastures, bare or grassy mountain slopes up to the snow-line, mainly 5000–6000m.

10 HIMALAYAN SNOWCOCK *Tetraogallus himalayensis* 58–62cm FIELD NOTES: Behaviour similar to Caucasian Snowcock. SONG/CALL: A high-pitched *shi-er shi-er* and a deeper *wai-wain-guar-guar*. When disturbed utters an accelerating *kuk kuk kuk....* HABITAT: Sparsely vegetated scree or grassy patches among or below crags on mountain slopes between scrub and snow-line, 3500–6000m.

36 PHEASANTS

1 **WHITE EARED-PHEASANT** *Crossoptilon crossoptilon* 86–96cm FIELD NOTES: Feeds on the ground in small groups, larger groups of 30 or so are formed in winter. SONG/CALL: A far-carrying, grating *gag gag gagerah gagerah gagerah gagerah*. HABITAT: Subalpine birch, rhododendron, coniferous and mixed forests in winter, from 2800–4300m.

2 **TIBETAN EARED-PHEASANT (HARMAN'S or ELWES'S EARED-PHEASANT)** *Crossoptilon harmani* 75–85cm FIELD NOTES: Usually found in small parties feeding on the ground. Sometimes considered a race of White-eared Pheasant. SONG/CALL: Very similar to White-eared Peasant. HABITAT: Subalpine meadows, alpine scrub and clearings in conifer and mixed forests, from 3000–5000m.

3 **BROWN EARED-PHEASANT (MANCHURIAN EARED-PHEASANT)** *Crossoptilon mantchuricum* 96–100cm FIELD NOTES: Rare. Feeds on the ground in small groups, with larger groups of up to 30 in winter. SONG/CALL: A deep *gu-gu-gu-gu* and a *gu-ji-gu-ji* when foraging. HABITAT: Deciduous and mixed conifer forests with shrubby understorey, from 1100–2600m.

4 **BLUE EARED-PHEASANT (PALLAS'S or MONGOLIAN EARED-PHEASANT)** *Crossoptilon auritum* 96cm FIELD NOTES: Feeds on the ground in small groups with larger groups of 50–60 in winter. SONG/CALL: A loud, hoarse *ka ka…la*, *krip krraah krraah* or *wu wu wu*. When alarmed utters a *ziwo-ge ziwo-ge*. HABITAT: Coniferous and mixed forests, juniper scrub and alpine meadows, from 2700–4400m.

5 **CHEER PHEASANT (CHIR or WALLICH'S PHEASANT)** *Catreus wallichii* Male 90–118cm, Female 61–76cm FIELD NOTES: Feeds on ground usually close to cover. Roosts on rocky outcrops or trees. SONG/CALL: A grating, accelerating *chir-a-pir chir-a-pir chir chir chirwa chirwa*, also a series of high whistles interspersed with harsh staccato and short *chut* notes. HABITAT: Rocky and grassy hillsides with scrub covering.

6 **COPPER PHEASANT (SOEMMERRING'S PHEASANT)** *Syrmaticus soemmerringii* Male 87–136cm, Female 51–54cm FIELD NOTES: Usually forages in deep cover. Roosts in trees. SONG/CALL: A hoarse *ko ko ko*. HABITAT: Coniferous and mixed forests with thick undergrowth. RACES: *S. s. ijimae* SE Kyushu, males have rump and lower back white. Not illustrated.

7 **REEVES'S PHEASANT (WHITE-CROWNED LONG-TAILED PHEASANT)** *Syrmaticus reevesii* Male 150–210cm Female 70–80cm FIELD NOTES: Forages at forest edge or on farmland early and late, otherwise keeps to forests. Roosts in trees. SONG/CALL: A series of high chirps accompanied by wing-whirring. Also a soft *pu pu pu*. HABITAT: Forests and areas of tall grass and bushes.

8 **PHEASANT (COMMON or RING-NECKED PHEASANT)** *Phasianus colchicus* Male 66–89cm, Female 53–63cm FIELD NOTES: Probably one of the most familiar birds. Two main forms, green-necked and ring-necked, very variable, especially where introduced. SONG/CALL: A harsh *korkk korrk KO OK korkk-kok*, often followed by wing-whirring. When alarmed gives a rapid *kut-UK kut-UK kut-UK*. HABITAT: Very varied including farmland, open woodland, woodland edge, open country and riverine scrub. RACES: *P. c. versicolor* (Green Pheasant) (fig 8b) Japan. Often considered to be a full species.

9 **GOLDEN PHEASANT** *Chrysolophus pictus* Male 100–115cm, Female 61–70cm FIELD NOTES: Male unmistakable. Forages early and late on tracks and clearings, otherwise keeps to thick cover. SONG/CALL: A loud *ka-cheek* or *cha-chak*. HABITAT: Bamboo and scrub on rocky hills. Introduced population in Britain, occurs mainly in rhododendron thickets.

10 **LADY AMHERST'S PHEASANT** *Chrysolophus amherstiae* Male 105–120cm, Female 60–70cm. FIELD NOTES: Male unmistakable. Skulking, usually keeps to thick cover. Forms in large groups in winter. SONG/CALL: A loud *cheek ker-chek* or *su-ik-ik*. HABITAT: Forest, bamboo and thick scrub on hills and mountains. Introduced population in Britain, frequents conifer plantations, mixed and deciduous woodland with undergrowth.

37 QUAILS AND BUTTONQUAILS

1 CALIFORNIA QUAIL *Callipepla californica* 24–28cm FIELD NOTES: Introduced to Corsica from America. Forages on the ground, usually in small groups. SONG/CALL: A loud *chi-ca-go* and various cackles, chuckles and grunts. HABITAT: Scrubby hills and farmland.

2 NORTHERN BOBWHITE (COMMON BOBWHITE) *Colinus virginianus* 21–26cm FIELD NOTES: Introduced to France from America. Shy, typically in small groups that usually keeps to cover. SONG/CALL: Male gives a rising *bob-WHITE* or *bob-bob-WHITE*, female answers with a thin *a-loie-a-hee*. Various other sounds noted, including a raucous squealing and a whistled *hoy*. HABITAT: Semi-open and open country, farmland also woodland edge.

3 QUAIL (COMMON, EUROPEAN or EUROPEAN MIGRATORY QUAIL) *Coturnix coturnix* 16–18cm FIELD NOTES: Shy and furtive, more often heard than seen. In flight long pointed wings distinguish quails from other gamebirds and button-quails. Some males have rufous tinged face and throat. SONG/CALL: Male has a rapid *quip quip-ip* often interpreted as *wet-my-lips*, female utters a low *bree-bree*. When flushed gives a shrill *tree-tree*. HABITAT: Open grasslands, pastures and weedy waste areas.

4 JAPANESE QUAIL (ASIAN MIGRATORY QUAIL) *Coturnix japonica* 17–19cm FIELD NOTES: Action and habits similar to Quail. SONG/CALL: A chattering *chrr-churrk-chrr*. Flushed notes similar to Quail. HABITAT: Rolling grasslands, fields, forest clearings and montane foothills.

5 HARLEQUIN QUAIL *Coturnix delegorguei* 16–19cm FIELD NOTES: Gregarious. Actions and habits similar to Quail. SONG/CALL: Male gives a rapid *whit-whit*, *whit-whit-whit* or *tswic-tswic-tswic*, female may respond with a soft *quick-ik*. When flushed utters a squeaky *skreeee*. HABITAT: Open grassland and fields.

6 SMALL BUTTONQUAIL (ANDALUSIAN HEMIPODE, LITTLE or COMMON BUTTONQUAIL) *Turnix sylvatica* 15–16cm FIELD NOTES: Rare and secretive, when alarmed prefers to run rather than fly. If seen in flight, has short blunt wings and buff upperwing-coverts that contrast with dark flight-feathers. Although crouched when feeding can be quite upright when crossing open ground. SONG/CALL: Female gives a low, droning *hoooo hoooo hooo* reminiscent of a distant foghorn or the lowing of cattle. Both sexes give a low-pitched *cree cree cree*, probably to keep contact while in cover. HABITAT: Dry grassland and heaths with low scrub and crop fields with rough grassy margins.

7 YELLOW-LEGGED BUTTONQUAIL *Turnix tanki blanfordii* 15–18cm FIELD NOTES: Shy and secretive. Actions and habits similar to Small Buttonquail. SONG/CALL: Female has a human-like, moaning hoot and a far-carrying *off-off-off*. Also recorded is a *pook-pook*, probably uttered by male. HABITAT: Scrub, grassland, slightly marshy areas and cultivated fields.

8 BARRED BUTTONQUAIL *Turnix suscitator okinavensis* 15–17cm FIELD NOTES: Secretive, actions and habits similar to Small Buttonquail. SONG/CALL: Female gives a *groo groo groo drr-r-r-r-r-r* said to sound like a distant motorbike, also a far-carrying *hoon-hoon-hoon-hoon*. HABITAT: Dry grasslands and cultivated fields.

38 CRANES

1 COMMON CRANE (EURASIAN CRANE) *Grus grus* 110–120cm FIELD NOTES: Gregarious, forms large flocks post breeding. In flight, from below, shows black primaries and secondaries. Juvenile more brownish-grey than adult and lacks the distinctive head and neck colours, these being replaced by plain brownish-ochre. SONG/CALL: A far-carrying *krooh* and a repeated, harsh *kraah*. During breeding utters a musical duet, *krrroo* (male) *kraw* (female). Juvenile gives a high *cheerp*. HABITAT: Breeds on bogs, marshes, damp heathland, swampy clearings in forests and steppe and semi-desert areas. Winters in open country with or without nearby lakes or marshes.

2 BLACK-NECKED CRANE *Grus nigricollis* 115cm FIELD NOTES: Gregarious. In flight, from below, shows black primaries, secondaries and tail. Juvenile generally greyish-ochre on head, neck and upperparts, white below. SONG/CALL: A series of loud trumpeting honks. HABITAT: Breeds in high-altitude grassy wetlands, lakeside marshes and pastures, 2950–4900m.

3 HOODED CRANE *Grus monacha* 100cm FIELD NOTES: Occurs in small parties. In flight, from below, wings dark with slightly darker primaries and secondaries. Juvenile has head and neck buffish-white with a dark eye patch. SONG/CALL: A loud *krurrk*. HABITAT: Breeds in high-altitude forested wetlands and isolated bogs. Non-breeders occur in open wetlands, grassland and agricultural fields, with wintering birds also using lake shores, river shores and paddyfields.

4 SANDHILL CRANE *Grus canadensis* 100–120cm FIELD NOTES: Gregarious. Older birds often stained rusty. In flight, from below, shows black primaries and secondaries. Juvenile generally sandy-brown lacking the red on head. SONG/CALL: A vibrant and rolling *karr-rooo*. HABITAT: Breeds in marshes, wet meadows and various open wetlands. Winters on similar types and also on agricultural land and coastal wetlands.

5 WHITE-NAPED CRANE *Grus vipio* 125–150cm FIELD NOTES: Gregarious, large flocks occur in some wintering areas. In flight, from below, shows black primaries and secondaries with a wide white bar on greater underwing-coverts that contrasts with grey body and lesser underwing-coverts. Juvenile has head brown with a pale throat. SONG/CALL: High-pitched bugling. HABITAT: Breeds in marshes, wet meadows and on vegetated lake shores, feeds on adjacent grasslands and agricultural land. On passage and on wintering grounds occurs on fields, wetlands, paddyfields and estuary mudflats.

6 JAPANESE CRANE (RED-CROWNED CRANE) *Grus japonensis* 150cm FIELD NOTES: Gregarious. More aquatic than other cranes. Rare. In flight, from below, shows white primaries and black secondaries. Juvenile has rusty head and neck, body mainly white tinged rusty on wings and mantle, elongated tertials brownish-black. SONG/CALL: Penetrating, high-pitched trumpeting. HABITAT: Breeds in marshes, bogs and wet meadows. In winter found in various freshwater wetlands, saltmarshes and mudflats and paddyfields.

7 SIBERIAN CRANE *Grus leucogeranus* 140cm FIELD NOTES: The most aquatic of cranes. Very rare. In flight, from below, shows black primaries. Juvenile generally rusty-buff, including face, underparts white. SONG/CALL: A soft musical *koonk koonk*. HABITAT: Breeds on tidal flats, bogs, marshes and open wetlands in the lowland tundra and taigia-tundra transition zone. On passage occurs on large isolated wetlands.

8 DEMOISELLE CRANE *Anthropoides vigo* 90–100cm FIELD NOTES: Gregarious, often in very large flocks during migration. In flight, from below, has black primaries and secondaries. Juvenile has head and neck pale grey lacking the distinctive colours of the adult. Tertials much shorter than adult. SONG/CALL: Similar to Common Crane although drier and higher pitched. Juvenile utters a thin, high, rolling whistle. HABITAT: Breeds on grassy steppe, often close to streams, shallow lakes or other wetlands also semi-desert and desert, if water is nearby, seems to be adapting to cultivated fields in some areas.

39 BUSTARDS

1 LITTLE BUSTARD *Tetrax tetrax* 43cm FIELD NOTES: Flight feathers of male upperwing are mainly white with prominent black tips to outer primaries and black primary coverts, which appear as a crescent. Female very similar with the addition of a few dusky bars on secondaries. During display inflates neck feathers, also indulges in leaps with wings held open. SONG/CALL: A dry *prrit* also a low grunt when disturbed. In flight wings make a whistling noise *sisisisisi*.... HABITAT: Open grasslands, rough plains, pastures and crop fields.

2 DENHAM'S BUSTARD *Neotis denhami* Male 100cm, Female 80cm (Vagrant) FIELD NOTES: Flight feathers of upperwing are black with a white patch at the base of inner primaries. Tips of secondary coverts white, forming a bar. Tail with two wide black and white bars. SONG/CALL: A barking *kaa-kaa*. HABITAT: In native Africa: grasslands with or without bushes.

3 NUBIAN BUSTARD *Neotis nuba* Male 70cm, Female 50cm. FIELD NOTES: Upperwing flight-feathers black with large white patch at base of primaries contiguous with white bar at base of secondaries. Primary coverts white with broad black tips also a black patch on the bend of the wing. SONG/CALL: A low *wurk*, otherwise little documented. HABITAT: Arid and semi-arid scrub or savanna.

4 HOUBARA BUSTARD (HOUBARA) *Chlamydotis undulata* Male 65–75cm, Female 55–65cm FIELD NOTES: Upperwing flight-feathers black with broad tips of outer primaries white. Primary coverts white with broad black tips, also a black alula. A white bar splits flight-feathers from brown coverts. Generally shy, when disturbed tends to hide rather than fly. During display neck and head feathers are erected, 'puffed-out', as bird runs around display ground. SONG/CALL: Generally silent. HABITAT: Open semi-desert and dry steppe, usually with grass or low scrub. RACES: *C. u. fuertaventurae* E Canary Islands. Much darker on wings and mantle. Not illustrated.

5 MACQUEEN'S BUSTARD *Chlamydotis macqueenii* Male 65–75cm, Female 55–65cm FIELD NOTES: Actions habits and wing pattern similar to Houbara Bustard, from which it has been recently split. SONG/CALL: Generally silent. HABITAT: Semi-desert and dry steppe with grass or low scrub.

6 ARABIAN BUSTARD *Ardeotis arabs* Male 100cm, Female 75cm FIELD NOTES: Upperwing flight-feathers black with indistinct grey-white bars on inner primaries and secondaries. Secondary coverts grey. During display neck feathers are 'puffed-out', tail cocked and spread and wings drooped. SONG/CALL: During display utters a *puk-puk*. HABITAT: Semi-desert, dry grasslands, arid bush and cultivated fields.

7 GREAT BUSTARD *Otis tarda* Male 105cm, Female 75cm FIELD NOTES: Upperwing appears mainly grey-white with black secondaries and blackish tips to primaries. During display male appears to turn itself inside out, due to inflated neck, cocked tail and erected white wing feathers. SONG/CALL: A low bark uttered during disputes or when alarmed. During display gives a hollow drone. HABITAT: Rolling or flat open grasslands, occasionally in cork oak areas and olive groves.

40 RAILS AND CRAKES

1 SLATY-LEGGED CRAKE (BANDED or RYUKYU CRAKE) *Rallina eurizonoides* 27cm FIELD NOTES: Shy. Often flies into trees when flushed. SONG/CALL: A persistent *kek-kek kek-kek...* or *ow-ow ow-ow....* HABITAT: Forest and forest edge.

2 OKINAWA RAIL *Gallirallus okinawa* 30cm FIELD NOTES: Runs when flushed. SONG/CALL: A *kwi kwi kwi ki-kwee ki-wee, kyip kyip kyip kyip* or *ki-kik-ki.* HABITAT: Broadleaf evergreen forest with dense undergrowth with wet areas.

3 SLATY-BREASTED RAIL (BLUE-BREASTED BANDED RAIL) *Gallirallus striatus* 29cm (Vagrant) FIELD NOTES: Very secretive. SONG/CALL: A sharp *terrik* and a noisy *ka-ka-ka.* HABITAT: In native India, S China and SE Asia: mangroves, marshes, paddyfields and grasslands.

4 WATER RAIL *Rallus aquaticus* 29cm FIELD NOTES: Secretive. More often heard than seen. Will feed in open if not disturbed. SONG/CALL: Various pig-like squeals and grunts, also utters a *kipp kipp kipp* during courtship. HABITAT: Dense reedbeds, marshes and overgrown ditches.

5 SPOTTED CRAKE *Porzana porzana* 22–24cm FIELD NOTES: Secretive, although will feed in open if undisturbed. SONG/CALL: A high-pitched, whiplash-like *whitt,* also a ticking *tik-tak* and a croaking *qwe-qwe-qwe.* HABITAT: Marshes, bogs, wet meadows and paddyfields.

6 SORA (SORA CRAKE, SORA RAIL) *Porzana carolina* 20–23cm (Vagrant) FIELD NOTES: Secretive but will feed in the open if not disturbed. SONG/CALL: A plaintive *ker-wee,* a *wee-ker,* also a high-pitched descending whinny. HABITAT: In native America: marshes, after breeding various wetland areas including pastures, mudflats and mangroves.

7 LITTLE CRAKE *Porzana parva* 18–20cm FIELD NOTES: Note long primary projection. SONG/CALL: A far-carrying, accelerating *qwek qwek qwek qwek-qwek-qwek kwa kwa-kwa-kwa....* HABITAT: Marshes and lakes with extensive aquatic vegetation.

8 BAILLON'S CRAKE *Porzana pusilla* 17–19cm FIELD NOTES: Note short primary projection. SONG/CALL: A dry, frog-like rattle. HABITAT: Marshes, wet grasslands and pastures with sedges.

9 RUDDY-BREASTED CRAKE (RUDDY CRAKE) *Porzana fusca* 21–23cm FIELD NOTES: Secretive. Occasionally feeds at the edge of reeds. SONG/CALL: A harsh *tewk,* often speeds up and ends with a grebe-like bubbling. HABITAT: Marshes, paddyfields and dry bush by lakes.

10 BAND-BELLIED CRAKE (SIBERIAN RUDDY CRAKE, CHINESE BANDED CRAKE) *Porzana paykullii* 20–22cm FIELD NOTES: Typical secretive crake behaviour, heard more than seen. SONG/CALL: Said to sound like intermittent drumbeats or the noise of a wooden rattle. HABITAT: Marshes, wet meadows, damp woodlands and paddyfields.

11 BLACK-TAILED CRAKE (ELWE'S or RUFOUS-BACKED CRAKE) *Porzana bicolor* 20–22cm FIELD NOTES: Secretive and crepuscular, although has been recorded feeding in the open. SONG/CALL: A rasping *waak-waak* followed by a descending trill. HABITAT: Swamp areas and paddyfields in or near forests, also wet grassland and small marshes.

12 STRIPED CRAKE *Aenigmatolimnas marginalis* 18–21cm (Vagrant) FIELD NOTES: Secretive, although sometimes found in the open. SONG/CALL: A sharp *tak-tak-tak-tak.* HABITAT: In native Africa: grassland, marsh edge, ponds and ditches.

13 SWINHOE'S RAIL (SWINHOE'S, ASIAN or SIBERIAN YELLOW RAIL) *Coturnicops exquisitus* 13cm FIELD NOTES: Very secretive. In flight shows white secondaries. SONG/CALL: A *tick-tick tick-tick-tick.* HABITAT: Wet meadows, grassy marshes or swamps.

14 AFRICAN CRAKE *Crex egregia* 20–23cm (Vagrant) FIELD NOTES: Skulking. Most active early and late. SONG/CALL: A trilled *kik-kik-kik-kik-ik-ik-ikikikikik.* HABITAT: In native Africa: wet grassy areas.

15 CORNCRAKE (CORN CRAKE) *Crex crex* 27–30cm FIELD NOTES: More often heard than seen. Most active early and late. SONG/CALL: A monotonous dry *krek-krek krek-krek.* HABITAT: Grasslands, dry or wet meadows.

41 CRAKES, WATERHEN, MOORHENS, GALLINULES, SWAMP-HEN, WATERCOCK AND COOTS

1 BROWN CRAKE *Amaurornis akool* 26–28cm (Vagrant) FIELD NOTES: Shy and skulking. SONG/CALL: A long, vibrating whistle. HABITAT: In native SE China, India: swamps and paddyfields.

2 WHITE-BREASTED WATERHEN *Amaurornis phoenicurus* 28–33cm FIELD NOTES: Often feeds in the open, also climbs about in bushes and small trees. SONG/CALL: Monotonous grunts, croaks and chuckles. HABITAT: Damp scrub, marshes, paddyfields, lake and pond edges.

3 BLACK CRAKE *Amaurornis flavirostris* 19–23cm (Vagrant) FIELD NOTES: Readily feeds in the open. SONG/CALL: A duet, one bird utters a harsh *krrok-krraaa* the other follows with a soft purring. HABITAT: In native Africa: marshes, swamps and lakeside vegetation.

4 MOORHEN (COMMON MOORHEN or GALLINULE) *Gallinula chloropus* 32–35cm FIELD NOTES: Often relatively tame. Regularly swims, with a jerky action. SONG/CALL: A bubbling *krrrruk* or *kurr-ik*, also *a kik-kik-kik* given when alarmed. HABITAT: Various wetland areas, including lake edges, ponds, rivers and ditches.

5 LESSER MOORHEN *Gallinula angulata* 22–23cm (Vagrant) FIELD NOTES: Shy. Actions similar to Moorhen. SONG/CALL: A soft *pyup*, a rapid clucking and when alarmed a *tek*. HABITAT: In native Africa: reedbeds, marshes, also lakes and rivers with fringing vegetation.

6 ALLEN'S GALLINULE *Porphyrula (Porphyrio) alleni* 22–24cm (Vagrant) FIELD NOTES: Secretive, swims but not usually far from cover. Climbs among reeds and bushes and often walks on floating vegetation. SONG/CALL: Various including a sharp *kik-kik-kik-kik-kik-kurr-kurr…*, a dry *keek* and a *kli-kli-kli* uttered in flight. HABITAT: In native Africa: well-vegetated marshes and lakes.

7 PURPLE GALLINULE (AMERICAN PURPLE GALLINULE) *Porphyrula (Porphyrio) martinica* 30–36cm (Vagrant) FIELD NOTES: Readily feeds in the open, although typically stays close to cover. Walks on floating plants, also clambers among reeds and bushes. SONG/CALL: A high-pitched *kyik*, also a wailing *ka-ka-ka* and a *kek-kek-kek* given in flight. HABITAT: In native America: well-vegetated lakes, pools and marshes.

8 PURPLE SWAMP-HEN (PURPLE GALLINULE) *Porphyrio porphyrio* 45–50cm FIELD NOTES: Unmistakable. Skulking. Clambers among dense reeds. SONG/CALL: A low *chuk* or *chuk-chuk* and when alarmed a *toot* said to sound like a toy trumpet. HABITAT: Dense reedbeds and the fringing vegetation by rivers and lagoons. RACES: *P. p. madagascariensis* (Green-backed Swamp-hen) Egypt, green upperparts, not illustrated; *P. p. caspius* (Grey-headed Swamp-hen) Caspian Sea, NW Iran and Turkey, head and neck greyish, not illustrated.

9 WATERCOCK *Gallicrex cinerea* 42–43cm FIELD NOTES: Mainly crepuscular. Skulking. Readily swims across open water. SONG/CALL: During the breeding season gives a deep booming, otherwise generally silent. HABITAT: Reed or grassy swamps, also paddyfields.

10 COOT (EURASIAN or COMMON COOT) *Fulica atra* 36–38cm FIELD NOTES: Often grazes on waterside grass. Gregarious. SONG/CALL: Various metallic, explosive notes including a short *kow* or *kowk* and a sharp *kick*. HABITAT: Lakes, ponds and rivers. In winter often occurs on estuaries or even sheltered sea bays.

11 AMERICAN COOT *Fulica americana* 31–37cm (Vagrant) FIELD NOTES: Note white undertail-coverts. Actions and habits as Coot. SONG/CALL: A harsh *krok*, also various cackling and clucking notes. HABITAT: In native America: lakes, ponds, rivers, estuaries and sea bays.

12 RED-KNOBBED COOT (CRESTED COOT) *Fulica cristata* 38–42cm FIELD NOTES: In winter red knob replaced by small red-brown spot. In all seasons note lack of pointed feather projection between bill and shield. SONG/CALL: Wide variety including a shrill *kik*, a double-clucking *klukuk*, also a metallic *krrook* and a groaning *euh*. HABITAT: Marshes and lakes with surrounding vegetation.

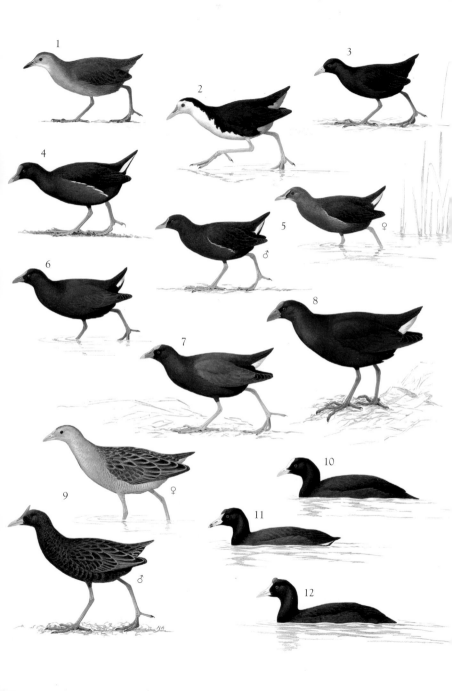

42 JACANA, PAINTED SNIPE, OYSTERCATCHER, IBISBILL, STILT, AVOCET AND CRAB PLOVER

1 PHEASANT-TAILED JACANA (WATER-PHEASANT) *Hydrophasianus chirurgus* 31–58cm (Vagrant) FIELD NOTES: In flight shows strikingly white wings. Walks on floating water-plants and readily swims. Often gregarious. Juvenile similar to non-breeding adult, but feathers of upperparts have pale fringes and black necklace is less distinct. SONG/CALL: A mewing *me-e-ou* or *me-onp* or similar, also in winter a nasal *tewn*. HABITAT: In native India, S China and SE Asia: lakes and ponds with floating and emergent vegetation.

2 PAINTED SNIPE (GREATER PAINTED SNIPE) *Rostratula benghalensis* 23–28cm FIELD NOTES: Mainly crepuscular. Secretive. Flies with dangling legs, much as rails. SONG/CALL: In display female utters a soft *koh koh koh*, likened to blowing across the top of an empty bottle, also various hisses and growls. HABITAT: Marshes and flooded fields, also feeds on nearby open grassland.

3 OYSTERCATCHER (EURASIAN OYSTERCATCHER) *Haematopus ostralegus* 40–46cm FIELD NOTES: In flight from above shows broad white wingbar and white rump. Juvenile like non-breeding adult but has upperparts browner with pale feather fringes, bill yellowish with darkish tip. SONG/CALL: A sharp *kleep* or *kle-eap*, also a quiet *weep*. In display gives a piping, trilling *ke-beep ke-beep ke-beep kwirrrrrr ee-beep ee-beep ee-beep*. In alarm utters a *kip* or *pick*. HABITAT: Saltmarshes, beaches, inland on farmland also by lakes and rivers.

4 CANARY ISLANDS OYSTERCATCHER (CANARY or CANARIAN BLACK OYSTERCATCHER) *Haematopus meadewaldoi* 43cm FIELD NOTES: Probably extinct. Very little known about habits. SONG/CALL: Probably similar to Oystercatcher. HABITAT: Rocky and sandy shores.

5 IBISBILL *Ibidorhyncha struthersii* 39–41cm FIELD NOTES: In flight from above shows white patch on inner primaries and white spots near tips of the other primaries. Feeds by probing among riverbed stones. SONG/CALL: A ringing *klew-klew* and a loud, rapid *tee-tee-tee-tee*. HABITAT: Mountain river valleys with flat stony floodplains.

6 BLACK-WINGED STILT *Himantopus himantopus* 35–40cm FIELD NOTES: Unmistakable. Some show blackish or greyish crown and hindneck. In flight from above shows plain black wings, white tail and rump. Juvenile has browner mantle and wings with buff feather fringes. SONG/CALL: A sharp *kek*, also a high-pitched *kikikikik* and a yelping *kee-ack*. HABITAT: Various wetland areas including saltmarshes, saltpans, lakes and marshes. RACES: *H. h. leucocephalus* (White-headed Stilt) (fig 6b) (Vagrant) SE Indonesia, Australasia.

7 AVOCET (PIED AVOCET) *Recurvirostra avosetta* 42–45cm FIELD NOTES: Unmistakable. Gregarious. Readily swims, upending to feed, like a dabbling duck. Juvenile has black areas replaced with brown and white of upperparts smudged with greyish-brown. SONG/CALL: A melodious *kluit-kluit-kluit*, a harsher *kloo-eet* or *krrree-yu* given in alarm. HABITAT: Shallow saline or brackish lakes, lagoons, saltpans and estuaries. During non-breeding season also occurs on tidal mudflats, freshwater lakes and locally agricultural land.

8 CRAB PLOVER *Dromas ardeola* 38–41cm FIELD NOTES: Adult unmistakable. Juvenile has black areas replaced with dark grey and white on wings more greyish, they can look quite gull-like due to greyish mantle and habit of resting on tarsi. SONG/CALL: A barking *ka-how ka-how….* At breeding sites utters various sharp whistles such as *kew-ki-ki* and *ki-tewk*. HABITAT: Sandy coasts, estuaries, lagoons, exposed coral reefs and mudflats.

43 STONE CURLEW, THICK-KNEES, EGYPTIAN PLOVER, CREAM-COLOURED COURSER AND PTRATINCOLES

1 COLLARED PRATINCOLE (COMMON or RED-WINGED PRATINCOLE) *Glareola pratincola* 23–26cm FIELD NOTES: In flight shows narrow white trailing edge to secondaries and reddish-chestnut underwing-coverts. In flight from above dark primaries contrast with paler coverts and mantle. Tail deeply forked. SONG/CALL: A harsh *kik* or *kirrik* and a rolling *kikki-kirrik-irrik*. HABITAT: Flat open areas, fields and steppe usually near water.

2 BLACK-WINGED PRATINCOLE *Glareola nordmanni* 23–26cm FIELD NOTES: In flight shows all dark underwing. Upperwing less contrasting than Collared Pratincole. Tail deeply forked. SONG/CALL: A low-pitched *chrr-chrr*, also a rapid *pwik-kik-kik* and a *kritt*, *krip* or *kikiip*. HABITAT: Saline and alkaline steppe, grasslands and lake shores.

3 ORIENTAL PRATINCOLE (EASTERN, EASTERN COLLARED or LARGE INDIAN PRATINCOLE) *Glareola maldivarum* 23–24cm FIELD NOTES: In flight has chestnut underwing-coverts and upperwing appears all dark. Tail deeply forked. SONG/CALL: A sharp *kyik*, *chik-chik* or *chet* often given in flight, also a *ter-ack* and a rising *trooeet*. HABITAT: Similar to Collared Pratincole.

4 SMALL PRATINCOLE (SMALL INDIAN, LITTLE or MILKY PRATINCOLE) *Glareola lactea* 17cm (Vagrant) FIELD NOTES: In flight, from below shows white secondaries with black tips and white inner primaries, from above has less white on inner primaries. Tail square-ended or shallowly forked. SONG/CALL: A *tuck-tuck-tuck*, also a high-pitched, rolling *prrip* or *tiririt* given in flight. HABITAT: In native India and SE Asia: sand bars and shingle banks on rivers, also coastal marshes and estuaries.

5 CREAM-COLOURED COURSER (DESERT COURSER) *Cursorius cursor* 19–22cm FIELD NOTES: In flight from below has mainly black underwing, from above pale body and wing contrast with dark primaries. Juvenile lacks dark head markings, upperparts have pale feather fringes. SONG/CALL: A harsh *praak-praak*, also a piping *quit quit quit* or *quit-quit-whow* when displaying. HABITAT: Arid open desert or semi-desert, gravel plains, open fields and saltflats.

6 EGYPTIAN PLOVER (EGYPTIAN COURSER, CROCODILE BIRD) *Pluvianus aegyptius* 19–21cm (Vagrant) FIELD NOTES: Unmistakable. In flight has broad black band on white flight-feathers, above and below, upperwing-coverts grey, underwing-coverts white. SONG/CALL: A harsh, high-pitched *cherk-cherk-cherk* and a soft *wheeup*. HABITAT: In native Africa: river banks and river islands, formerly bred along the Nile.

7 STONE-CURLEW (EUROPEAN STONE-CURLEW, THICK-KNEE) *Burhinus oedicnemus* 40–44cm FIELD NOTES: Timid. Mainly crepuscular. During the day often stands motionless. SONG/CALL: A *cur-lee* or *churrrreee*, often repeated. HABITAT: Steppe, dry fields, heathland and semi-desert. RACES: *B. o. harterti* (fig7b) south and east of the Caspian Sea.

8 SENEGAL THICK-KNEE (SENEGAL STONE-CURLEW) *Burhinus senegalensis* 32–38cm FIELD NOTES: Actions similar to Stone-curlew, although tends to be less timid. SONG/CALL: Similar to Stone-curlew, although more nasal and metallic. HABITAT: River banks and islands, also open areas near water. In Egypt recorded nesting on flat roofs.

9 SPOTTED THICK-KNEE (SPOTTED or CAPE DIKKOP) *Burhinus capensis* 37–44cm FIELD NOTES: Tends to stay near bush cover, especially during the day. Mainly nocturnal. SONG/CALL: A plaintive *tche-uuuu* and a rapid *pi-pi-pi-pi* when alarmed. HABITAT: Bushy areas on broken ground and savanna grasslands, also rocky river beds.

10 GREAT THICK-KNEE (GREAT STONE-PLOVER, GREAT STONE-CURLEW) *Esacus recurvirostris* 49–54cm FIELD NOTES: Shy. Mainly nocturnal or crepuscular. SONG/CALL: A wailing, whistled *see* or *see-ey*, also a harsh *see-eek* when alarmed. HABITAT: Shingle and rocky riverbeds, rocky beaches, estuaries and reefs.

44 PLOVERS

1 LITTLE RINGED PLOVER *Charadrius dubius* 14–17cm FIELD NOTES: Obvious pale wingbar on upperwing. SONG/CALL: A *pee-oo*, descending in pitch, a *pip-pip-pip* when alarmed and a harsh *cree-ah* during display. HABITAT: Margins of rivers, lakes or gravel-pits.

2 RINGED PLOVER (GREAT or COMMON RINGED PLOVER) *Charadrius hiaticula* 18–20cm FIELD NOTES: Bold white wingbar on upperwing. SONG/CALL: A *too-lee*, rising in pitch, a soft *too-weep* when alarmed. HABITAT: Coasts, lakes and rivers, also Arctic tundra.

3 SEMIPALMATED PLOVER *Charadrius semipalmatus* 17–19cm (Vagrant) FIELD NOTES: Narrow white bar on upperwing. SONG/CALL: A sharp *tu-wee* or *che-wee*. In alarm gives a rapidly repeated *chip* or *tewit*. HABITAT: In native America: as Ringed Plover.

4 LONG-BILLED PLOVER (LONG-BILLED RINGED PLOVER) *Charadrius placidus* 19–21cm FIELD NOTES: Poorly-defined pale wingbar on upperwing. SONG/CALL: A clear *piwee*, also a pleasant *tudulu*. HABITAT: Edges of lakes and rivers also on mudflats.

5 KILLDEER *Charadrius vociferous* 23–26cm (Vagrant) FIELD NOTES: Prominent white bar on upperwing and chestnut-orange rump. SONG/CALL: A shrill *kill-dee*, *kill-diu* or variants. HABITAT: In native America: mainly grasslands and agricultural land.

6 KITTLITZ'S PLOVER (KITTLITZ'S SAND PLOVER) *Charadrius pecuarius* 12–14cm FIELD NOTES: Long legged. White bar on upperwing, broad white edges to tail. SONG/CALL: A *pipeep* or *prit* given in alarm. HABITAT: Edges of lakes, coastal lagoons and nearby grassland.

7 THREE-BANDED PLOVER *Charadrius tricollaris* 18cm (Vagrant) FIELD NOTES: Narrow white bar on upperwing and long, white-sided tail. SONG/CALL: A high-pitched *weee- weet*, *pi-peep* and a *wick-wick* when alarmed. HABITAT: In native Africa: edges of rivers, lakes and pools.

8 KENTISH PLOVER (SNOWY PLOVER) *Charadrius alexandrinus* 15–17cm FIELD NOTES: White bar on upperwing, white sides to rump and tail. SONG/CALL: In flight a soft *pit*, a hard *prrr* or *too-eet* when alarmed. HABITAT: Sandy shores of coasts, brackish lakes, lagoons and saltpans.

9 CHESTNUT-BANDED PLOVER (CHESTNUT-BANDED SAND PLOVER) *Charadrius pallidus* 15cm (Vagrant) FIELD NOTES: Narrow white bar on upperwing, white sides to tail and rump. SONG/CALL: A soft *chup*, also a *drreet* or *dweeu* and a *hweet* given in alarm. HABITAT: In native Africa: alkaline lakes, saltpans and coastal lagoons.

10 LESSER SAND PLOVER (MONGOLIAN SAND PLOVER) *Charadrius mongolus* 19–21cm FIELD NOTES: Usually shows a narrow white bar on upperwing. SONG/CALL: A short *drrit* also a sharp *chitik* or *chiktik*. HABITAT: Mountain steppes and elevated tundra near water, also coastal shingle and sand-dunes in north east of region. Winters on coasts.

11 GREATER SAND PLOVER (LARGE SAND PLOVER, GEOFFROY'S PLOVER) *Charadrius leschenaultii* 22–25cm FIELD NOTES: In flight toes project beyond tail, an obvious white bar on upperwing. SONG/CALL: A soft *trrri* also a melodious *pipruirr*. HABITAT: Open, dry treeless areas with nearby water. Winters mainly on coasts.

12 CASPIAN PLOVER (LESSER ORIENTAL PLOVER) *Charadrius asiaticus* 18–20cm FIELD NOTES: In flight toes project beyond tail, restricted white bar on upperwing. SONG/CALL: A *tup*, a *tik-tik-tik* and a repeated *tyurlee* during song-flight. HABITAT: Saltpans on dry lowland plains, sometimes far from water.

13 ORIENTAL PLOVER (ORIENTAL DOTTEREL, EASTERN SAND PLOVER) *Charadrius veredus* 22–25cm FIELD NOTES: Inconspicuous white bar on upperwing. SONG/CALL: In flight a *chip-chip-chip* also a piping *klink*. HABITAT: Margins of lakes and rivers and arid inland areas.

14 DOTTEREL (EURASIAN or MOUNTAIN DOTTEREL) *Charadrius morinellus* 20–24cm FIELD NOTES: No white bar on upperwing. SONG/CALL: A *pweet-pweet-pweet* or *kwip-kwip* also a trilling *skeer*. HABITAT: Open mountain tops, tundra. On passage hills, mountains, farmland.

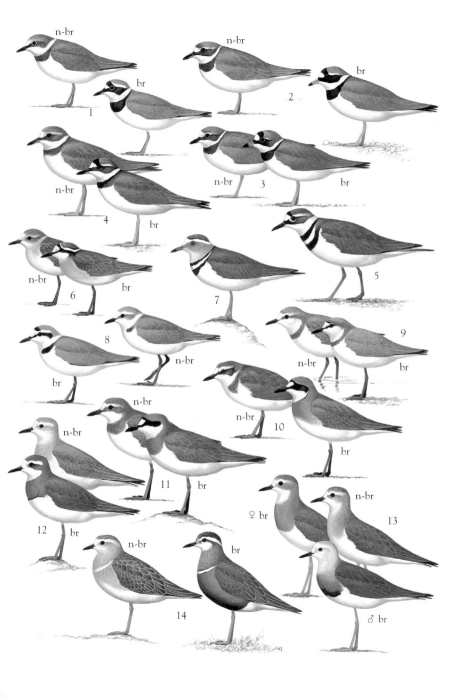

45 PLOVERS AND LAPWINGS

1 AMERICAN GOLDEN PLOVER (LESSER GOLDEN PLOVER) *Pluvialis dominica* 24–28cm (Vagrant) FIELD NOTES: Wing tips project beyond tail. Longer-legged than Golden Plover. Underwing-coverts dusky grey. SONG/CALL: A sharp *klu-eet*, *kleep* and *klu-ee-uh*. HABITAT: In native N America: breeds on well-drained tundra, otherwise occurs on fallow fields, short grassland also coastal mud and lakesides.

2 GOLDEN PLOVER (EUROPEAN GOLDEN PLOVER) *Pluvialis apricaria* 26–29cm FIELD NOTES: Wing tips slightly projecting or level with tail. Underwing-coverts white. SONG/CALL: A mellow *too-ee* or *tloo*. HABITAT: Breeds on dry tundra, moorland and heathland. Winters on fields, short grasslands, saltmarsh and coastal mudflats.

3 PACIFIC GOLDEN PLOVER (ASIAN GOLDEN or EASTERN GOLDEN PLOVER) *Pluvialis fulva* 23–26cm FIELD NOTES: Wing tips project beyond tail. Longer-legged and longer tertials than both Golden and American Golden Plover. Underwing-coverts dusky grey. SONG/CALL: A rapid *chu-wit* and drawn-out *klu-ee*. HABITAT: Breeds on dry tundra, on migration occurs on coastal lagoons, mudflats, also lake shores, river edges and sometimes fields.

4 GREY PLOVER (BLACK-BELLIED PLOVER) *Pluvialis squatarola* 27–30cm FIELD NOTES: In flight shows white rump and white upperwing bar. Underwing white with black axillaries. SONG/CALL: A mournful *tlee-oo-ee*. HABITAT: Breeds on lowland tundra, usually in damp areas. On migration and in winter found mainly on coastal mudflats and beaches.

5 GREY-HEADED LAPWING *Vanellus cinereus* 34–37cm FIELD NOTES: In flight tail with wide black tip, rump white. Upperwing shows large white area on secondaries and secondary coverts, rest of coverts brown, primaries black. Underwing white with black primaries. SONG/CALL: A plaintive *chee-it* and a rasping *cha-ha-eet* or *pink* when alarmed. HABITAT: Marsh, swampy grassland and rice fields.

6 SPUR-WINGED PLOVER (SPUR-WINGED LAPWING) *Vanellus spinosus* 25–28cm FIELD NOTES: In flight tail mainly black, rump white. Upperwing has black flight-feathers and brown coverts split by a bold white wingbar. Underwing black with white coverts. SONG/CALL: When alarmed a fast, repeated *kitt-kitt-kitt* or *tik-tik-tik*. Territorial call often transcribed as *did-ye-do-it*. HABITAT: Lakes, marshes, edges of large rivers, coastal lagoons, irrigated fields etc.

7 BLACK-HEADED PLOVER (BLACKHEAD PLOVER or BLACK-HEADED LAPWING) *Vanellus tectus* 25cm (Vagrant) FIELD NOTES: In flight upperwing similar to Spur-winged Plover except primary coverts white. SONG/CALL: When disturbed gives a piercing *kir*. Also utters a harsh *kwairr* and a shrill *kiarr*. HABITAT: In native Africa: dry plains.

8 RED-WATTLED LAPWING (RED-WATTLED PLOVER) *Vanellus indicus* 32–35cm FIELD NOTES: In flight similar to Spur-winged Plover but tail has a broad white tip. SONG/CALL: A shrill *treent-trint teen-ty-too-int trinti-too-int*. When alarmed gives a sharp, repeated *trint*. In display a prolonged *trint-trint-tee-int tee-int trinti-too-int too-int too-int*. HABITAT: Open areas such as farmland and grassland with nearby water.

9 WHITE-TAILED PLOVER (WHITE-TAILED LAPWING) *Vanellus leucurus* 26–29cm FIELD NOTES: Upperwing similar to Grey-headed Lapwing, tail white. SONG/CALL: A high-pitched *pet-eewit pet-ee-wit* and a plaintive *pee-wick*. HABITAT: Margins of marshes, lakes, rivers etc.

10 SOCIABLE PLOVER (SOCIABLE LAPWING) *Vanellus gregarius* 27–30cm FIELD NOTES: Upperwing shows white secondaries, black primaries and secondary coverts, rest of the coverts brown. Rump white. SONG/CALL: A harsh *kretsch kretsch kretsch* and a rapid rattling *rekrekrekrekrek*. HABITAT: Breeds on open steppe, otherwise mainly on grasslands and fields.

11 LAPWING (NORTHERN LAPWING, GREEN PLOVER, PEEWIT) *Vanellus vanellus* 28–31cm FIELD NOTES: Unmistakable. In flight above looks black with white on uppertail and wing-tips. SONG/CALL: A plaintive *wee-ip* or *pee-wit*. In display-flight gives a drawn out medley of *coo-wee-ip* and *wee-willuch-coo-wee-up*. HABITAT: Breeds and winters on grasslands, sometimes on estuaries in cold winters.

46 *CALIDRIS* SANDPIPERS AND STINTS

1 GREAT KNOT (GREATER or EASTERN KNOT, GREAT SANDPIPER) *Calidris tenuirostris* 26–28cm FIELD NOTES: In flight shows narrow white bar on upperwing, lower rump is white sparsely marked with black, appears white. SONG/CALL: A low *nyut-nyut* also reported are a low *chucker-chuker-chuker* and a soft *prrt*. HABITAT: Slopes or plateaux in sub-Arctic highlands. Winters mainly on sandy or muddy coastal shores.

2 KNOT (RED or LESSER KNOT) *Calidris canutus* 23–25cm FIELD NOTES: In flight shows narrow white bar on upperwing, lower rump is white barred black, appears greyish. SONG/CALL: A soft, nasal *knut*, *wutt* or *whet*. In display gives a plaintive *poor-me* and in alarm a *kikkik*. HABITAT: Open stony tundra near water. Winters mainly on sandy or muddy coastal shores.

3 SANDERLING *Calidris alba* 20–21cm FIELD NOTES: In flight, from above shows a broad white bar on upperwing and a dark leading edge when in non-breeding plumage. Feeds along the waters edge, typically with rapid runs interspersed with quick dips to pick up prey. SONG/CALL: In flight gives a *twick* or *kip*, often repeated or forming a quick trill. During display utters various trills, purrs and churring notes. HABITAT: Barren stony tundra near water. Winters mainly on sandy or muddy coastal shores.

4 SEMIPALMATED SANDPIPER *Calidris pusilla* 13–15cm (Vagrant) FIELD NOTES: Difficult to separate from other stints, especially in non-breeding plumage, note bill shape and calls. Slightly slower feeding action than Little Stint. SONG/CALL: A harsh *chrup* or *kreet*. HABITAT: In native America: damp grassy tundra. Winters on coastal, lake and pool shores.

5 WESTERN SANDPIPER *Calidris mauri* 14–17cm FIELD NOTES: Difficult to separate from other stints, especially in non-breeding plumage, note bill shape and calls. Often feeds in water. SONG/CALL: A thin, high-pitched *jeet* or *cheet*. HABITAT: Tundra with damp areas, pools and lakes. Winters on coastal and pool shores.

6 RED-NECKED STINT (RUFOUS-NECKED STINT) *Calidris ruficollis* 13–16cm FIELD NOTES: Difficult to separate from other stints, especially in non-breeding plumage, note bill shape and calls. Feeding actions similar to Little Stint. SONG/CALL: A coarse *chit*, *kreep*, *creek* or *chritt*. HABITAT: Dry tundra with damp areas near pools or lakes. Winters on coastal and pool shores.

7 LITTLE STINT *Calidris minuta* 12–14cm FIELD NOTES: Difficult to separate from other stints, especially in non-breeding plumage, note shape of bill and calls. Grey-sided tail. Has quick, running around, feeding action. SONG/CALL: A short *stit-tit*, others similar to Red-necked Stint. During display utters a *swee-swee-swee*. HABITAT: High-Arctic tundra near swampy areas. After breeding occurs on coastal mudflats and the shores of lakes, pools and rivers.

8 TEMMINCK'S STINT *Calidris temminckii* 13–15cm FIELD NOTES: At rest white-sided tail projects beyond wing. Has slow, deliberate feeding action. SONG/CALL: A rapid *tiririririr* or a trilled *trirr*. In display gives a reeling *kililililililili*. HABITAT: Sandy, stony and grassy areas near inlets, rivers and streams. After breeding occurs on marshes, lakes, ponds and estuaries.

9 LONG-TOED STINT *Calidris subminuta* 13–16cm FIELD NOTES: When alarmed often stands upright with neck extended. Usually feeds among waterside vegetation. SONG/CALL: A soft *prrt*, *chrrup* or *chulip*, also a sharp *tik-tik-tik*. HABITAT: Marshy tundra and pools in meadows or forests. After breeding edges of pools and lakes, also on marshes and tidal mudflats.

47 *CALIDRIS* SANDPIPERS

1 LEAST SANDPIPER *Calidris minutilla* 13–15cm (Vagrant) FIELD NOTES: Difficult to separate from Long-toed Stint (Plate 46), usually looks more compact or crouched. SONG/CALL: A shrill *kreeep* or a lower, purring *prrrt*. HABITAT: In native America: open tundra with nearby lakes and pools, after breeding frequents the edges of lakes and pools, also marshes and coastal mudflats.

2 WHITE-RUMPED SANDPIPER *Calidris fuscicollis* 15–18cm (Vagrant) FIELD NOTES: At rest wings project beyond tail. In flight has white uppertail-coverts. SONG/CALL: A high-pitched *jeeet* or *eeet* also a short *tit* or *teep*. HABITAT: In native America: grassy tundra near coasts, after breeding various inland and coastal wetland areas.

3 BAIRD'S SANDPIPER *Calidris bairdii* 14–17cm FIELD NOTES: At rest wings project beyond tail. Less gregarious than most of the genus. SONG/CALL: A low *preeet*, also a grating *krrt* and a sharp *tsick*. In display gives a guttural trill. HABITAT: Dry upland tundra, after breeding occurs on lakes, pools and reservoirs that are bordered with short grassland, less so on estuaries or beaches.

4 PECTORAL SANDPIPER *Calidris melanotos* 19–23cm FIELD NOTES: In flight has narrow white bar on upperwing and clear white sides to lower rump and uppertail-coverts. SONG/CALL: A reedy *churk* or *trrit*. During display gives hooting, repeated *oo-ah*. HABITAT: Dry areas of vegetated wetlands in Arctic tundra, after breeding frequents coastal and inland wetlands.

5 SHARP-TAILED SANDPIPER (SIBERIAN PECTORAL SANDPIPER) *Calidris acuminate* 17–21cm FIELD NOTES: In flight has narrow white bar on upperwing and black streaked white sides to lower rump and uppertail-coverts. SONG/CALL: A soft *wheep*, *pleep* or *trrt*, also a twittering *prrt-wheep-wheep*. During display gives a low *hoop* and a muffled trill. HABITAT: Tundra with wet peaty hollows and drier hummocks. After breeding lakes, lagoons, wet grasslands and coastal mudflats.

6 CURLEW SANDPIPER *Calidris ferruginea* 18–23cm FIELD NOTES: In flight has prominent white bar on upperwing and white lower rump and uppertail-coverts. Regularly wades, often up to belly, in shallow water. SONG/CALL: A rippling *chirrup*. In display utters a series of chatters, trills and whinnies. HABITAT: Arctic coastal tundra. After breeding frequents coastal mudflats, lagoons, estuaries and saltmarshes, also inland on marshes, lakes, rivers and flooded areas. (COX'S SANDPIPER *Calidris paramelanotos*: discovered in 1982 is now thought to be hybrid between Curlew Sandpiper and probably Pectoral Sandpiper. Not illustrated.)

7 DUNLIN (RED-BACKED SANDPIPER) *Calidris alpina* 16–22cm FIELD NOTES: In flight shows prominent white bar on upperwing and white sides to rump and uppertail-coverts. When feeding walks quickly, often with short runs, probing and pecking vigorously. SONG/CALL: A rasping *kreeeep*, also a low *beep*. During display gives a descending, reedy trill. HABITAT: Arctic tundra, upland moorland, saltmarsh and coastal grassland.

8 ROCK SANDPIPER *Calidris ptilocnemis* 20–23cm FIELD NOTES: Often considered conspecific with Purple Sandpiper. In flight shows prominent white bar on upperwing and white sides to rump. SONG/CALL: Similar to Purple Sandpiper. HABITAT: Coastal, upland tundra. Winters mainly on rocky and stony shores.

9 PURPLE SANDPIPER *Calidris maritima* 20–22cm FIELD NOTES: Often considered conspecific with Rock Sandpiper. In flight shows narrow white bar on upperwing and white sides to rump. SONG/CALL: A short *whit* or *kut*. During display utters various buzzing and wheezing trills along with low moans. HABITAT: Stony, upland tundra. Winters on rocky shores and man-made jetties etc.

48 SNIPE AND WOODCOCK

1 JACK SNIPE *Lymnocryptes minimus* 17–19cm FIELD NOTES: Secretive, tends to wait until nearly trodden on before being flushed, flies away with less erratic movements than Snipe. SONG/CALL: May utter a weak *gah* when disturbed. On breeding grounds gives a muffled *ogogok-ogogok-ogogok*. HABITAT: Breeds in bogs of boreal forest and bushy tundra. Winters in marshes, flooded fields and in wet grassy areas surrounding lakes, pools and rivers etc.

2 SNIPE (COMMON SNIPE) *Gallinago gallinago* 25–27cm FIELD NOTES: When flushed flies off in an erratic manner. In flight wings show a white trailing edge, underwing usually shows white mid-wing patch and white bar. SONG/CALL: In display utters a repeated *chipper-chipper-chipper-chipper*. When disturbed gives a harsh *scaap*. HABITAT: Breeds in various marshy or boggy places. After breeding spreads to flooded fields and ditches.

3 GREAT SNIPE *Gallinago media* 27–29cm FIELD NOTES: Actions usually more sluggish than Snipe. Has extensive white on outer-tail, underwing uniformly dark barred. SONG/CALL: Utters a weak *aitch-aitch-aitch* when flushed. Various bubbling, twittering and gurgling sounds given when displaying. HABITAT: Breeds on open, damp grasslands usually with nearby bushes, less often in dry woodland. On migration occurs mainly in wet pastures, marsh and swamp edges.

4 SWINHOE'S SNIPE (CHINESE SNIPE) *Gallinago megala* 27–29cm FIELD NOTES: In flight shows small amount of toe projection. Underwing uniformly dark barred. Tertials shorter than primaries. SONG/CALL: Sometimes utters a gruff *scaap* when flushed. During display gives a repeated *tchiki*. HABITAT: Breeds in swamps and damp forest clearings, after breeding occurs in similar haunts as Pin-tailed Snipe.

5 PIN-TAILED SNIPE (PÍNTAIL SNIPE) *Gallinago stenura* 25–27cm FIELD NOTES: In flight toes project well beyond tail. Underwing uniformly dark barred. Supercilium wider at base of bill than Snipe. Tertials overlap primaries. Short tail. SONG/CALL: May utter a short *scaap* when flushed. During display-flight utters a repeated, hoarse *terre* or *tcheka*. HABITAT: Usually breeds in marshes, muddy pools and moist pastures etc. in tundra forest. On migration and winter occurs in similar situations to Snipe although may also visit dryer areas.

6 SOLITARY SNIPE *Gallinago solitaria* 29–31cm FIELD NOTES: Underwing uniformly dark barred. SONG/CALL: Gives a harsh *kensh* when flushed. During display utters a deep *choka-choka*. HABITAT: Breeds in mountain bogs and river valleys. On migration and winter found in a variety of damp places such as marshes, paddyfields, pastures etc.

7 LATHAM'S SNIPE (JAPANESE SNIPE) *Gallinago hardwickii* 28–30cm FIELD NOTES: Underwing uniformly dark barred. Tertials overlap primaries. Longer-tailed than Pin-tailed Snipe. SONG/CALL: Gives a short *chak* when flushed. Utters a *ji-ji-ji-zubiykahk-zubiyahk-zubiyahk* during circling display-flight, followed by a *ga-ga-ga* as bird dives. HABITAT: Breeds on heathland and moorland, often amid light woodland. Frequents freshwater margins in winter.

8 WOOD SNIPE (HIMALAYAN SNIPE) *Gallinago nemoricola* 28–32cm FIELD NOTES: Little-known, said to recall Woodcock in flight. Underwing closely barred dark. Barred belly. SONG/CALL: Occasionally utters a low, croaking *chock-chock* when flushed. HABITAT: Thought to breed in woodland at high altitude, during non-breeding season occurs at lower altitudes in mountain marshes, swamps and pools.

9 WOODCOCK (EURASIAN WOODCOCK) *Scolopax rusticola* 33–35cm FIELD NOTES: Usually encountered when flushed or during display-flight (roding) when flies above territory with slow wingbeats giving squeaks and grunts. SONG/CALL: Apart from display, see above, occasionally gives a snipe-like *schaap* or *schaap schaap*. HABITAT: Breeds in mixed, coniferous and broadleaved woodland with glades and damp areas for feeding.

10 AMANI WOODCOCK *Scolopax mira* 34–36cm FIELD NOTES: Often treated as conspecific to the very similar Woodcock. SONG/CALL: Little-recorded other than a continuous shrill *reep-reep-reep* given during distraction display. HABITAT: Evergreen forests and surrounding areas such as sugar cane fields.

49 WILLET, DOWITCHERS AND GODWITS

1 SHORT-BILLED DOWITCHER (COMMON DOWITCHER) *Limnodromus griseus* 25–29cm (Vagrant) FIELD NOTES: In non-breeding plumage difficult to separate from Long-billed Dowitcher, note call. In flight shows white oval from upper rump to mid-back. SONG/CALL: In flight gives a mellow, rapid *tututu* or *chu-du-du*. HABITAT: In native America: wet meadows, bogs and swampy coastal tundra. Winters on inland and coastal wetlands. RACES: *L. g. hendersoni* (fig 1b) west of Hudson Bay to Alaska.

2 LONG-BILLED DOWITCHER *Limnodromus scolopaceus* 27–30cm FIELD NOTES: In non-breeding plumage difficult to separate from Short-billed Dowitcher, note call. In flight shows white oval from upper rump to mid back. SONG/CALL: A sharp *kik* or *kik-kik-kik-kik* also *kreeek* when alarmed. In display, although recorded at other times, gives a rapid, repeated *pee-ter-wee-too*. HABITAT: Marshes and swamps on Arctic tundra. On migration frequents various wetlands both inland and coastal.

3 ASIAN DOWITCHER (ASIATIC or SNIPE-BILLED DOWITCHER) *Limnodromus semipalmatus* 33–36cm FIELD NOTES: Often associates with godwits. Lacks the contrasting white back of other dowitchers. SONG/CALL: A yelping *chep-chep* or *chowp* also a soft *kiaow*. At breeding site utters a soft, repeated *kewick* or *kru-ru*. HABITAT: Lake shores, flooded meadows and grassy bogs. On passage mainly coastal wetlands.

4 BLACK-TAILED GODWIT *Limosa limosa* 40–44cm FIELD NOTES: In flight has bold white bar on upperwing a white rump and black tail, underwing mainly white. SONG/CALL: A *kek*, *tuk* or *kip* often repeated. During display gives an excited *wick-a wick-a-wick-a*, a *tititit* and a hoarse *wee-eeh*. HABITAT: Damp moorland or pastures, lowland water-meadows and grassy marshes. Winters on estuaries, mudflats, lake shores and grassland. RACES: *L. l. islandica* Iceland, Shetland, Faeroes and Lofoten Island; *L l. melanuroides* E Asia. Both races are darker chestnut, the latter much smaller than nominate. Not illustrated.

5 HUDSONIAN GODWIT *Limosa haemastica* 36–42cm (Vagrant) FIELD NOTES: In flight has narrow white bar on upperwing, shorter than shown by Black-tailed Godwit, white rump and black tail, underwing-coverts and axillaries black. SONG/CALL: A nasal *toe-wit* or *wit* or similar, also a soft *chow-chow*. HABITAT: In native America: marshlands near coasts or rivers.

6 BAR-TAILED GODWIT *Limosa lapponica* 37–41cm FIELD NOTES: In flight shows white from rump to upper back, no white wingbar, tail barred, underwing mainly white. SONG/CALL: A high-pitched *kik* or *kiv-ik* often repeated, also a nasal *ke-wuh*. During display utters various phrases including a rapid *a-wik a-wik a-wik* and a *ku-wew*. HABITAT: Lowland tundra, forest tundra and rolling uplands. Winters mainly on estuaries and sandy or muddy coastal shores.

7 WILLET *Catoptrophorus* (*Tringa*) *semipalmatus* 33–41cm (Vagrant) FIELD NOTES: In flight, above and below, shows a broad white wingbar, primary tips, underwing-coverts and axillaries black, rump white. Actions much like Redshank. SONG/CALL: A loud *kip* or *wiek*, often repeated, given when alarmed. In flight gives a harsh *wee-wee-wee*. The *pill-will-willet* uttered during display is unlikely to heard in the region. HABITAT: In native America: saltmarsh, brackish lakes, also sandy beaches and tidal mudflats.

50 CURLEWS AND UPLAND SANDPIPER

1 **UPLAND SANDPIPER (UPLAND PLOVER)** *Bartramia longicauda* 28–32cm (Vagrant) FIELD NOTES: Juvenile similar to adult but looks more scaly and with plain, dark unbarred scapulars. SONG/CALL: Flight call is a piping *quip-ip-ip* or a *kwee-lip*. HABITAT: In native N America: various grasslands in both breeding and non-breeding seasons.

2 **LITTLE CURLEW (LITTLE WHIMBREL)** *Numenius minutus* 29–32cm FIELD NOTES: In display flies to a considerable height whilst singing, then dives producing a whistling from tail and wings. In flight underwing-coverts buff with dark bars. Wing tips level with tail. SONG/CALL: Song is a rising *corr-corr-corr* followed by a level *quee-quee-quee*. Flight call is a whistled *te-te-te* or a rougher *tchew-tchew-tchew*, also, when alarmed, a harsh *kweek-ek*. HABITAT: Breeds in clearings in Larch woodland, at other times occurs on various types of short grassland.

3 **ESKIMO CURLEW** *Numenius borealis* 29–34cm (Vagrant) FIELD NOTES: Almost extinct? Wing tips project beyond tail. In flight underwing-coverts cinnamon with dark bars. SONG/CALL: Not well documented some said to recall both Little Curlew and Upland Sandpiper. HABITAT: In native Canada and America: breeds on Arctic tundra. Frequents various types of short grassland during non-breeding season.

4 **BRISTLE-THIGHED CURLEW** *Numenius tahitiensis* 40–44cm (Vagrant) FIELD NOTES: In flight shows bright cinnamon rump and uppertail. Generally more cinnamon than Whimbrel. SONG/CALL: A rippling *whe-whe-whe-whe* a ringing *whee-wheeoo* and whistled *chi-u-it*. HABITAT: In native Alaska: barren tundra, winters on coasts of tropical islands.

5 **WHIMBREL** *Numenius phaeopus* 40–46cm FIELD NOTES: In flight shows white rump and lower back. American race lacks white on rump and back. SONG/CALL: On breeding grounds utters an accelerating bubbling that rises in pitch. A rippling *pupupupupupupu* is the most frequently heard call. HABITAT: Breeds on moorland and tundra, on migration frequents coastal areas and nearby pastures. RACES: *N. p. hudsonicus* (Hudsonian Curlew) (fig 5b) (Vagrant) N and S America and Australasia.

6 **SLENDER-BILLED CURLEW** *Numenius tenuirostris* 36–41cm FIELD NOTES: Endangered. In flight shows white rump and lower back. Generally slightly paler than Curlew. Juvenile has streaks on flanks in place of the spots of adult. SONG/CALL: A short *cour-lee* higher pitched than Curlew, also a sharp *cu-wee* given when disturbed. HABITAT: Breeds on bogs and marshland in Siberian taiga forest. Winters on fresh or brackish waters and near-by grassland.

7 **CURLEW (EURASIAN, WESTERN or COMMON CURLEW)** *Numenius arquata* 50–60cm FIELD NOTES: In flight shows white rump and lower back. Females slightly larger and longer-billed than males. SONG/CALL: A far carrying *cour-lee* and a stammering *tutututu* when disturbed, also a sequence of bubbling or rippling notes given mainly during the breeding season. HABITAT: Breeds on moorland, heathland and grassy meadows, winters mainly at coastal sites but also visits pastures and arable land.

8 **FAR-EASTERN CURLEW (EASTERN or AUSTRALIAN CURLEW)** *Numenius madagascariensis* 60–66cm FIELD NOTES: Shy. Sometimes mixes with flocks of Curlew. In flight lacks white markings of Curlew. Female slightly larger and longer-billed than male (longest bill of any wader). SONG/CALL: Similar to Curlew but bubbling notes are said to be less melodic and contact *cour-lee* flatter. When disturbed gives a strident *ker ker-ee-ker-ee*. HABITAT: Breeds in bogs and marshes, winters mainly on estuaries and beaches less so on inland wetlands.

51 SHANKS AND *TRINGA* SANDPIPERS

1 SPOTTED REDSHANK (DUSKY REDSHANK) *Tringa erythropus* 29–32cm FIELD NOTES: Moulting birds have non-breeding plumage blotched with black. In flight shows white oval in centre of back. Often wades up to belly. SONG/CALL: In flight gives a distinctive *chu-it*. When alarmed utters a short *chip*. During display gives a series of creaking, grinding notes. HABITAT: Open Arctic tundra with nearby bogs and marshes. After breeding occurs on upper reaches of estuaries, also on lagoons, lakes and marshes.

2 REDSHANK (COMMON REDSHANK) *Tringa tetanus* 27–29cm FIELD NOTES: Noisy and timid. In flight shows white oval in centre of back and striking white secondaries and inner primaries. SONG/CALL: A piping *teu-hu* or *teu-hu-hu* or similar. When alarmed utters a loud *tli-tli-tli-tli*. During display-flight gives a musical yodelling. HABITAT: Wide variety of coastal and inland wetlands.

3 MARSH SANDPIPER *Tringa stagnatilis* 22–25cm FIELD NOTES: In flight looks like a small Greenshank, but toes project well beyond tail. SONG/CALL: A plaintive *keeuw* or *kyu-kyu-kyu*. When flushed utters a loud *yip*. During display has a yodelling *tu-ee-u tu-ee-u tu-ee-e…* and a twittering *chip chip chip-ipepepepepepe*. HABITAT: Open freshwater marshland. After breeding frequents marshes, ponds, saltmarshes and estuaries.

4 GREENSHANK (COMMON or GREATER GREENSHANK) *Tringa nebularia* 30–35cm FIELD NOTES: In flight shows white rump and back, toes project slightly beyond tail. SONG/CALL: A ringing *chew-chew-chew* and a *kiu kiu kiu* when alarmed. During display gives a repeated musical *too-hoo-too-hoo…* HABITAT: Taiga and forest areas with clearings, wooded moorland, marshes and bogs. Winters on a large variety of coastal and inland wetlands.

5 SPOTTED GREENSHANK (NORDMANN'S GREENSHANK) *Tringa guttifer* 29–32cm FIELD NOTES: Rare. In flight shows white rump and back, tail pale grey. Toes do not project beyond tail. SONG/CALL: A piercing *keyew*, also recorded is a harsh *gwark*. HABITAT: Coastal lowland swamp and marshy areas in sparse larch forests. On passage occurs mainly on coastal mudflats, sandflats and lagoons.

6 GREATER YELLOWLEGS *Tringa melanoleuca* 29–33cm (Vagrant) FIELD NOTES: In flight shows square white rump, toes project well beyond tail. SONG/CALL: A clear, slightly descending *teu-teu-teu*, very like that of Greenshank. HABITAT: In native America: forest bogs. After breeding frequents a variety of freshwater or brackish wetlands.

7 LESSER YELLOWLEGS *Tringa flavipes* 23–25cm (Vagrant) FIELD NOTES: In flight looks very similar to, but smaller than, Greater Yellowlegs. SONG/CALL: A flat, harsh *tew-tew* or *tew*. HABITAT: In native America: forest bogs and grassy clearings. After breeding occurs on a wide variety of coastal and inland wetlands.

8 WOOD SANDPIPER *Tringa glareola* 19–21cm FIELD NOTES: In flight shows white rump and narrow barring on tail. SONG/CALL: A high-pitched *chiff-iff-iff* and a *chip* or *chip-chip-chip* when alarmed. Gives a series of yodelling notes during display. HABITAT: Forest bogs and lightly wooded marshes. After breeding occurs on inland lakes, pools, flooded grasslands and marshes.

9 SOLITARY SANDPIPER *Tringa solitaria* 18–21cm (Vagrant) FIELD NOTES: In flight shows dark rump and barred outer tail feathers. SONG/CALL: An excited *peet*, *peet-weet-weet* or *tewit-weet*. HABITAT: In native America: similar to Green Sandpiper.

10 GREEN SANDPIPER *Tringa ochropus* 21–24cm FIELD NOTES: In flight shows white rump and broad bars on tail. SONG/CALL: A musical *tlueet-wit-wit* and a sharp *wit-wit-wit* when alarmed, variations of both these used in display. HABITAT: Damp areas in woodlands. After breeding frequents pools, lake edges, stream sides and ditches.

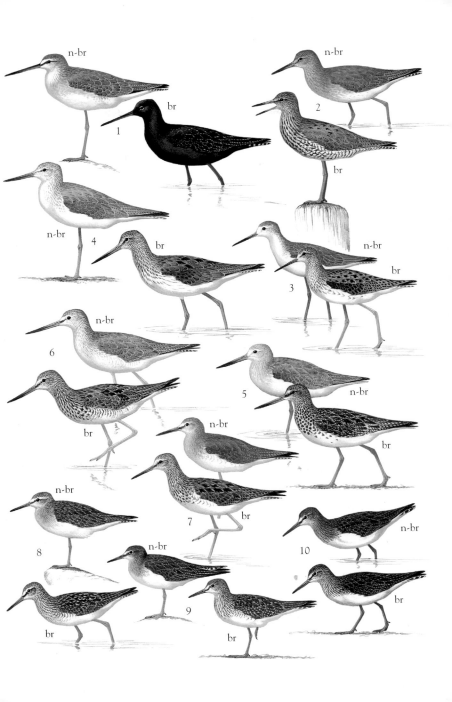

52 TEREK SANDPIPER, *ACTITIS* SANDPIPERS, TATTLERS AND PHALAROPES

1 TEREK SANDPIPER *Xenus cinereus* 22–25cm FIELD NOTES: In flight shows a wide, white trailing edge. Often feeds in active, dashing manner. SONG/CALL: In flight gives a rippling *du-du-du-du-du*, or a mellow Redshank-like *chu-du-du*. During display repeats a melodious *ka-klee-rree ka-klee-rree ka-klee-rree*. HABITAT: Breeds by upland rivers and streams, otherwise usually encountered in a variety of wetland areas such as lakes, marshes, estuaries and saltpans.

2 COMMON SANDPIPER *Actitis hypoeucos* 19–21cm FIELD NOTES: In flight shows white bar on upperwing. Flies low with flicking wings. Bobs tail when walking. SONG/CALL: Gives a piping *tswee-wee-wee* in flight, also a *sweeet-eet* when alarmed. During breeding display-flight, although often heard in winter and migration, utters a repeated *kittie-needie*. HABITAT: Breeds by upland rivers and streams otherwise occurs on various freshwater and saltwater areas.

3 SPOTTED SANDPIPER *Actitis macularius* 18–20cm (Vagrant) FIELD NOTES: In flight white wingbar on upperwing shorter and less distinct than on Common Sandpiper. Flies with flicking wings. Bobs tail when walking. SONG/CALL: In flight gives a rising *peet-weet* or a single *peet*. HABITAT: In native N America: haunts are similar to those of the Common Sandpiper.

4 GREY-TAILED TATTLER (POLYNESIAN, SIBERIAN or GREY-RUMPED TATTLER, GREY-RUMPED SANDPIPER) *Heteroscelus* (*Tringa*) *brevipes* 24–27cm FIELD NOTES: In non-breeding plumage shows slate-grey underwing that contrasts with white belly when in flight. Bobs tail when walking. SONG/CALL: In flight utters a *tu-whip* and when alarmed a *klee*, *klee-klee* or *weet-eet*. HABITAT: Breeds on rocky upland rivers, on migration usually occurs on sandy or muddy shorelines.

5 WANDERING TATTLER *Heteroscelus* (*Tringa*) *incanus* 26–29cm FIELD NOTES: Possibly breeds in extreme east of Palearctic. Only safely distinguished from Grey-tailed Tattler in non-breeding season by voice. SONG/CALL: In flight gives a ringing *pew-tu-tu-tu-tu-tu*. HABITAT: Breeds by mountain streams, at other times on rocky coasts and adjoining beaches.

6 WILSON'S PHALAROPE *Steganopus tricolor* 22–24cm (Vagrant) FIELD NOTES: In flight shows white patch on lower rump. Tends to swim less than other phalaropes. When feeding on land often uses a hurried walk with a feverish pecking action or adopts an attitude with tail up and breast almost touching the ground. SONG/CALL: A soft *aangh* sometimes given in flight. HABITAT: In native N America: small lakes and pools in prairie or taiga region, winters on various types of inland waters.

7 RED-NECKED PHALAROPE (NORTHERN PHALAROPE) *Phalaropus lobatus* 18–19cm FIELD NOTES: In flight upperwing shows white wingbar. Regularly swims. Thin billed. SONG/CALL: At breeding grounds utters various warblings and twitterings. In flight gives a short *kip*, a harsh *cherp* and a *kerrek*. HABITAT: Breeds on bogs and pools in moorland and tundra, on migration occurs on lakes and pools and coastal waters, winters at sea.

8 GREY PHALAROPE (RED PHALAROPE) *Phalaropus fulicaria* 20–22cm FIELD NOTES: In flight upperwing shows wide white wingbar. Regularly swims. Short, thick bill. SONG/CALL: At breeding grounds gives a buzzing *prrrt* and various chirrupings and twitterings. In flight utters a sharp *pik*. HABITAT: Breeds in coastal tundra marshes. On migration sometimes found on coastal pools or lakes, otherwise strictly pelagic.

53 SANDPIPERS, RUFF AND TURNSTONES

1 SPOON-BILLED SANDPIPER (SPOONBILL SANDPIPER) *Eurynorhynchus pygmaeus* 14–16cm FIELD NOTES: Rare. In flight has prominent white bar on upperwing, sides of rump white. Sweeps bill from side to side while feeding in shallow water. SONG/CALL: A rolling *preep* or a shrill *wheet*. During display gives a descending, cicada-like trill *preer-prr-prr*. HABITAT: Coastal tundra, usually near freshwater lakes, pools and marshes. On passage occurs on muddy coasts and coastal lagoons.

2 BROAD-BILLED SANDPIPER *Limicola falcinellus* 16–18cm FIELD NOTES: In flight shows narrow white bar on upperwing, in non-breeding plumage shows a dark leading edge, much like non-breeding Sanderling. SONG/CALL: A buzzing *chrrreet* or *trrreet*. During display-flight gives rhythmical, buzzing trills *sprrr-sprrr-sprrr* and a fast *swirrirrirrirr…*. HABITAT: Wettest parts of open bogs. On passage frequents inland and coastal wetlands.

3 STILT SANDPIPER *Micropalama* (*Calidris*) *himantopus* 18–23cm (Vagrant) FIELD NOTES: In flight has inconspicuous white bar on upperwing and white rump, feet project well beyond tail. Often wades up to belly. SONG/CALL: A soft *drrr*, *kirrr* or *grrrt*, also a hoarse *djew* and a clear *whu*. HABITAT: In native America: dry or wet tundra, after breeding frequents inland and coastal wetlands.

4 BUFF-BREASTED SANDPIPER *Tryngites subruficollis* 18–20cm FIELD NOTES: Often very tame. In flight from below shows dark tips to primary coverts, forming a crescent mark. SONG/CALL: Generally silent, occasionally utters a short *prrreet* when flushed. During display makes rapid clicking sounds. HABITAT: Arctic tundra. On passage frequents grasslands or dry mud surrounds of lakes and rivers.

5 RUFF (REEVE: female only) *Philomachus pugnax* 26–32cm FIELD NOTES: Breeding males unmistakable but very variable. In moult males have non-breeding type plumage splattered with dark blotches on the breast. In flight shows narrow white bar on upperwing and prominent white sides to long uppertail-coverts. Large numbers gather in leks to display, spreading ruffs, jumping and jostling or standing motionless in an effort to attract a female. SONG/CALL: Generally silent although may give a low *kuk* in flight. HABITAT: Coastal tundra, marsh fringes and damp meadows. In non-breeding season frequents lake, pool and river margins, wet grasslands and marshes.

6 TURNSTONE (RUDDY TURNSTONE) *Arenaria interpres* 21–26cm FIELD NOTES: Unmistakable. In flight, from above, wing shows prominent white bar and white patch on innerwing-coverts. Centre of back and lower rump white split by dark band on upper rump. SONG/CALL: A rapid, staccato *trik-tuk-tuk-tuk*, *tuk-e-tuk* or *chit-uk*. When alarmed utters a sharp *chick-ik*, *kuu* or *teu*. During display gives a long rolling rattle. HABITAT: Mainly stony coastal plains or lowlands. After breeding mostly coastal, frequenting stony and rocky shores.

7 BLACK TURNSTONE *Arenaria melanocephala* 22–25cm (Vagrant) FIELD NOTES: Actions, habits and flight patterning very similar to Turnstone. SONG/CALL: A trilling *skirrr*. HABITAT: In native America: breeds on Alaska's coastal plain, winters mainly on rocky coasts.

1

n-br

br

2

n-br

br

4

3

n-br

br

♂ br
varieties

5

♀ br

♂ br

♂ n-br

6

n-br

7

n-br

br

br

54 SKUAS

1 POMARINE SKUA (POMARINE JAEGER) *Stercorarius pomarinus* 46–51cm FIELD NOTES: In flight the bulkiest of all 'smaller' skuas. Aggressively pursues seabirds in a bid to steal food, has been known to go as far as killing the victim. Juvenile has upperparts variable from mid-brown to dark brown, barred paler. Underparts paler barred dark. Head uniform in colour, from grey-brown to dark brown. Wings show distinct white flash at base of primaries. SONG/CALL: During disputes at breeding colonies gives a series of nasal screams, otherwise generally silent. HABITAT: Breeds on coastal tundra, after breeding mainly pelagic.

2 ARCTIC SKUA (PARASITIC JAEGER) *Stercorarius parasiticus* 41–46cm FIELD NOTES: Aerobatically chases and harries seabirds in an attempt to make them disgorge food. Juveniles very variable, many similar to juvenile Pomarine Skuas, especially dark individuals, pale forms usually show a buff or grey-buff head. Wings show distinct white flash at base of primaries. SONG/CALL: On breeding grounds utters a loud, nasal mewing *eh-glow*. Also recorded are a harsh *kek* or *kook* and in flight a nasal *gi-ooo*. Otherwise generally silent. HABITAT: Breeds on coastal tundra, coastal moorland and barren islands. After breeding mainly pelagic.

3 LONG-TAILED SKUA (LONG-TAILED JAEGER) *Stercorarius longicaudus* 48–53cm FIELD NOTES: In flight often gives the impression of being heavy chested. Less piratical than other skuas, when does indulge tends to chase terns. Juvenile very variable and similar in plumage to juvenile Arctic Skua, best told by lack of extensive white flash at base of primaries and general lighter structure. SONG/CALL: On breeding grounds gives a rattling *krr-krr-krr-kri-kri-kri* followed by a repeated, mournful *pheeeu*. Also, when alarmed, utters a *krik* or *kreek*. Otherwise mainly silent. HABITAT: Breeds on coastal and inland tundra. After breeding mainly pelagic.

4 GREAT SKUA (BONXIE) *Stercorarius skua* 53–58cm FIELD NOTES: Very aggressive to seabirds, recorded killing victims when attempting to rob them of food. Juvenile has underparts uniform rufous, upperparts grey-brown with paler rufous spots and fringes, head grey-brown. SONG/CALL: On breeding grounds gives a plaintive, wailing *piah-piah-piah-piah….* In alarm utters a harsh *tuk* or *gek* and when attacking intruders at breeding site gives a strangled *kayaya*. HABITAT: Breeds on coastal moorland and offshore islands. After breeding mainly pelagic.

5 SOUTHERN SKUA (ANTARCTIC SKUA) *Stercorarius antarctica* 61–66cm (Vagrant) FIELD NOTES: Habits similar to its northern counterpart the Great Skua. Juveniles probably inseparable in the field. SONG/CALL: Generally silent. HABITAT: In native Falkland Islands and SE Argentina: breeds in grassy or rocky areas near sea. Winters at sea. RACES: *S. a. lonnbergi* (Brown Skua) (fig 5b) Subantarctic Islands.

6 SOUTH POLAR SKUA (MACCORMICK'S SKUA) *Stercorarius maccormicki* 50–55cm FIELD NOTES: Various morphs, grading from pale to dark, all tend to lack any rufous in plumage. Much care is needed when trying to separate darker forms from other large skuas. Juveniles of pale and dark forms similar to respective adult, apart from some pale feather edges on upperparts and blue bill with a black tip. SONG/CALL: Generally silent during the non-breeding season. HABITAT: Pelagic. Regular non-breeding visitor to the N Atlantic and N Pacific probably much overlooked in Palearctic.

55 GULLS

Due to the complex plumages of young gulls (often a four year process to get from the brown of juveniles to the grey of adults) and the difficulty in explaining such within a limited text, it was thought better to refer the reader to books that cover this area more fully. (*See Further Reading.*)

1 GREAT BLACK-HEADED GULL (PALLAS'S GULL) *Larus ichthyaetus* 57–61cm FIELD NOTES: Flight action ponderous with a prominent projecting head. Upperwing shows a narrow black subterminal band on white outer primaries. SONG/CALL: A low *kyow-kyow* and a nasal *kraagh*. HABITAT: Open country by freshwater or brackish lakes. In winter mainly coastal.

2 RELICT GULL (MONGOLIAN GULL) *Larus relictus* 44cm FIELD NOTES: Gregarious, breeds in large colonies. Has similar upperwing pattern to Great Black-headed Gull. SONG/CALL: A laughing *ka-ka ka-ka kee-aa*. HABITAT: Shores or islands of saline mountain lakes.

3 MEDITERRANEAN GULL *Larus melanocephalus* 36–38cm FIELD NOTES: Upperwing of adult very pale silvery-white, primaries entirely white. Colonial. In some areas pairs frequently breed amid Black-headed Gull colonies. SONG/CALL: A *yeah*, *jeeah* or *ga-u-a*, also a cooing *kyow*. HABITAT: Brackish and freshwater lakes, lagoons and marshes. Winters mainly in coastal areas.

4 LITTLE GULL *Larus (Hydrocoloeus) minutus* 25–30cm FIELD NOTES: Buoyant, tern-like flight. In flight adult upperwing silvery-grey, while the underwing is dark grey, both show a white trailing edge. SONG/CALL: A short nasal *keck* or *keck-keck-keck*. During display gives a shrill *ke-kay ke-kay ke-kay*. HABITAT: Well-vegetated, lowland freshwater lakes, rivers and marshes. Winters mainly on coasts or nearby lakes and lagoons, sometimes seen inland on migration.

5 SABINE'S GULL *Larus (Xema) sabini* 27–33cm FIELD NOTES: Distinctive tricoloured upperwing pattern, grey coverts, black outer primaries and primary coverts, white inner primaries and secondaries. Tail forked. Juvenile Kittiwake can show similar pattern but usually shows black band between coverts and secondaries. SONG/CALL: A grating *krrr*. HABITAT: Near marshes and pools in Arctic tundra. During migration mainly pelagic.

6 SAUNDERS'S GULL (CHINESE BLACK-HEADED GULL) *Larus (Chroicocephalus) saundersi* 29–32cm FIELD NOTES: Buoyant tern-like flight. Inner primaries form a black wedge, making underwing pattern diagnostic. Upperwing is grey with black tips, white outer primaries. SONG/CALL: A shrill *eek eek*. HABITAT: Coastal wetlands. Winters on coasts.

7 BONAPARTE'S GULL *Larus (Chroicocephalus) philadelphia* 28–30cm (Vagrant) FIELD NOTES: Underwing grey with white outer primaries, all primaries black-tipped. Upperwing pattern similar to Saunders's Gull. SONG/CALL: A nasal *chirp*, also a tern-like *tee-er*. HABITAT: In native America: tree-lined marshes, ponds and lakes. Winters in coastal areas.

8 BLACK-HEADED GULL (COMMON BLACK-HEADED GULL) *Larus (Chroicocephalus) ridibundus* 37–43cm FIELD NOTES: Upperwing grey with black-tipped white outer primaries. Underwing pale grey, leading primary white, tipped black, other outer primaries are dark grey with black tips. SONG/CALL: A high-pitched *karr*, *kreeay* or *krreearr*, also a sharp *kek-kek*. HABITAT: Brackish and freshwater lakes, lagoons and marshes. Very cosmopolitan post breeding, including coasts, lakes, towns, also many types of field and grassland.

9 BROWN-HEADED GULL (INDIAN BLACK-HEADED GULL) *Larus (Chroicocephalus) brunnicephalus* 41–45cm FIELD NOTES: Upperwing grey, outer primaries white with broad black tips, broken by white subterminal 'mirrors'. Underwing grey, primaries blackish the outer most having white subterminal 'mirrors'. SONG/CALL: A harsh *gek gek* or *grarhh*, also a wailing *ko-yek ko yek* and a raucous *kreeak*. HABITAT: Islands in high-altitude lakes or marshes. Winters on coasts, large lakes and rivers.

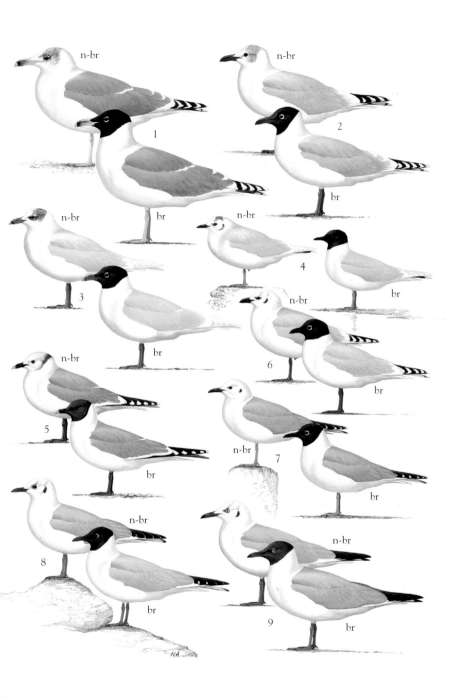

56 GULLS

See note on plate 55 referring to young gulls.

1 SOOTY GULL (HEMPRICH'S or ADEN GULL) *Larus hemprichii* 43–48cm FIELD NOTES: Sociable, often occurs with White-eyed Gull. Upper and underwing very dark with a white trailing edge. SONG/CALL: A mewing *kaarr*, *keee-aaar* or laughing *veeeaah ve vah veeeaah*, also a high-pitched *kee-kee-kee*. HABITAT: Coastal, including harbours and ports.

2 WHITE-EYED GULL *Larus leucophthalmus* 39–43cm FIELD NOTES: Sociable, often occurs with Sooty Gull. Upper and underwing dark grey with a white trailing edge. SONG/CALL: Similar to Sooty Gull but less harsh and slightly lower pitched. HABITAT: Coastal, including harbours.

3 LAUGHING GULL *Larus atricilla* 36–41cm (Vagrant) FIELD NOTES: Upperwing grey with a white trailing edge and black outer primaries. SONG/CALL: A laughing *ha-ha-ha....* HABITAT: In native America: coastal beaches, islands and saltmarshes.

4 FRANKLIN'S GULL *Larus pipixcan* 32–38cm (Vagrant) FIELD NOTES: In flight shows grey centre to tail, upperwing grey with white trailing edge and broad white tips on outer primaries, broken by black subterminal band. SONG/CALL: A soft *kruk* and a shrill *guk*, usually uttered while feeding. HABITAT: In native America: inland lakes, river valleys, marshes, coastal lagoons and sandbanks.

5 GREY-HEADED GULL (GREY-HOODED GULL) *Larus* (*Chroicocephalus*) *cirrocephalus* 38–43cm FIELD NOTES: Occasionally shows a pinkish tinge to underparts. Upperwing grey, base of outer primaries white otherwise black with white subterminal 'mirrors' on outer most pair. Underwing dusky, primaries blackish with white 'mirrors' on outermost pair. SONG/CALL: A harsh *garr*, a querulous *kwarr* or drawn-out *caw-caw*. HABITAT: Mainly coasts also on inland lakes and rivers.

6 GREAT BLACK-BACKED GULL (GREATER BLACK-BACKED GULL) *Larus marinus* 64–78cm FIELD NOTES: Can be aggressive and predatory. Heavy and powerful flight. Black upperwing shows white trailing edge and extensive white tips to outermost primaries. SONG/CALL: A hoarse *oow-oow-oow*, also a deep *owk*, all notes gruffer than other large gulls. HABITAT: Coasts, locally on inland lakes.

7 SLATY-BACKED GULL (KAMCHATKA GULL) *Larus schistisagus* 55–67cm FIELD NOTES: Some show paler grey mantle. In flight shows a broad white trailing edge and often has an indistinct white band dividing the slaty upperwing from the black-tipped outer primaries, the latter has a white subterminal 'mirror' on outermost feather. SONG/CALL: Similar to Herring Gull. HABITAT: Sea cliffs, rocky islets and sandy shores. Winters in coastal areas.

8 LESSER BLACK-BACKED GULL *Larus fuscus* 51–61cm FIELD NOTES: Gregarious, often mixes with other gull species. Upperwing has white trailing edge, black outer primaries have white subterminal 'mirror' on outermost feather. SONG/CALL: Similar to Herring Gull, although usually deeper. HABITAT: Coastal and inland wetlands, including cliffs, dunes, moorland and islands in lakes or rivers. Winters mainly in coastal areas although often occurs inland on wetlands and farmland. RACES: *L. f. graellsii* (fig 8b) Britain, France, Iberia, Iceland and Faeroes; *L. f. heuglini* (Heuglin's or Siberian Gull) (fig 8c) N Siberia, sometimes considered to be a full species.

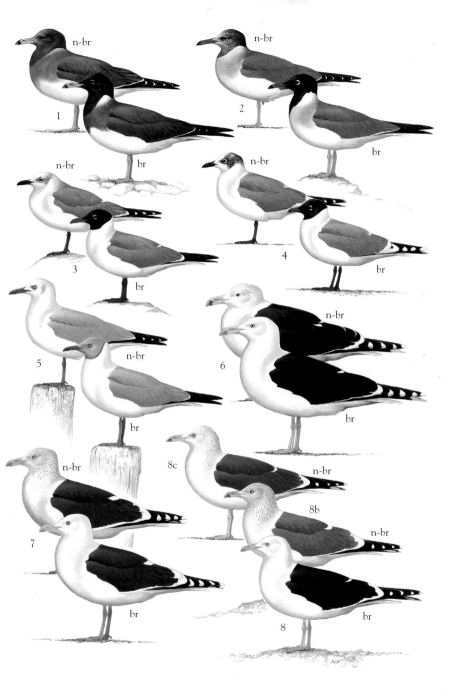

57 GULLS

See note on plate 55 referring to young gulls.

1 HERRING GULL *Larus argentatus* 55–67cm FIELD NOTES: The familiar gull of NW Europe. Gregarious. Upperwing shows black-tipped outer primaries with white subterminal 'mirrors' on two outermost feathers. SONG/CALL: A loud, laughing *keeah-keeah-keeah-keah-kau-kau…*, also a short *keeah*, *keeow* or *kyow*. When alarmed utters *gag-ag-ag*. HABITAT: Coastal and near coastal areas, also locally on inland moorland. After breeding very cosmopolitan including coasts, farmland, landfill sites, cities and towns. RACES: *L. a. vegae* (Vega Gull) (fig 1b) NE Siberia, sometimes considered a full species.

2 YELLOW-LEGGED GULL *Larus michahellis* 52–58cm FIELD NOTES: Actions, habits and upperwing pattern very similar to Herring Gull. SONG/CALL: Similar to Herring Gull, although slightly deeper and more nasal. HABITAT: Coastal areas, also locally on inland lakes and rivers. Post breeding frequents coasts, inland wetlands, fields and rubbish dumps. RACES: *L. m. cachinnans* (Caspian Gull) Black Sea to Kazakhstan and Caspian Sea, paler above with large subterminal 'mirrors' on two outermost primary feathers. Not illustrated. At the time of writing the placement of this race is unsure, it may well be a race of Herring Gull or more probably a full species.

3 CALIFORNIA GULL *Larus californicus* 47–54cm (Vagrant) FIELD NOTES: Gregarious scavenger. Actions, habits and wing pattern similar to Herring Gull. SONG/CALL: A scratchy *aow* and *uh-uh-uh*, also a squealing *kiarr*. Laughing call much as Herring Gulls, but higher pitched. HABITAT: In native America: breeds on inland lakes, winters on coasts, inland wetlands, farmland and towns and cities.

4 ARMENIAN GULL *Larus armenicus* 54–62cm FIELD NOTES: Gregarious. Upperwing pattern similar to Herring Gull but with one white subterminal 'mirror' on outermost primary feather. SONG/CALL: Similar to Yellow-legged Gull. HABITAT: Inland lakes, rivers and marshes, winters on coasts and inland wetlands.

5 ICELAND GULL (GREENLAND GULL) *Larus glaucoides* 55–64cm FIELD NOTES: Winter visitor. Often encountered within flocks of other gull species. Upperwing very pale grey with white outer primaries. SONG/CALL: Similar to Herring Gull but higher pitched. HABITAT: Coastal areas including harbours and ports, also on inland lakes and rubbish dumps. RACES: *L. g. kumlieni* (Kumlien's Gull) (Vagrant) (fig 5b) NE Canada, sometimes considered a full species.

6 GLAUCOUS-WINGED GULL *Larus glaucescens* 61–68cm FIELD NOTES: Aggressive predator. Slow powerful flight. Upperwing pattern resembles Herring Gull but outer primaries grey. SONG/CALL: A low *kak-kak-kak* or *klook-klook-klook*, a deep *kow-kow*, a high-pitched *keer-keer*, also a screamed *ka-ka-ako*. HABITAT: Mostly coastal including ports and harbours, also visits rubbish dumps.

7 GLAUCOUS GULL *Larus hyperboreus* 64–77cm FIELD NOTES: Can be an aggressive scavenger. In flight broad-winged and more lumbering than the otherwise similar and smaller Iceland Gull. SONG/CALL: Generally silent but most notes as Herring Gull, although more hoarse. HABITAT: Coastal and inland cliffs, also offshore islands and open land near coasts. Winters mainly on coasts, including harbours, also inland on rubbish dumps.

8 THAYER'S GULL *Larus thayeri* 56–63cm (Vagrant) FIELD NOTES: Actions and habits similar to Herring Gull. Upperwing shows dark grey outer primaries with white subterminal 'mirrors' on the two outermost feathers. Often considered to be a race of Iceland Gull or Herring Gull. SONG/CALL: Similar to Herring Gull? HABITAT: In native America: breeds on coastal cliffs, winters mainly in coastal areas, including harbours and nearby rubbish dumps.

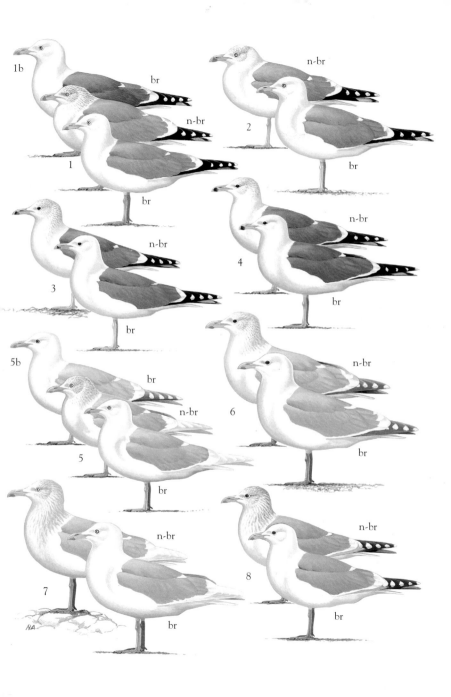

1b

br

n-br

1

br

2

n-br

br

3

n-br

br

4

n-br

br

5b

br

n-br

5

br

6

n-br

br

7

n-br

br

8

n-br

br

NA

58 GULLS

See note on plate 55 referring to young gulls.

1 SLENDER-BILLED GULL *Larus (Chroicocephalus) genei* 42–44cm FIELD NOTES: Often encountered in small parties. Upperwing shows white outer primaries tipped black, which resembles non-breeding Black-headed Gull, but present species always looks longer-necked. SONG/CALL: A harsh rolling *krerrr*, other notes as Black-headed Gull but lower pitched. HABITAT: Saline and freshwater lakes, coasts and inland seas. Winters mainly on coasts.

2 BLACK-TAILED GULL (TEMMINCK'S or JAPANESE GULL) *Larus crassirostris* 44–47cm FIELD NOTES: Often in large colonies. Upperwing primaries are black with small white tips, outermost feather may have a small white subterminal 'mirror'. SONG/CALL: A plaintive mewing. HABITAT: Seashores, sea cliffs and rocky islands, winters in coastal areas.

3 AUDOUIN'S GULL *Larus audouinii* 48–52cm FIELD NOTES: Colonial breeder. Usually feeds at sea on fish, less of a scavenger than other gulls. Upperwing shows black outer primaries with small white tips and tiny white subterminal 'mirror' on outermost feather. SONG/CALL: A nasal *gleh-i-eh*, a low *ug-ug-uk* and a raucous *argh argh argh....* HABITAT: Rocky islands. Post breeding occurs on coastal bays, estuaries and beaches.

4 RING-BILLED GULL *Larus delawarensis* 43–47cm (Vagrant) FIELD NOTES: Sociable usually mixes with other gulls. Upperwing has black outer primaries with small, white subterminal 'mirror' on outermost feather. SONG/CALL: A mellow *kowk*, other notes like Herring Gull but higher pitched and more nasal. HABITAT: In native America: breeds on inland lakes and wet pastures, winters on estuaries, bays, coastal pools, lakes, fields and rubbish dumps.

5 COMMON GULL (MEW GULL) *Larus canus* 40–46cm FIELD NOTES: Often associates with other gulls, especially in winter. Upperwing shows black outer primaries with prominent white subterminal 'mirrors' on outermost feathers. SONG/CALL: A high-pitched, laughing *ke ke ke kleeeh-a...kleeeh-a...kay-a kay-a kay-a kay-a ke ke*, also a yelping *keea keea*. When alarmed gives a persistent *glee-u glee-u glee-u....* HABITAT: Coastal marshes and cliffs, beaches and inland moorland. Winters in a wide variety of locations including coasts, lakes, reservoirs, farmland and town parks. RACES: *L. c. kamtschatschensis* (Kamchatka Gull) (fig 5b) NE Siberia.

6 ROSS'S GULL (ROSY GULL) *Rhodostethia rosea* 29–32cm FIELD NOTES: In flight, which is light and buoyant, shows pointed tail and pale grey upperwing with black edged outermost primary, underwing mid-grey with white secondaries and tips of inner primaries. SONG/CALL: A melodic *a-wo a-wo a-wo* and *claw claw claw*. Also a squabbling *miaw miaw miaw* and a soft *kew*. HABITAT: Marshy areas in tundra and taiga. Winters at the edge of pack ice and at sea, occasionally blown into coastal areas.

7 KITTIWAKE (BLACK-LEGGED KITTIWAKE) *Rissa tridactyla* 38–40cm FIELD NOTES: Colonial breeder, sometimes in very large numbers. Outer primaries on upper and underwing black-tipped, underwing white. Slightly forked tail. At sea often scavenges around fishing boats. SONG/CALL: A nasal, wailing *kitt-i-waak kitt-i-waak*, a harsh *vek-vek-vek* or *kek-kek-kek* a thin *zeep* and a short *kya*. HABITAT: Coastal cliffs and islands, also locally on buildings and piers. Winters at sea, unless blown inshore.

8 RED-LEGGED KITTIWAKE *Rissa brevirostris* 36–38cm FIELD NOTES: Habits much as Kittiwake. Wing pattern similar to Kittiwake, although underwing grey. SONG/CALL: Similar to Kittiwake, although said to be higher pitched. HABITAT: Cliffs on remote islands. Winters at sea.

9 IVORY GULL *Pagophila eburnea* 40–43cm FIELD NOTES: Unmistakable. Aggressive scavenger, especially around animal carcasses. Juvenile white with black mask and black spots at tips of mantle and wing feathers. SONG/CALL: A shrill, tern-like *kree-ar* or *keeer*. Other notes said to be like Black-headed Gull. HABITAT: Sea cliffs, also rocky or flat shores. Winters around pack ice.

59 TERNS

1 BLACK TERN *Chlidonias niger* 22–24cm FIELD NOTES: Buoyant foraging flight, regularly dipping down to pick insects from water surface. Rump grey. Underwing pale grey. Tail shallowly forked. SONG/CALL: A weak *kik* or *kik-kik*. Also shrill, nasal *kyeh*, *kreek* or *ki ki ki* when alarmed. HABITAT: Vegetated inland lakes, ponds and marshes. On migration, lakes, marshes and estuaries.

2 WHITE-WINGED TERN (WHITE-WINGED BLACK TERN) *Chlidonias leucopterus* 23–27cm FIELD NOTES: Actions similar to Black Tern. Rump white. Underwing-coverts black. Tail very shallowly forked, appears square. SONG/CALL: A harsh high-pitched *kreek*, a soft *kek* and a rasping *kesch* or *chr-re re*. HABITAT: Vegetated inland lakes, ponds, marshes and rice fields. On migration, estuaries, lagoons and lakes.

3 WHISKERED TERN *Chlidonias hybridus* 23–29cm FIELD NOTES: Actions similar to Black Tern, although sometimes uses plunge-diving to feed. Rump grey, paler in non-breeding plumage. Tail shallowly forked. SONG/CALL: A rasping *cherk* also a *kek* or *kek kek*. HABITAT: Vegetated lakes, pools, rivers and marshes. On migration, lakes, estuaries and coastal lagoons.

4 WHITE-CHEEKED TERN *Sterna repressa* 32–34cm FIELD NOTES: Feeds by plunge-diving and also by dipping to pick food from water surface. Deeply forked tail, and rump grey, contiguous with rest of upperparts. SONG/CALL: A short *kep* or *keep*, also a rasping *kee-arrh*. HABITAT: Breeds on offshore islands, occurs along coasts, very rarely inland.

5 ARCTIC TERN *Sterna paradisaea* 33–38cm FIELD NOTES: Feeds mainly by plunge-diving. In flight has deeply forked tail with long streamers. From below all primaries appear translucent. SONG/CALL: A piping *pee-pee-pee* or similar, also a *prree-eh* and a rattling *kt-kt-kt-krrr-kt*. When alarmed gives a high *kree-ah* or *kree-err*. HABITAT: Coastal beaches and islands, also inland on lakes, heaths and pastures. On migration mainly coastal.

6 COMMON TERN *Sterna hirundo* 32–39cm FIELD NOTES: Feeds mainly by plunge-diving. In flight has deeply forked tail with longish streamers. From below inner primaries translucent. SONG/CALL: A rapid *kye-kye-kye-kye…*, also a *kirri-kirri-kirri* or similar. In alarm gives a screeching *kreeeah* or *kree-eer* and a sharp *kik*. HABITAT: Coastal and inland areas, including beaches, estuaries, islands, lakes and rivers. On migration mainly coastal. RACES: *S. h. longipennis* (fig 6b) NE Siberia south to NE China.

7 ROSEATE TERN *Sterna dougallii* 33–38 cm FIELD NOTES: Feeds mainly by plunge-diving, hovers less and tends to 'fly into water'. Tail deeply forked with very long streamers. SONG/CALL: A rasping *kraak* or *zraaach*, also a short, soft *cher-vik*. HABITAT: Low-lying islands or beaches. On migration mainly coastal.

8 FORSTER'S TERN *Sterna forsteri* 33–36cm (Vagrant) FIELD NOTES: Feeds mainly by plunge-diving. Usually looks bulkier than Common Tern. Tail deeply forked, grey centred with long streamers. SONG/CALL: A rolling, nasal *kyarr*, *kwarr* or *kreerr*, also a rapid *kek-kek-kek….* HABITAT: In native America: freshwater lakes and marshes, also coastal areas.

9 LEAST TERN (AMERICAN LITTLE TERN) *Sternula antillarum* 22–34cm (Vagrant) FIELD NOTES: Actions and habits similar to Little Tern. Deeply forked tail, and rump, grey. SONG/CALL: A *kid-ick kid-ick kid-ick*, also a shrill *kip kip kip* and a rasping *zr-e-e-e-p*. HABITAT: In native America: beaches, estuaries, lakes and rivers.

10 LITTLE TERN *Sternula albifrons* 22–28cm FIELD NOTES: Very active when foraging, feeds by plunge-diving, with much hovering. Upperwing has outer pair of primaries dark. Tail deeply forked. SONG/CALL: A rapid *kirrikikki kirrikiki*, a sharp *kik-kik* and a rasping *kyik* or *kriet* given in alarm. HABITAT: Sand bars and shingle banks on coasts or lakes and rivers. On migration mainly coastal.

11 SAUNDERS'S TERN *Sternula saundersi* 20–28cm FIELD NOTES: Actions as Little Tern. Upperwing has three outer primaries dark. Tail deeply forked. SONG/CALL: As Little Tern, although said to be less chattering. HABITAT: Mainly coastal.

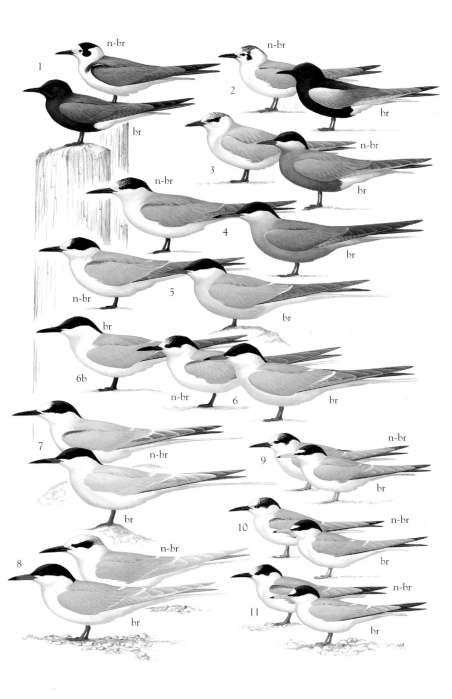

60 TERNS

1 CASPIAN TERN *Hydroprogne caspia* 47–54cm FIELD NOTES: Feeds mainly by hovering then plunge-diving. Upperwing shows grey outer primaries with darker tips. Underwing shows dark outer primaries. Tail forked. SONG/CALL: A loud, croaking *kraah, krah-krah* or *kree-ahk*. HABITAT: Coasts, lakes and reservoirs. Winters in coastal areas.

2 ROYAL TERN *Sterna maxima* 45–50cm FIELD NOTES: Feeds mainly by plunge-diving. Upperwing similar to Caspian Tern. Underwing pale with dark trailing edge to outer primaries. Tail deeply forked. SONG/CALL: A low-pitched grating *kerriup, krree-it* or *kirruck*. HABITAT: Breeds on offshore islands. Winters on coasts.

3 ELEGANT TERN *Sterna elegans* 39–43cm (Vagrant) FIELD NOTES: Feeds by plunge-diving. Bill colour varies from deep yellow to orange-red. Outer primaries on upperwing often appear dark grey. Pale underwing has dark tips to outer primaries with the outermost feather mainly blackish. Tail deeply forked. SONG/CALL: A nasal, rasping *karreek* or *ka-zeek*. HABITAT: In native America: sandy beaches and islands, after breeding occurs in estuaries, coastal lagoons, mudflats and harbours.

4 CRESTED TERN (GREATER CRESTED or SWIFT TERN) *Sterna bergii* 43–53cm FIELD NOTES: Feeds mainly by plunge-diving. Wing pattern similar to Royal Tern. Rump and tail pale grey, the latter deeply forked. SONG/CALL: A grating *krrik* or *kee-rit*, also a high-pitched *kree-kree*. HABITAT: Offshore islands, sandy and rocky shores.

5 LESSER CRESTED TERN *Sterna bengalensis* 36–41cm FIELD NOTES: Feeds mainly by hovering and plunge-diving. Wing pattern similar to Sandwich Tern. Rump and tail pale grey, the latter deeply forked. SONG/CALL: A harsh *krrik-krik* or *kerrick*. HABITAT: Offshore low-lying islands. Winters on coasts and at sea.

6 CHINESE CRESTED TERN *Sterna bernsteini* 42cm FIELD NOTES: Very rare. Little-recorded of actions, suspected to be much like Crested Tern. Upperwing has outer webs of outer primaries blackish. Underwing white. Tail deeply forked. SONG/CALL: Little-recorded other than harsh high-pitched cries. HABITAT: Offshore islets. During migration occurs on coasts.

7 BLACK-NAPED TERN *Sterna sumatrana* 34–35cm FIELD NOTES: Feeds mainly by plunge-diving but also by skimming low over water picking food from surface. Outer web of outermost primary blackish. Tail deeply forked with longish streamers. SONG/CALL: A sharp *tsii-chee-chi-chip* and a *chit-chit-chitrer* uttered when excited or alarmed. HABITAT: Breeds on small offshore islands, feeds in nearby coastal bays, lagoons and inlets.

8 SANDWICH TERN *Sterna sandvicensis* 36–41cm FIELD NOTES: Usually occurs in noisy parties. Feeds mainly by plunge-diving, often from considerable height, up to 10m. Inner webs of outer primaries on upperwing form a silver-grey wedge. Underwing primaries show dusky tips. Tail deeply forked. SONG/CALL: A grating *kirrruk* or *kerRICK*, also a short *krik* or *krik krik*. HABITAT: Undisturbed sandy shores and low coastal islands, during migration and winter mainly in coastal areas.

9 GULL-BILLED TERN *Gelochlidon nilotica* 33–43cm FIELD NOTES: Feeds by hawking insects or dipping to pick from surface of ground or water. Flight gull-like. In flight mid to outer primaries show a dark trailing edge above and below. Rump and forked tail pale grey. SONG/CALL: A nasal *kay-did, kay-tih-did, gur-WICK, ger-erk* or *kay-vek*, also a metallic *kak-kak* and when alarmed a *kvay-kvay*. On breeding grounds utters a *br-r-r-r....* HABITAT: Fresh and brackish lakes, saltmarsh and rivers, often feeds over nearby grasslands. On migration frequents coastal areas.

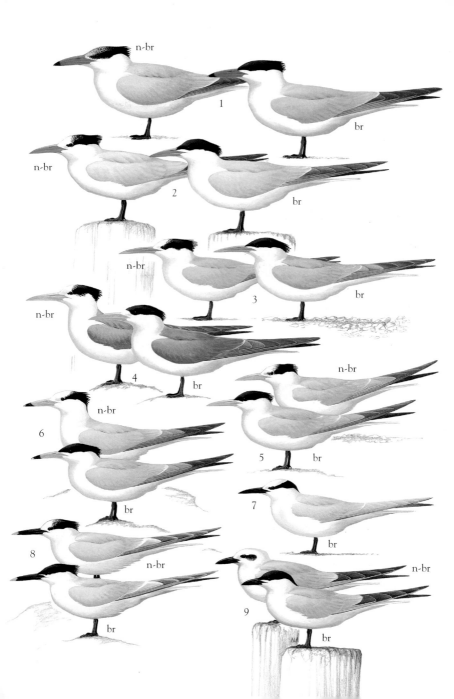

61 TERNS, NODDIES, FAIRY TERN AND SKIMMERS

1 GREY-BACKED TERN (SPECTACLED TERN) *Onychoprion lunata* 38cm FIELD NOTES: Feeds mainly by plunge-diving. Underwing shows grey-brown primaries and secondaries, coverts white. Tail grey, white-edged and deeply forked. SONG/CALL: High-pitched screeching, less harsh than Sooty Tern. HABITAT: Sandy beaches, coral islands and low sea cliffs. Winters at sea.

2 ALEUTIAN TERN (KAMCHATKA TERN) *Onychoprion aleutica* 32–34cm FIELD NOTES: Feeds by dipping to pick from water surface. Underwing white with dark trailing edge to secondaries and dusky outer primaries. White rump and tail, the latter deeply forked. SONG/CALL: A soft, wader-like *twee-ee-ee*. HABITAT: Coastal plains, sandy beaches and marshes on rocky islands.

3 BRIDLED TERN (BROWN-WINGED TERN) *Onychoprion anaethetus* 34–36cm FIELD NOTES: Feeds by plunge-diving and dipping to pick from water surface. Underwing mainly white with dusky tips to primaries and secondaries. Rump and tail dark grey, the latter deeply forked and white edged. SONG/CALL: A yapping *wep-wep* or *wup-wup*. HABITAT: Rocky or sandy islands, post breeding maritime.

4 SOOTY TERN (WIDEAWAKE TERN) *Onychoprion fuscata* 36–45cm FIELD NOTES: Feeds mainly by dipping to pick food from water surface also occasionally plunge-dives. Underwing white with dusky primaries and dusky tips to secondaries. Rump and tail blackish, the latter deeply forked and white-edged. SONG/CALL: A distinctive *ker-wacki-wah*, *ker-wacki-wack* or *wide-awake*, also a short *kraark*. HABITAT: Rocky, stony or sandy islands, post breeding maritime.

5 BLUE-GREY NODDY (BLUE NODDY) *Procelsterna cerulea* 25–28cm (Vagrant) FIELD NOTES: Often hovers then dips to pick prey from water surface, also paddles on water. Tail forked. SONG/CALL: Generally silent although sometimes gives a loud squeal. HABITAT: In native tropical Pacific islands: cliffs or rocky areas on islands.

6 BLACK NODDY (WHITE-CAPPED NODDY) *Anous minutus* 35–39cm (Vagrant) FIELD NOTES: May be conspecific with Lesser Noddy. Feeds mainly by hovering and dipping to pick prey from water surface. Tail forked. SONG/CALL: A distinctive *tik-tikoree* and a staccato rattle. HABITAT: In native tropical islands: sea cliffs or on trees on offshore islands.

7 LESSER NODDY *Anous tenuirostris* 30–34cm FIELD NOTES: Non-breeding visitor. Actions and habits similar to Black Noddy. Tail forked. SONG/CALL: A purring, also rattling notes when alarmed, otherwise generally silent away from breeding colonies. HABITAT: Mainly maritime.

8 COMMON NODDY (BROWN NODDY) *Anous stolidus* 38–45cm FIELD NOTES: Feeds by hovering and dipping to pick prey from water surface, also foot patters. Tail forked. SONG/CALL: A crow-like *kwok-kwok*, *karruuk* or *krao*. HABITAT: Sea cliffs and rocky islets.

9 FAIRY TERN (WHITE TERN) *Gygis alba* 25–30cm (Vagrant) FIELD NOTES: Feeds by diving. Tail forked. Juvenile has tips of mantle and wing feathers tinged brownish. SONG/CALL: Silent away from breeding sites. HABITAT: In native Tropics: trees and bushes on coral islands, post breeding maritime.

10 AFRICAN SKIMMER *Rynchops flavirostris* 36–42cm (Vagrant) FIELD NOTES: Feeds by 'ploughing' water with lower mandible whilst in skimming-flight. Non-breeding plumage is browner with a whitish collar on lower hindneck. Rump and tail black, the latter forked and white-edged. SONG/CALL: A sharp *kik kik kik…* or *kip kip kip…* and a harsh *kreeee*. HABITAT: In native Africa: lakes, coastal lagoons and rivers.

11 INDIAN SKIMMER (SCISSORBILL) *Rynchops albicollis* 38–43cm (Vagrant) FIELD NOTES: Feeding actions and habits similar to African Skimmer. Tail forked, white with black central streak. SONG/CALL: A nasal, yapping *kap kap kap*. HABITAT: In native India: mainly large rivers.

62 GUILLEMOTS AND MURRELETS

1 GUILLEMOT (COMMON GUILLEMOT or MURRE) *Uria aalge* 38–43cm FIELD NOTES: During breeding season often occurs in huge numbers at cliff face colonies. Rapid, whirring flight. Underwing has white wing-coverts with a dark axillary area and small dark 'arm-pit' bar. Feet project slightly beyond tail. SONG/CALL: At colonies utters a *ha ha ha* that leads into a guttural *ha-rrrhr*, also a rumbling *mmm….* At sea juveniles give a plaintive *peeeooee*. HABITAT: Coastal cliffs, winters at sea.

2 BRÜNNICH'S GUILLEMOT (THICK-BILLED GUILLEMOT or MURRE) *Uria lomvia* 39–43cm FIELD NOTES: Actions and habits similar to Guillemot. Underwing has white wing-coverts and dark axillary area, no dark bar on 'arm-pit'. Feet project slightly beyond tail. SONG/CALL: Similar to Guillemot. HABITAT: Coastal cliffs, winters at sea.

3 RAZORBILL *Alca torda* 37–39cm FIELD NOTES: Usually breeds in small groups on rocky cliffs or among boulders. Flight rapid and whirring. Underwing pattern similar to Brünnich's Guillemot. Feet do not project beyond tail. SONG/CALL: At breeding sites utters a guttural *goarrr* or *urrr*. At sea juveniles give a piping whistle. HABITAT: Coastal cliff faces and rocky or boulder pile areas below. Winters at sea.

4 BLACK GUILLEMOT (TYSTIE) *Cepphus grylle* 30–36cm FIELD NOTES: Rapid, whirring flight. In flight shows white underwing-coverts and large white patch on upperwing. Usually breeds in small scattered groups. SONG/CALL: At breeding areas gives a high *peeeeeh* or *seeeeeuu*, also *sipp-sipp-sipp* series. HABITAT: Rocky coasts. Winters near breeding sites, northern populations often more dispersive. RACES: *C. g. islandicus* (fig 4b) Iceland.

5 PIGEON GUILLEMOT (SEA PIGEON) *Cepphus columba* 30–37cm FIELD NOTES: Rapid, whirring flight. In flight shows greyish-brown underwing-coverts and a large white patch with broad black bar on upperwing. Usually breeds in small colonies. SONG/CALL: A wheezy *peeeeee*. HABITAT: Sea cliffs and rocky slopes. Winters at sea near rocky coasts and in sheltered coves. RACES: *C. c. snowi* (fig 5b) S Kamchatka, Kurile Islands.

6 SPECTACLED GUILLEMOT (SOOTY GUILLEMOT) *Cepphus carbo* 38cm FIELD NOTES: Rapid, whirring flight. Underwing blackish-brown. Usually breeds in small colonies, rarely in colonies of 200 or more pairs. SONG/CALL: Similar to Pigeon Guillemot? HABITAT: Sea cliffs, rocky slopes or boulder fields. Winters at sea, usually near coasts.

7 LONG-BILLED MURRELET *Brachyramphus perdix* 26cm FIELD NOTES: Actions and habits similar to Marbled Murrelet, from which it has recently been split. SONG/CALL: As Marbled Murrelet? HABITAT: Mainly coastal forests. Winters at sea, more dispersive than Marbled Murrelet.

8 MARBLED MURRELET *Brachyramphus marmoratus* 24cm FIELD NOTES: The recent split from Long-billed Murrelet may mean that this species becomes a vagrant, or may not occur at all? Flight rapid and whirring. In flight winter birds show white scapulars. SONG/CALL: A high-pitched *peeeaah-peeeaah* or *meer-meer-meer*. HABITAT: Breeds in coastal forests, feeds at sea. Winters along sea coasts.

9 KITTLITZ'S MURRELET (SHORT-BILLED MURRELET) *Brachyramphus brevirostris* 22–23cm FIELD NOTES: Actions, habits and wing pattern similar to Marbled Murrelet. SONG/CALL: A hoarse, drawn-out *squak*. HABITAT: Breeds on coastal mountain slopes, feeds at sea. Winters at sea.

10 ANCIENT MURRELET *Synthliboramphus antiquus* 24–27cm FIELD NOTES: Flight rapid and whirring. Underwing-coverts white contrasting with dusky flanks. Colonial breeder. SONG/CALL: Low whistles and chirping or clinking notes. HABITAT: Well-vegetated offshore islands, feeds at sea. Winters at sea.

11 JAPANESE MURRELET (CRESTED MURRELET) *Synthliboramphus wumizusume* 26cm FIELD NOTES: Rare. Actions and underwing pattern very similar to Ancient Murrelet. Colonial breeder. SONG/CALL: Shrill whistles. HABITAT: Rocky islets and coasts. Winters at sea.

63 LITTLE AUK, AUKLETS AND PUFFINS

1 LITTLE AUK (DOVEKIE) *Alle alle* 17–19cm FIELD NOTES: Rapid, whirring flight. Underwing dusky, contrasting with white body. Breeds in large colonies. SONG/CALL: At colonies gives a chattering *krrii-ek ak ak ak ak ak* or similar. When alarmed utters a whinnying *whuwhuwhu.* Generally silent after breeding. HABITAT: Breeds on rock scree of coastal slopes. Winters at sea.

2 CASSIN'S AUKLET (ALEUTIAN AUK) *Ptychoramphus aleuticus* 20–23cm (Vagrant) FIELD NOTES: No marked difference in non-breeding plumage. Rapid, whirring flight. SONG/CALL: Generally silent away from breeding sites. HABITAT: In native N Pacific: coastal islands. Winters at sea.

3 CRESTED AUKLET *Aethia cristatella* 23–27cm FIELD NOTES: Typical auk flight, rapid and whirring. Juvenile lacks crest and face plumes, otherwise similar to non-breeding adult. Usually breeds in large colonies, often mixed with other auks. SONG/CALL: At breeding grounds utters honking and grunting sounds, otherwise generally silent. HABITAT: Scree slopes and cliffs on islands and mainland coasts. Winters at sea.

4 WHISKERED AUKLET (PYGMY AUKLET) *Aethia pygmaea* 17–18cm FIELD NOTES: Flight rapid and whirring. Juvenile lacks crest, but may show 'ghost' head plumes, otherwise similar to non-breeding adult. Breeds in large colonies, often mixed with other auks. SONG/CALL: A high-pitched *eeaah ah ah ah…* or *eeaah ik eah.* HABITAT: Rocky islands and sea cliffs. Winters at sea, usually near coasts.

5 LEAST AUKLET (KNOB-BILLED AUKLET) *Aethia pusilla* 12–14cm FIELD NOTES: Typical auk flight, rapid and whirring. Juvenile lacks head plumes, otherwise similar to non-breeding adult. Breeds in very large colonies, often with other auk species. SONG/CALL: At breeding colonies gives various chattering, twittering and squealing notes. HABITAT: Rocky coasts, cliffs and islands. Winters at sea.

6 PARAKEET AUKLET *Cyclorrhynchus psittacula* 23–25cm FIELD NOTES: In flight shows dark underwing. Flight as other auks, although often at greater height. Colonial breeder, often mixed with other auk species. SONG/CALL: At breeding colonies gives a whistle or trill, rising in pitch. HABITAT: Cliffs and rocky slopes on offshore islands. Winters at sea.

7 RHINOCEROS AUKLET *Cerorhinca monocerata* 35–38cm FIELD NOTES: Rapid, whirring flight. Juvenile lacks head plumes, otherwise similar to non-breeding adult. Colonial breeder, often in association with other auk species. SONG/CALL: At breeding colonies utters growling and shrieking cries. HABITAT: Grassy slopes at coasts or inland. Winters at sea.

8 PUFFIN (COMMON or ATLANTIC PUFFIN) *Fratercula arctica* 26–36cm FIELD NOTES: Rapid, whirring flight. Underwing dusky, contrasting with white body. Red-orange feet often conspicuous in flight. Juvenile has small, dark, reddish-tipped bill otherwise similar to non-breeding adult. Colonial breeder. SONG/CALL: At breeding sites utters a growling *arr* or *arr-uh.* Generally silent post breeding. HABITAT: Rocky and grassy slopes, on coasts and islands. Winters at sea.

9 HORNED PUFFIN *Fratercula corniculata* 36–41cm FIELD NOTES: Typical auk flight, rapid and whirring. Underwing dusky. Red-orange feet often conspicuous in flight. Juvenile has small dull bill, otherwise similar to non-breeding adult. Colonial breeder. SONG/CALL: At breeding sites utters harsh grunting and growling notes. HABITAT: Rocky coastal cliffs and offshore islands. Winters at sea.

10 TUFTED PUFFIN *Fratercula cirrhata* 36–41cm FIELD NOTES: Unmistakable, especially in breeding plumage. Actions much as other puffins. Juvenile like non-breeding adult but has small dusky yellow bill, dark eye and sometimes paler underparts. Colonial breeder. SONG/CALL: At breeding grounds utters soft grunts and growls. HABITAT: Rocky coasts and islands. Winters at sea.

64 SANDGROUSE

1 LICHTENSTEIN'S SANDGROUSE *Pterocles lichtensteinii* 24–26cm FIELD NOTES: Mainly crepuscular or nocturnal. Usually encountered in pairs or small groups, larger parties recorded during watering-flights and daytime roosts. In flight upperwing shows pale buff wingbar on greater coverts, underwing plain greyish-buff. SONG/CALL: A whistling *qewheeto*, *chee-weeup* or *witch-ouuu* given in flight or from the ground. When alarmed utters a *kerrek-kerrek-kerrek*, *krre-krre-kree* or *qua-qua-qua*. HABITAT: Deserts, semi-deserts, scrubby hillsides and dry wadis.

2 CROWNED SANDGROUSE (CORONETED SANDGROUSE) *Pterocles coronatus* 27–29cm FIELD NOTES: Watering-flights usually made in mornings, with flocks of up to 50, at waterholes much larger numbers recorded. In flight upperwing has dark flight-feathers and primary covert, rest of coverts sandy. Underwing shows white coverts contrasting with dark flight-feathers. SONG/CALL: A rolling *ch-ga ch-gar-ra*, *que quet querrooo* or *chiruk-chirugaga*, also a *wok tu wok kock* and a *wheeek* that descends in pitch. HABITAT: Stony desert and semi-desert, dry hills and mountains.

3 SPOTTED SANDGROUSE *Pterocles senegallus* 30–35cm FIELD NOTES: Watering flights usually made during morning, with flocks of around 20. In flight upperwing pale sandy, underwing pale buff with dark secondaries and dusky tips to primaries. Note elongated central tail feathers. SONG/CALL: A musical *whitoo whitoo*, *wicko wicko* or *waqu waqu*. HABITAT: Desert and semi-desert with sparse vegetation.

4 CHESTNUT-BELLIED SANDGROUSE *Pterocles exustus* 31–33cm FIELD NOTES: Most watering-flights, small flocks join up to make large congregations at waterholes, take place in mornings with extra evening flights made in hot dry weather. In flight appears dark, due to blackish underwing and belly. SONG/CALL: In flight utters a chuckling *kt-arr kt-arr* or longer *whit kt-arr wit wit-ee-er kt-arrr-arr*, also a *chocka chocka* or *wot worp wot worp*. HABITAT: Semi-desert with sparse vegetation, fallow fields and dry cultivations.

5 BLACK-BELLIED SANDGROUSE *Pterocles orientalis* 33–39cm FIELD NOTES: Occurs in small flocks, up to 25, makes morning flights to waterholes where congregation can number several hundred. In flight white underwing-coverts contrast with black belly. SONG/CALL: A bubbling *tchowrrr rerr-rerr*, *churr-churr-rur* or *durrrll*. HABITAT: Dry steppe and semi-desert with sparse, low vegetation, also occasionally in dry cultivated areas.

6 PIN-TAILED SANDGROUSE *Pterocles alchata* 31–39cm FIELD NOTES: Often in massive flocks. Watering-flights usually take place in mornings. In flight underwing-coverts white contrasting with black flight-feathers. Note elongated central tail feathers. SONG/CALL: A nasal *arrrh-arrrh*, *catar-cater*, *guettarr* also a *ga-hg ga-ng arrr* and *arrk-arrk-arrk*. HABITAT: Arid and semi-arid plains with sparse vegetation.

7 PALLAS'S SANDGROUSE *Syrrhaptes paradoxus* 40cm FIELD NOTES: Flies to waterholes in small flocks, mainly during the morning. Post breeding often forms flocks of several hundreds. In flight underwing pale with dark trailing edge to secondaries. Note elongated central tail feathers. SONG/CALL: A low-pitched *cu-ruu cu-ruu cu-ou-ruu*, also a rapid, bubbling *kukerik-kukerik* and a sharp *tchep* or *kep*. HABITAT: Steppe and semi-desert with sparse, low vegetation, also fallow and abandoned fields.

8 TIBETAN SANDGROUSE *Syrrhaptes tibetanus* 40–48cm FIELD NOTES: Gregarious. Does not make regular watering-flights. In flight upperwing-coverts sandy, contrasting with black flight-feathers, underwing mainly black. SONG/CALL: A loud, deep *guk-guk* or *caga-caga*, also a *koonk-koonk*. HABITAT: Stony or rocky areas of semi-desert or desert uplands, up to 6000m.

65 DOVES AND PIGEONS

1 ROCK DOVE (ROCK PIGEON) *Columba livia* 31–34cm FIELD NOTES: The ancestor of feral town pigeons. In flight shows white rump, black subterminal band on tail and broad black bars on upperwing. Underwing white with dark trailing edge. SONG/CALL: A moaning *oorh*, or *oh-oo-oor*, also a hurried *oo-roo-coo t coo* given during display. HABITAT: Sea and inland cliffs, caves, ruined buildings and deep wells. Feral populations use mainly city and town buildings as nest sites.

2 HILL PIGEON (EASTERN ROCK PIGEON) *Columba rupestris* 33–35cm FIELD NOTES: In flight very similar to Rock Dove, generally paler with white mid-band on tail. SONG/CALL: A rolling *gut-gut-gut-gut*. HABITAT: Cliffs, gorges and caves in open rugged country, also in towns.

3 SNOW PIGEON *Columba leuconota* 31–34cm FIELD NOTES: Gregarious. In flight shows white upper rump, lower rump and tail black, the latter with broad crescent-shaped white band. SONG/CALL: A hiccough-like note followed by a *cuck-cuck* and then another hiccough-like note, also a prolonged *coo-ooo-ooo*. HABITAT: High-altitude rocky cliffs, steep gorges and snow-fields.

4 STOCK DOVE (STOCK PIGEON) *Columba oenas* 32–34cm FIELD NOTES: In flight shows broad black terminal band on tail, two small black bars on inner part of upperwing. Underwing grey with dark trailing edge. Often occurs in flocks of Wood Pigeons. SONG/CALL: A low *ooo-uh* or *ooo-er*. HABITAT: Open country, cultivated areas, open woodland, forest edge and parks, all with old trees for use as nest sites.

5 YELLOW-EYED DOVE (EASTERN STOCK DOVE, PALE-BACKED PIGEON) *Columba eversmanni* 29–31cm FIELD NOTES: In flight shows white upper rump, black bars on inner part of upperwing and broad black terminal band on tail. Underwing pale grey with dusky trailing edge. SONG/CALL: A subdued *quooh quooh quooh-cuu-gooh-cuu-gooh-cuu-gooh*. HABITAT: Light woodland in cultivated areas, also soil cliffs and ruins. Occurs on floodplains in winter.

6 WOOD PIGEON (COMMON WOOD PIGEON, RINGDOVE) *Columba palumbus* 41–45cm FIELD NOTES: Often in very large flocks. In flight, from above unmistakeable due to white wing crescent that stretches back from alula area. Juvenile lacks white neck patch. SONG/CALL: A mellow *coo COOO coo coo-coo cook* or similar, also a *coo ooo, coo coo coo* or *coo ke ke coo coo* given during display. HABITAT: Forest and forest edge, cultivated areas with nearby woodland or hedgerows, town parks and gardens. RACES: *C. p. casiotis* (fig 6b) N Oman, SE Iran to NW and C Himalayas and W China.

7 TROCAZ PIGEON (LONG-TOED PIGEON) *Columba trocaz* 38–40cm FIELD NOTES: The only pigeon on Madeira, apart from feral Rock Doves. In flight generally grey with darker flight-feathers, tail with broad black tip and pale grey subterminal band. SONG/CALL: A soft *coo-coo coooo cook*. HABITAT: Cliffs and crags in laurel forest.

8 BOLLE'S PIGEON (BOLLE'S LAUREL PIGEON) *Columba bollii* 35–37cm FIELD NOTES: Often in fast flight over treetops, otherwise shy. In flight generally dark grey with a pale subterminal band to dark-tipped tail. SONG/CALL: A guttural *ruk ruk gruuuk guk* or *ruor ruor ruor rup*. HABITAT: High-altitude laurel forest also recorded in nearby cultivated areas.

9 LAUREL PIGEON *Columba junoniae* 37–40cm FIELD NOTES: White terminal tail band diagnostic. Often flies with a slow, floppy flight. SONG/CALL: A hoarse *pu-pu-pooo* or *up- poooo*. HABITAT: Crags and gorges in high-altitude laurel forest, also recorded in nearby cultivated areas.

10 ASHY WOOD PIGEON (BUFF-COLLARED PIGEON) *Columba pulchricollis* 31–36cm FIELD NOTES: In flight generally dark grey. Usually in pairs or small flocks. SONG/CALL: A deep *coo coo coo*. HABITAT: High-elevation forests.

feral
varieties

66 DOVES AND PIGEONS

1 OLIVE PIGEON (AFRICAN OLIVE, RAMERON or YELLOW-EYED PIGEON) *Columba arquatrix* 38–41cm. FIELD NOTES: In flight from above looks uniform dark grey. Often skulks in trees. SONG/CALL: A rolling *coo-coo croo-croo croo-croo croo-croo*. HABITAT: Highland forest.

2 SPECKLED WOOD PIGEON (HODGSON'S PIGEON) *Columba hodgsonii* 38–40cm FIELD NOTES: In flight appears uniform dark grey-brown. Usually occurs in pairs or small flocks. Mainly arboreal. SONG/CALL: A deep *whock-whrroo-whrroo*. HABITAT: Evergreen and semi-evergreen hill forests, from 1800–4000m.

3 JAPANESE WOOD PIGEON (BLACK PIGEON) *Columba janthina* 37–43cm FIELD NOTES: Unmistakeable. Usually solitary although sometimes occurs in small flocks. SONG/CALL: A drawn-out *oo-woo oo-woo*. HABITAT: Dense evergreen forest.

4 NAMAQUA DOVE (LONG-TAILED DOVE) *Oena capensis* 26–28cm FIELD NOTES: In flight underwing chestnut with dark trailing edge, upperwing flight-feathers mainly chestnut with a dark trailing edge. Usually encountered in pairs or small groups, feeding mainly on the ground. Juvenile generally buff-grey with pale spots on tips of wing feathers. SONG/CALL: A soft, rising *hoo-ooooo*. HABITAT: Thorn-bush, scrub and palm groves.

5 BLACK-BILLED WOOD DOVE (ABYSSINIAN WOOD DOVE) *Turtur abyssinicus* 20cm (Vagrant) FIELD NOTES: In flight shows rufous inner webs to primaries. Usually solitary or in pairs, feeding mainly on the ground. SONG/CALL: A *cuwoo cuwoo co-oo-cuwoo coo cuwoo cu-cu-cu-cu-cucucucucucucucucu......*, which starts slowly then quickens and descends in pitch. HABITAT: In native Africa: savanna woodland, woodland around marsh or water, also woodland edge.

6 EMERALD DOVE (GREEN-WINGED DOVE) *Chalcophaps indica* 23–27cm FIELD NOTES: Usually encountered in singles, pairs or small groups, feeding on the ground in thick cover. In flight shows dark lower back crossed by two pale bars. SONG/CALL: A soft, drawn-out *tuk-hoop*, *hoo-hoo*. HABITAT: Forests, also in nearby plantations and agriculture.

7 AMERICAN MOURNING DOVE (MOURNING or CAROLINA DOVE) *Zenaida macroura* 30–31cm (Vagrant) FIELD NOTES: Feeds mainly on the ground. Flight swift, with wings producing a whistling sound. SONG/CALL: A mournful *oowoo-woo-woo-woo*. HABITAT: In native America: farmland with scattered trees, open woodland, parks and large gardens.

8 BRUCE'S GREEN PIGEON (YELLOW-BELLIED GREEN PIGEON) *Treron waalia* 28–30cm FIELD NOTES: Shy. Usually found in small groups feeding in tree canopy, at fruiting fig trees may be seen in larger flocks. SONG/CALL: A crooning whistle and a quarrelsome chatter. HABITAT: Wooded wadis, open country with scattered trees and gardens with large trees.

9 WEDGE-TAILED GREEN PIGEON (SINGING GREEN PIGEON) *Treron sphenura* 30–33cm FIELD NOTES: Usually found singly, in pairs or small parties feeding in typical clambering fashion on tree fruits and berries. SONG/CALL: A series of musical whistling or fluting notes, also a curious grunting. HABITAT: Forest and wooded areas in mountains.

10 WHITE-BELLIED GREEN PIGEON (JAPANESE GREEN PIGEON) *Treron sieboldi* 33cm FIELD NOTES: Feeds mainly in fruiting trees although also recorded feeding on the ground. Usually found in small parties. SONG/CALL: A mournful *oaooh oaooh* or *o-vuuo-vuuo-vuuo-vououo-oo*. HABITAT: Wooded hills and mountain slopes.

11 WHISTLING GREEN PIGEON (FORMOSAN or RED-CAPPED GREEN PIGEON) *Treron formosae* 35cm FIELD NOTES: Little-recorded, actions and habits said to be much as others of the genus. SONG/CALL: *Po-po-peh*, the last note higher pitched. HABITAT: Sub-tropical broadleaved evergreen forests, trees surrounding cultivated areas and town gardens.

67 DOVES

1 COLLARED DOVE (EUROPEAN COLLARED DOVE) *Streptopelia decaocto* 31–33cm
FIELD NOTES: Feeds mainly on the ground. From above all outer-tail feathers show broad white terminal band. Juvenile lacks black and white collar. SONG/CALL: A loud, low-pitched *koo-KOOO-kook* or *koo-KOOO-koo* or similar. On landing gives a harsh *kreair* or *whaaa*.
HABITAT: Semi-desert with scattered trees, farmyards, parks and gardens.

2 AFRICAN COLLARED DOVE (PINK-HEADED DOVE) *Streptopelia roseogrisea*
29–30cm FIELD NOTES: Feeds mainly on the ground. In flight appears very similar to Collared Dove, but note white undertail-coverts. Juvenile lacks black and white collar. SONG/CALL: A descending, rolling *crooo cro-cro-crococo*, *cruu currruuu* or *KOOK r-r-r-r-r-OOooooooooo*. Also a nasal *heh heh heh*. HABITAT: Semi-desert and savanna with trees, mangroves and town parks.

3 AFRICAN MOURNING DOVE (MOURNING or MOURNING COLLARED DOVE) *Streptopelia decipiens* 28–30cm FIELD NOTES: In flight like a darker version of Collared Dove, although white of tail less broad. Feeds mainly on the ground. SONG/CALL: A pleasant *WHOO-woooo wu-WOO-oo wu-WOO-wu wu-WOO-oo*, also a rolling *churrrrrrrrrrooooooooo*, on landing gives a throaty *oo-rrrrrrrrrr*. HABITAT: Savanna thickets and woodlands, also around cultivated areas and villages.

4 RED-EYED DOVE *Streptopelia semitorquata* 30cm FIELD NOTES: Feeds mainly on the ground. In flight uppertail shows black base and broad grey-buff terminal band. Juvenile has black collar indistinct, or lacking. SONG/CALL: A slow, hoarse *coo coo coo-coo coo* or similar. Often transcribed as *I-am-a-red-eyed-dove*. HABITAT: Well-wooded areas usually near water.

5 RED TURTLE DOVE (RED COLLARED DOVE) *Streptopelia tranquebarica* 23cm
FIELD NOTES: Feeds mainly on the ground. In flight uppertail is dark grey with prominent white terminal band and white sides. SONG/CALL: A deep *cru-u-u-u-u*. HABITAT: Open country with wooded or scrubby areas.

6 TURTLE DOVE (EUROPEAN or COMMON TURTLE DOVE) *Streptopelia turtur*
26–28cm FIELD NOTES: Feeds mainly on the ground. In flight appears dark, uppertail dark grey with white outer edges and prominent white terminal band on all outer feathers. SONG/CALL: A purring *turrrrr turrrrrr turrrrrr*. HABITAT: Open woodland, forest edge, copses, groves and hedgerows. RACES: *S. t. rufescens* (Isabelline Turtle Dove) (fig 6b) Egypt.

7 ORIENTAL TURTLE DOVE (RUFOUS TURTLE DOVE) *Streptopelia orientalis*
30–35cm FIELD NOTES: In flight darker than similar Turtle Dove with grey terminal tail band. Feeds on the ground. Juvenile very similar to juvenile Turtle Dove. SONG/CALL: A mournful *coo-cooroo-coocoo* or *gur-grugroo*. HABITAT: Open wooded areas near to cultivation, open areas with scattered trees and bushes, parks and large gardens. RACES: *S. o. meena* (fig 7b) W Siberia to Nepal and Himalayas, uppertail shows white terminal band.

8 DUSKY TURTLE DOVE (PINK-BREASTED DOVE) *Streptopelia lugens* 28–31cm
FIELD NOTES: In flight appears very dark with dull greyish terminal band on outer tail feathers. Juvenile lacks black neck patch and is paler and browner with pale rufous feather fringes. SONG/CALL: A deep, slow *coo-oor coo-oor*. HABITAT: Wooded areas mainly from 1000–2800m, also agriculture surrounded by trees and acacia wadis.

9 LAUGHING DOVE (PALM DOVE) *Streptopelia senegalensis* 25–27cm FIELD NOTES: In flight uppertail mainly grey, outer feathers white with black bases. Feeds mainly on the ground. SONG/CALL: A bubbling *do do dooh dooh do*. HABITAT: Around human habitation, cultivated areas and savanna with scattered trees. RACES: *S. s. cambayensis* (fig 9b) E Arabia, E Iran to India.

10 SPOTTED DOVE (NECKLACE DOVE) *Streptopelia chinensis* 30cm FIELD NOTES: In flight uppertail dark with broad white terminal band on outer feathers. Feeds on the ground. SONG/CALL: A melodious *coo croo-oo croo-oo* or *coocoo croor-croor*. HABITAT: Around human habitation and cultivated areas.

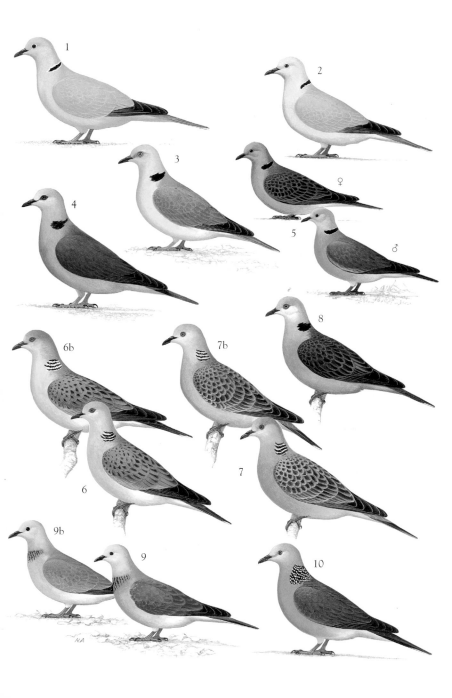

68 CUCKOOS

1 JACOBIN CUCKOO (PIED or BLACK AND WHITE CUCKOO) *Clamator jacobinus* 34cm FIELD NOTES: In flight from above shows white patch at base of primaries. Juvenile duller, brownish above buffy below. SONG/CALL: A loud, fluting *piu piu pee-pee piu pee-pee-piu*, also when alarmed a harsh *chu-chu-chu-chu*. HABITAT: Open scrub, woodland, also cultivated areas with bushes or trees.

2 CHESTNUT-WINGED CUCKOO (RED-WINGED CRESTED CUCKOO) *Clamator coromandus* 46cm FIELD NOTES: Retiring. Often hunts in low vegetation in search of insects. Juvenile duller with rufous fringes on mantle feathers. SONG/CALL: A harsh *chee-ke-kek*, also a hoarse whistle. HABITAT: Bush and scrub country, also broadleaved forest.

3 GREAT SPOTTED CUCKOO *Clamator glandarius* 35–39cm FIELD NOTES: Presence of hidden bird often given away by Magpies, the main parasitised host. Juvenile has black cap and rufous primaries with dark tips. SONG/CALL: A loud rattling, cackling *cherr-cherr-che-che-che-che-che*. Female utters a bubbling *gi-gi-gi-gi-gi-gi-gi-gi-ku-ku-ku-ku*. Advertising call is a clear *kleeok*. HABITAT: Savanna-like heathland with cork oak and stone pine, also olive groves and cultivation with bushes and trees.

4 LARGE HAWK-CUCKOO *Hierococcyx sparverioides* 38–40cm FIELD NOTES: Secretive. Arboreal. Juvenile barred brown and rufous above, forehead grey, nape pale rufous. Underparts whitish with dark spotting. SONG/CALL: A shrill, screaming *pi-pee-ha* that increases in speed and pitch leading to a frantic climax. HABITAT: High-elevation, open forests, especially oak.

5 COMMON HAWK-CUCKOO (BRAIN-FEVER BIRD) *Hierococcyx various* 33cm (Vagrant) FIELD NOTES: Arboreal. Juvenile upperparts barred brown and rufous underparts whitish with dark streaks. SONG/CALL: A monotonous, high-pitched *wee-piwhit*, often written as *brainfever* with the accent on the *fe*. HABITAT: In native India: wooded country, forest, gardens and groves of cultivated trees.

6 HODGSON'S HAWK-CUCKOO (HORSFIELD'S or FUGITIVE HAWK-CUCKOO) *Hierococcyx fugax hyperythus* 28–30cm FIELD NOTES: Illustrated race has been considered a full species (Northern Hawk-Cuckoo). Juvenile has whitish underparts with dark streaks, upperpart and wing feathers with buffish fringes. SONG/CALL: A shrill *ju-ichi ju-ichi*, repeated up to 20 times. HABITAT: Evergreen and deciduous forests, bamboo thickets and plantations.

7 DIDRIC CUCKOO (DIEDERIK or DIDERIC CUCKOO) *Chrysococcyx caprius* 18–20cm FIELD NOTES: In flight from below shows black and white barred underwing and tail. Juvenile similar to adult female but with streaking on throat and breast. Bill reddish. SONG/CALL: Male calls with the onomatopoeic *dee-dee-dee-dee-deederik*. Female utters a *deea-deea-deea*. HABITAT: Dry scrub and open woodland.

8 KLAAS'S CUCKOO *Chrysococcyx klaas* 18cm FIELD NOTES: In flight from below has white underwing-coverts and mainly white tail. Juvenile similar to adult female but more heavily barred above and below. SONG/CALL: A mournful *whit-jeh whit-jeh whit-jeh*. HABITAT: Open bush-land, open woodland and forest edge.

9 DRONGO CUCKOO *Surniculus lugubris* 25cm (Vagrant) FIELD NOTES: Secretive. Arboreal. Movements sluggish. Perches more horizontal when calling. Juvenile dull black with white spotting on head, back, breast and wings. SONG/CALL: A rising *pip-pip-pip-pip-pip-pip*. HABITAT: In native S China and SE Asia: open secondary forest, plantations, orchards etc.

69 CUCKOOS, KOEL AND COUCALS

1 CUCKOO (COMMON or EURASIAN CUCKOO) *Cuculus canorus* 32–34cm FIELD NOTES: Often perches horizontally with tail cocked and wings drooped. Female has brownish tinge to breast. Juvenile has conspicuous white nape patch otherwise similar to rufous female, although some are more grey, with pale fringes on mantle and wings and dark barring on throat and breast. SONG/CALL: Main call is the well-known *cu-coo* or variants. Also when excited utters a harsh *gowk gowk gowk*. Female delivers a bubbling *puhuhuhuhuhuhuhuhuhu*. HABITAT: Wide-ranging including woodland, forest edge, moorland, farmland with trees and bushes, scrub, open country, coastal dunes and heathland.

2 INDIAN CUCKOO *Cuculus micropterus* 33cm FIELD NOTES: Note wider spaced barring on underparts and broad blackish subterminal bar to tail. Juvenile barred white and rufous on head and neck, mantle and wings grey-brown with pale fringes. Underparts pale buff barred black. SONG/CALL: A loud, hollow, persistently repeated 4-note whistle, often transcribed as *crossword puzzle* or *one more bottle*. HABITAT: Deciduous, evergreen and secondary forests.

3 ORIENTAL CUCKOO (HIMALAYAN CUCKOO) *Cuculus saturatus* 30–32cm FIELD NOTES: Only safely separated from Cuckoo by voice. SONG/CALL: A distinctive, resonant *poo-poo-poo-poo* also a muted, hoopoe-like *poo-poo poo-poo poo-poo poo-poo*. HABITAT: Forests, forest edge and clearings, also open woodland.

4 LESSER CUCKOO (SMALL CUCKOO) *Cuculus poliocephalus* 26cm FIELD NOTES: Note small size and wider spaced barring on underparts. Juvenile very similar to juvenile Cuckoo, but smaller and lacks white nape patch. SONG/CALL: A loud, cheery *pretty-peel-lay-ka-beet* or *that's-your-choky-pepper..... choky-pepper*. HABITAT: Broadleaved and pine forests, also secondary growth and scrub.

5 PLAINTIVE CUCKOO (GREY-BELLIED CUCKOO) *Cacomantis (merulinus) passerinus* 22cm (Vagrant) FIELD NOTES: Restless feeder, usually in tree canopy. Noted making aerial flycatcher-like sallies. SONG/CALL: A clear *pee-pipee-pee...pipe-pee*. HABITAT: In native India and SE Asia: open woodland, secondary forest, bush, scrub and cultivated areas.

6 KOEL (COMMON, ASIAN or INDIAN KOEL) *Eudynamys scolopacea* 42cm (Vagrant) FIELD NOTES: Unobtrusive, usually keeping to cover. First sighting is generally of bird flying silently from tree to tree. SONG/CALL: A loud *kooyl* or a bubbling *kwow-kwow-kwow-kwow*. HABITAT: In native India: open forest, forest edge, scrub, gardens and orchards.

7 BLACK-BILLED CUCKOO *Coccyzus erythrophthalmus* 27–31cm (Vagrant) FIELD NOTES: Skulking. Undertail of adult is grey with narrow white tips each with a narrow black subterminal bar. In flight, above, shows large chestnut patch on base of primaries. Juvenile tail lacks black bars and has smaller white tips. SONG/CALL: A repeated *cu-cu-cu*. Unlikely to be heard in Palearctic. HABITAT: In native N American: woodland, forest edge and thickets.

8 YELLOW-BILLED CUCKOO *Coccyzus americanus* 28–32cm (Vagrant) FIELD NOTES: Very similar to Black-billed Cuckoo, except undertail dark with wide white tips in both adult and juvenile. SONG/CALL: A hollow *ka-ka-ka-ka-ka-ka......kow-kow-kowlp-kowlp-kowlp*. Unlikely to be heard in Palearctic. HABITAT: In native N America: woodland, forest edge, thickets and open country with trees and bushes.

9 SENEGAL COUCAL *Centropus senegalensis* 40–42cm FIELD NOTES: Often cumbersome. Feeds in trees and on the ground, when can recall a long-tailed gamebird. Juvenile very similar to adult White-browed Coucal but with buffy underparts and only a slight pale supercilium. SONG/CALL: A hollow, hooting *hoo-hoo* then a falling *hu-hu-hu-hu-hu-hu-hu*. HABITAT: Thickets, cultivated land with bushes and trees, orchards and reedbeds.

10 WHITE-BROWED COUCAL *Centropus superciliosus* 36–42cm FIELD NOTES: Habits similar to Senegal Coucal. Juvenile a duller version of adult. SONG/CALL: A hollow series of notes, often described as sounding like water being poured from a bottle. Also a variety of harsh *kak* and *hok* notes. HABITAT: Dense scrub and palms, usually near water.

70 OWLS

1 BARN OWL *Tyto alba* 33–35cm FIELD NOTES: Appears strikingly white in flight. Nocturnal, although often seen hunting during the day. SONG/CALL: A shrill, hoarse *shrrreeeeee*. HABITAT: Open country and farmland with scattered trees, woodland edge and also around human habitation. RACES: *T. a. guttata* (fig 1b) C and E Europe.

2 GRASS OWL (EASTERN GRASS OWL) *Tyto capensis longimembris* 32–38cm (Vagrant) FIELD NOTES: In flight upperwing shows ochre patch at base of primaries. Hunts from just before dusk to mid-morning. Sometimes considered to be a full species. SONG/CALL: Generally silent, although a screech, said to be similar to that of the Barn Owl has been recorded. HABITAT: Open grassland.

3 SNOWY OWL *Bubo scandiacus* 53–65cm FIELD NOTES: Usually hunts at dusk or dawn, although hunts throughout the day during summer. SONG/CALL: Male gives a booming *goo goo* or *gawh gawh*, female similar but higher pitched. When alarmed male utters a cackling *kre-kre-kre*, female gives loud whistling or mewing notes. HABITAT: Tundra with rocks or hummocks and low vegetation. In winter occurs on grassland, marshes and fields.

4 EAGLE OWL (EURASIAN or NORTHERN EAGLE OWL) *Bubo bubo* 60–75cm FIELD NOTES: Usually nocturnal or crepuscular, although in summer often hunts during daylight hours. SONG/CALL: Male gives a deep, muffled *HOO-o* or *BOO-ho*, female's much the same but higher pitched and more hoarse. Female also utters a barking scream. When alarmed gives a shrill *ka-ka-kaKAYu*. HABITAT: Rocky areas, cliffs, gorges and caves in grassland, open woodland and semi-desert, also locally around ruined buildings and farmland. RACES: *B. b. sibiricus* (Siberian Eagle Owl) (fig 4b) SW and C Ural area, W Siberia to River Ob; *B. b. ascalaphus* (Pharaoh or Desert Eagle Owl) (fig 4c) NW Africa, N Egypt, Arabia and Iraq, has a *WAHa* or *hooWAHa* call; *B. b. bengalensis* (Rock or Indian Eagle Owl) (fig 4d) Himalayas. The latter two are often considered full species.

5 SPOTTED EAGLE OWL *Bubo africanus* 45cm FIELD NOTES: Mainly nocturnal, usually feeds by dropping on prey from a perch, also recorded catching bats in flight. SONG/CALL: A soft *hoo-hoo-hoo* and a fluty, nasal *wheeoo*. HABITAT: Open woodland, rocky hills and ravines, locally around human habitation.

6 BLAKISTON'S FISH OWL (BLAKISTON'S EAGLE OWL) *Bubo blakistoni* 60–72cm FIELD NOTES: Feeds mainly on fish, crabs or frogs, dropping on prey from a perch, hunts mostly at night or dusk. SONG/CALL: A deep *boo-bo-voo*, *shoo-hoo* or *foo-fooroo*. HABITAT: Forested rivers.

7 BROWN FISH OWL *Bubo zeylonensis* 50–57cm FIELD NOTES: Crepuscular and nocturnal. From a perch swoops on fish, catching them in talons. SONG/CALL: A deep *boom boom* or *boo-o-boom*, a subdued *hu-who-hu* and a harsh *we-aaah*. HABITAT: Tree-lined rivers or lakes.

8 HAWK OWL (NORTHERN HAWK OWL) *Surnia ulula* 36–39cm FIELD NOTES: Mainly diurnal. Often perches on exposed treetops scanning surrounding area, also hovers to look for prey or chases prey like a Sparrowhawk. SONG/CALL: A bubbling *uluulululululu….* When alarmed gives a shrill *ki-ki-kikikikiki*. HABITAT: Forest edges and clearings near bogs, moorland or cultivation. Some winters often erupts south.

9 BROWN HAWK OWL (ORIENTAL HAWK OWL) *Ninox scutulata* 27–33cm FIELD NOTES: Mainly nocturnal, but shortly before dusk seen to hunt insects in mid-air in the manner of a nightjar. Roosts deep in tree canopy. SONG/CALL: A mellow, rising *coo-coo* repeated monotonously. HABITAT: Woodlands, parks and gardens with large trees.

10 TENGMALM'S OWL (BOREAL OWL) *Aegolius funereus* 24–26cm FIELD NOTES: Nocturnal. Feeds on a variety of prey especially voles and mice. SONG/CALL: A soft, rapid *po-po-po-po-po-po-po…*, also a nasal *kuwake* and a short *chiak*. HABITAT: Mature mixed forest with tall conifers, clearings and marshy areas.

71 OWLS AND OWLETS

1 MOUNTAIN SCOPS OWL *Otus spilocephalus* 17–21cm FIELD NOTES: Nocturnal. Said to hunt beneath the canopy, reported as keeping close to the ground. SONG/CALL: A far-carrying, metallic *plew plew* with about a 5–10 second interval between notes. HABITAT: Dense broadleaved montane forest. RACES: *O. s. huttoni* (fig 1b) W Himalayas.

2 INDIAN SCOPS OWL *Otus bakkamoena deserticolor* 20–24cm FIELD NOTES: This and the next two species are often considered conspecific. Nocturnal. Daytime roost is often on a branch close to trunk. SONG/CALL: A frog-like *wuk* or *whut* repeated at 4–6 second intervals. HABITAT: Woodlands on mountains, hills and plains, also orchards and large gardens.

3 COLLARED SCOPS OWL *Otus lettia ussuriensis* 23–25cm FIELD NOTES: Nocturnal. Often sits on low perch scanning ground for prey. SONG/CALL: A *koog-koog* or *kgook-kgook* given at long intervals. HABITAT: Forests, scrub near cultivation and gardens.

4 JAPANESE SCOPS OWL *Otus semitorques* 23–25cm FIELD NOTES: Nocturnal. Actions and habits much as Indian Scops Owl. SONG/CALL: A deep *whook* repeated at long intervals, also recorded are a *koo* or *kwe* and a repeated *kwee-kwee* or *pwe-u pew-u*. HABITAT: Forests on hills and plains, in winter also in parks and gardens.

5 BRUCE'S SCOPS OWL (STRIATED, PALE or PALLID SCOPS OWL) *Otus brucei* 21cm FIELD NOTES: Nocturnal, although also recorded hunting before dusk and during the day. SONG/CALL: A hollow, low-pitched *boo…boo…boo…* given at about one second intervals. HABITAT: Fairly open areas with bushes and trees including orchards, groves, riverine woodland, parks and large gardens. RACES: *O. b. exiguous* (fig 5b) NE Arabia, S Iraq and Israel.

6 SCOPS OWL (EUROPEAN or COMMON SCOPS OWL) *Otus scops* 19–20cm FIELD NOTES: Nocturnal. Often roosts on a branch up against tree trunk. SONG/CALL: A monotonous, plaintive whistle *tyuu* repeated about every 3 seconds, often confused with frog or toad calls, although these usually have shorter notes. HABITAT: Broadleaved woodland, copses, orchards, groves, churchyards and large gardens.

7 AFRICAN SCOPS OWL *Otus senegalensis* 16–19cm FIELD NOTES: Nocturnal. Best distinguished from similar Scops Owl by call. SONG/CALL: A *da-pwoorp* repeated at 12–20 second intervals. HABITAT: Hilly wooded areas.

8 ORIENTAL SCOPS OWL (EASTERN or ASIAN SCOPS OWL) *Otus sunia* 18–21cm FIELD NOTES: Nocturnal. Roosts high in tree amongst dense foliage. SONG/CALL: A toad-like *oot-to-ta* or *oot-ta*. HABITAT: Deciduous and mixed forests, orchards, parkland and gardens.

9 RYUKYU SCOPS OWL (ELEGANT SCOPS OWL) *Otus elegans* 20cm FIELD NOTES: Actions and habits similar to Oriental Scops Owl, which is often considered conspecific. SONG/CALL: A hoarse, cough-like *uhu*, *kuru* or *u-kuruk* repeated at 2–4 second intervals. HABITAT: Dense evergreen forest.

10 PYGMY OWL (EURASIAN PYGMY OWL) *Glaucidium passerinum* 16–17cm FIELD NOTES: Active during daytime, especially at dawn or dusk, when often located calling from top of tall tree. Often hunts shrike-like from a prominent perch, feeding mainly on voles and birds. SONG/CALL: A mellow, fluting *peeu* or *hyew* given at about 1–2 second intervals, when excited often adds short, low vibrating hoots between normal notes. Also gives a squeaky *cheek-cheek-cheek…* when setting-up a winter territory. HABITAT: Coniferous and mixed forests.

11 COLLARED OWLET (COLLARED PYGMY OWL) *Glaucidium brodiei* 16cm FIELD NOTES: Diurnal. Actions appear to be similar to Pygmy Owl. SONG/CALL: A mellow, bell-like *hoo hoo-hoo hooo* or *toot-toottoot-toot*. HABITAT: Forest edge, woodland and scrub.

12 ASIAN BARRED OWLET (BARRED or CUCKOO OWLET) *Glaucidium cuculoides* 22–25cm FIELD NOTES: Mainly diurnal. Actions much as Pygmy Owl. SONG/CALL: A rapid trill, descending in pitch, also a loud *hooloo-hooloo-hooloo kok-kok chirrr*. HABITAT: Open pine and oak forest, scrub also near human habitation.

1 LITTLE OWL *Athene noctua* 21–23cm FIELD NOTES: Mainly crepuscular, although often seen in the open perched on posts, wires or buildings. SONG/CALL: A sharp *KEE-ew* also a mellow *goooek* repeated every 5–10 seconds. When alarmed utters a loud *kyitt kyitt*. HABITAT: Various, including steppe, semi-desert, open woodland, farmland and around human habitation. RACES: *A. n. lilith* (fig 1b) Cyprus, inland Middle East from SE Turkey to S Sinai.

2 SPOTTED LITTLE OWL (SPOTTED OWLET) *Athene brama* 19–21cm FIELD NOTES: Nocturnal and crepuscular, although often seen basking in the sun during the day. SONG/CALL: A medley of screeching and chattering notes, transcribed as *chirurrr chirurrr chirurrr* interspersed with *cheevah cheevah cheevah*. Also a rapid *kuerk-kuerk-kuerk* said to sound like fighting cats. HABITAT: Agricultural areas, around human habitation and semi-desert.

3 HUME'S OWL (HUME'S TAWNY OWL) *Strix butleri* 35–38cm FIELD NOTES: Nocturnal. Hunts mainly from a perch, often near tracks or roads. SONG/CALL: A soft *hoooo hoo-u hoo-u*. HABITAT: Arid mountains and gorges in rocky deserts with nearby water and trees.

4 TAWNY OWL *Strix aluco* 37–39cm FIELD NOTES: Nocturnal. Hunts from a perch or by quartering over grassland, marshland or bushes, also chases prey in flight. SONG/CALL: A shrill *kewick* and a haunting *hooooo.......hu huhuhu hooooooo*, also a tremulous low trill. HABITAT: Open forest or woodland, agricultural areas with trees, parks and large gardens.

5 GREAT GREY OWL (DARK WOOD OWL) *Strix nebulosa* 65–70cm FIELD NOTES: Mainly crepuscular. Feeds mostly on rodents, dropping on them from a branch, stump or pole perch. SONG/CALL: A soft, deep *hoo-hoo-hoo-hoo*, female answering with a mellow *whoop* or *woo woo*. When alarmed gives a growling *grrrrrrrrrrrok*, a harsh *grrook-grrook-grrook* or a high *kjah-kjah-kjah*. HABITAT: Coniferous or mixed forests with clearings, nearby pastures or bogs.

6 URAL OWL *Strix uralensis* 50–62cm FIELD NOTES: Nocturnal, although often active during daytime. Can be very aggressive, especially when tending young. Hunts mostly from a perch. SONG/CALL: A deep *whooho…woohoo-uwoohoo*, also a rising *hoohoohoohoohoohoo* that falls away at the end. When alarmed utters an explosive, barking *waff*. HABITAT: Coniferous, mixed or deciduous forests with clearings and nearby fields or bogs. RACES: *S. u. davidi* (Pere David's Owl or Sichuan Wood Owl) (fig 6b) C China. Often considered a full species.

7 BROWN WOOD OWL (HIMALAYAN BROWN OWL) *Strix leptogrammica newarensis* 40–55cm FIELD NOTES: Nocturnal. Rare. Pairs said to call to each other at dusk. SONG/CALL: A low, Rock Dove-like *to-hooh*. HABITAT: Dense montane forests.

8 MARSH OWL (AFRICAN MARSH OWL) *Asio capensis* 29–36cm FIELD NOTES: Nocturnal and crepuscular. Hunts mainly by quartering just above vegetation, often hovers or uses a perch before dropping onto prey. SONG/CALL: A croaking *kaaa-kaaa* or *quark-quark*. When alarmed gives a high squeal. HABITAT: Grassland, marshland and fields.

9 SHORT-EARED OWL *Asio flammeus* 37cm FIELD NOTES: Often active during daytime, especially early mornings and evenings. Hunts by quartering close to vegetation, often hovers before pouncing on prey. In flight outer primaries look dark-tipped compared to Long-eared Owl. SONG/CALL: During display gives a muffled *hoo-hoo-hoo-hoo-hoo….* A *kee-ow* often used as to keep contact. In winter gives various barking notes. HABITAT: Tundra, grassland, marshland, moorland and forest plantations. In winter often occurs on farmland and coastal grassland.

10 LONG-EARED OWL *Asio otus* 35–37cm FIELD NOTES: Nocturnal. When relaxed 'ear tufts' are laid flat. In flight outer primaries show 4 or 5 dark bars. SONG/CALL: During breeding season gives a series of 10 or more *hoo* notes. When alarmed utters a barking *ooack ooack ooack*. HABITAT: Woodland, copses and plantations in open country. In winter often on moorland and farmland with hedgerows.

grey
morph

1b

1

2

3

4

rufous
morph

5

6b

6

7

8

9

10

HA

73 NIGHTJARS AND NIGHTHAWK

1 PLAIN NIGHTJAR *Caprimulgus ignoramus* 22–23cm FIELD NOTES: Nocturnal. In flight male shows white spots on four outer primaries and broad white tips to outermost tail feathers. Female has buff wing spots and no white in tail. SONG/CALL: A high-pitched churr. HABITAT: Dry mountain areas with scattered vegetation and barren lowlands.

2 MOUNTAIN NIGHTJAR (ABYSSINIAN NIGHTJAR) *Caprimulgus poliocephalus* 22–24cm FIELD NOTES: Nocturnal. In flight male has white spots on four outer primaries and broad white tips to outermost tail feathers. Female has smaller white wing spots and less white on tail. SONG/CALL: A shrill *peeyoo-pirrrr* or *wee-oo-wee weerrr*. HABITAT: Rocky mountains with juniper.

3 NUBIAN NIGHTJAR *Caprimulgus nubicus* 21–22cm FIELD NOTES: Nocturnal. In flight shows pale rufous underwing and broad white spots on four outer primaries and broad white tips to outermost tail feathers. Female wing and tail spots smaller. SONG/CALL: A barking *ow-wow* or *ow-wow-wow*. HABITAT: Desert areas with scattered scrub often near water.

4 VAURIE'S NIGHTJAR (CENTRAL ASIAN or CHINESE NIGHTJAR) *Caprimulgus centralasicus* 19cm FIELD NOTES: Very little-known, only specimen recorded is thought to be an immature female. SONG/CALL: Unrecorded. HABITAT: Probably scrub covered sandy foothills and arid plains.

5 SYKES'S NIGHTJAR (SIND NIGHTJAR) *Caprimulgus mahrattensis* 23cm FIELD NOTES: Nocturnal. In flight male shows similar pattern to Nightjar. Female spots smaller and more buff. SONG/CALL: A soft, even churr. HABITAT: Semi-desert with scattered thorn scrub or tamarisks.

6 INDIAN NIGHTJAR *Caprimulgus asiaticus* 24cm FIELD NOTES: Nocturnal. In flight male has similar pattern to Nightjar. Female spots a little smaller and tinged buff. SONG/CALL: A far-carrying *chuck-chuck-chuck-chuck-k-k-k-roo*. HABITAT: Open plains and cultivation with sparse vegetation, also large gardens.

7 GREY NIGHTJAR (JUNGLE NIGHTJAR) *Caprimulgus indicus* 28–32cm FIELD NOTES: Nocturnal. In flight male has large white spots on four outer primaries and white tips to all tail feathers apart from central pair. Female wing and tail spots are tawny-buff. SONG/CALL: A rapid *tuk tuk tuk tuk....* HABITAT: Open woodlands on mountains and hills with clearings.

8 NIGHTJAR (EUROPEAN or EURASIAN NIGHTJAR) *Caprimulgus europaeus* 26–28cm FIELD NOTES: Nocturnal. In flight male shows white spots on outer three or four primaries and white tips to outermost tail feathers. Female lacks white wing and tail markings and white throat patches often smaller and more buff. SONG/CALL: A prolonged churr that regularly changes in pitch. HABITAT: Woodland edge, clearings, heathland and moorland with scattered trees or bushes, also young forest plantations. RACES: *C. e. plumipes* (fig 8b) NW China, W and NW Mongolia.

9 RED-NECKED NIGHTJAR *Caprimulgus ruficollis* 30–32cm FIELD NOTES: Nocturnal. Flight pattern of male very similar to Nightjar, female with smaller white markings on wings and tail. SONG/CALL: A prolonged *kuTOK kuTOK kuTOK....* HABITAT: Dry open woodland or scrub, scrubby hillsides and semi-desert. RACES: *C. r. desertorum* (fig 9b) NE Morocco, N Algeria and N Tunisia.

10 EGYPTIAN NIGHTJAR *Caprimulgus aegyptius* 24–26cm FIELD NOTES: Nocturnal. Underwing pale, wing spots very small or lacking. Tail with small white or buff tips on outermost feathers. SONG/CALL: A rapid, purring *kowrr-kowrr-kowrr...* that slows towards the end. HABITAT: Desert and semi-desert with scattered trees or scrub often near water.

11 NIGHTHAWK (COMMON or BOOMING NIGHTHAWK) *Chordeiles minor* 23–25cm (Vagrant) FIELD NOTES: In flight male shows prominent white band on primaries also white subterminal band on all outer tail feathers. Female white markings less distinct. SONG/CALL: A nasal *peent*, *pee-ik* or *beerp*. HABITAT: In native America: open woodland or scrub, also towns.

74 SWIFTS

1 HIMALAYAN SWIFTLET *Aerodramus brevirostris* 13–14cm FIELD NOTES: Regularly seen in flocks flying around mountain peaks and ridges. Flight often interspersed with bat-like fluttering. Forms large roosts, usually in caves. SONG/CALL: A twittering *chit chit*, also a low rattle. HABITAT: Over wooded river valleys in mountainous areas.

2 CHIMNEY SWIFT *Chaetura pelagica* 12–13cm (Vagrant) FIELD NOTES: Usually gregarious. Flight typical of family, with bat-like fluttering when feeding low down. SONG/CALL: A chattering *chip chip chip chip....* HABITAT: In native America: woodland, farmland, villages and towns.

3 WHITE-THROATED NEEDLETAIL (NEEDLE-TAILED SWIFT) *Hirundapus caudacutus* 19–20cm FIELD NOTES: Flight fast and powerful. Below shows white throat and large white horseshoe-shaped area from tail to flanks. SONG/CALL: A high-pitched twittering. HABITAT: Wooded lowlands, thinly vegetated hills, feeding over river valleys and pastures.

4 PLAIN SWIFT *Apus unicolor* 14–15cm FIELD NOTES: Very difficult to separate from Swift, flight usually more erratic and fluttering. SONG/CALL: A hoarse *sriii*, very similar to Swift. HABITAT: Over any area in Canaries from sea-level to 2500m.

5 CAPE VERDE SWIFT (ALEXANDER'S SWIFT) *Apus alexandri* 13cm FIELD NOTES: Flight much as Swift although often more fluttering. SONG/CALL: As Swift, but harsher and less piercing. HABITAT: Over all areas of Cape Verde Islands.

6 SWIFT (COMMON or EUROPEAN SWIFT) *Apus apus* 16–17cm FIELD NOTES: Flight fast and powerful interspersed with long glides. Forked tail not always noticeable during fast direct flight. SONG/CALL: A screaming *srreeee*. HABITAT: Cities, towns, villages and cliffs, feeds over large variety of locations especially lakes.

7 PALLID SWIFT (MOUSE-COLOURED SWIFT) *Apus pallidus* 16–17cm FIELD NOTES: Very difficult to separate from Swift, if seen well note blunt wingtips, larger white throat patch and paler secondaries. SONG/CALL: A screaming *srreeeeu* lower pitched than Swift. HABITAT: Sea and inland cliffs, gorges, towns and villages.

8 ALPINE SWIFT *Apus melba* 20–22cm FIELD NOTES: Flight fast and powerful, less agile than Swift with slower wingbeats. SONG/CALL: A high-pitched twittering *trrr-titititititititititititi-ti-ti-ti-ti....* HABITAT: Mountain, hill and sea cliffs, also locally in towns.

9 FORK-TAILED SWIFT (PACIFIC SWIFT) *Apus pacificus* 17–18cm FIELD NOTES: Below shows pale fringes, especially on belly and undertail-coverts. Usually in flocks mixed with other swift species. SONG/CALL: A high-pitched *skree-ee-ee*. HABITAT: Towns, villages, sea and inland cliffs, forages over same and around cultivated areas, mountains, forests and lakes.

10 WHITE-RUMPED SWIFT (AFRICAN WHITE-RUMPED SWIFT) *Apus caffer* 14cm FIELD NOTES: Flight fast and agile with fluttering wingbeats. Tail deeply forked, although when held closed appears as a single spike. From below appears quite dark with, when seen under good conditions, pale tips to secondaries. SONG/CALL: A rapid, chattering. HABITAT: Valleys and gorges in craggy hills and mountains, sometimes in open country.

11 LITTLE SWIFT *Apus affinis* 12–13cm FIELD NOTES: Fluttering bat-like flight combined with short glides. From below appears black with prominent white throat. SONG/CALL: A high-pitched rippling trill and a rapid *siksiksiksik...*, usually used during chases. HABITAT: Towns, villages, cliffs and ravines, forages over nearby country.

12 HOUSE SWIFT *Apus nipalensis* 15cm FIELD NOTES: Actions and habits as Little Swift, which is often considered conspecific. SONG/CALL: A shrill whickering scream, similar to Little Swift? HABITAT: Towns, cities and mountain areas, feeds over surrounding country.

13 AFRICAN PALM SWIFT (PALM SWIFT) *Cypsiurus parvus* 16cm FIELD NOTES: Tail deeply forked but usually kept closed. Flight fast, fluttering and agile, glides with wings held below the horizontal. SONG/CALL: A high-pitched *sisisi-soo-soo* or *skiiirrrrrrr*. HABITAT: Open country, towns and villages with nearby palms.

75 KINGFISHERS

1 RUDDY KINGFISHER *Halcyon coromanda* 25cm FIELD NOTES: Shy and secretive. Juvenile duller with dark bill with paler tip. SONG/CALL: A rapid, mellow disyllabic or trisyllabic note. Also a tremulous *pyorr pyorr*. HABITAT: Occurs on or near mountain streams in dense evergreen forests. Also, in parts of Japan, found in wet *Cryptomeria* groves.

2 WHITE-BREASTED KINGFISHER (WHITE-THROATED or SMYRNA KINGFISHER) *Halcyon smyrnensis* 27–28cm FIELD NOTES: Often encountered far from water. In flight from above shows large bluish-white patch on base of primaries. Juvenile duller, bill orange-yellow with darker tip. SONG/CALL: A loud, rapid trilling *kilililililili…*, repeated, often quite incessantly. Also a cackling *chake ake ake-ake-ake-ake* usually given as bird takes flight. HABITAT: Very cosmopolitan, including roadside trees, plantations, bamboo, farmland, gardens, dams, ponds, canals, creeks, mudflats and light industrial areas.

3 BLACK-CAPPED KINGFISHER *Halcyon pileata* 28cm FIELD NOTES: Perches conspicuously. In flight, from above, shows large white patch on base of primaries. Juvenile duller with an orange-buff loral spot and slight scaling on breast. Bill brownish-orange. SONG/CALL: A ringing cackle, *kikikikikiki*. HABITAT: Occurs mainly in riverbank woodland and deciduous forests near water.

4 GREY-HEADED KINGFISHER (CHESTNUT-BELLIED KINGFISHER) *Halcyon leucocphala* 22cm FIELD NOTES: Usually encountered on a prominent perch. In flight, from above, shows large white patch at base of primaries. Juvenile duller with head and breast scaly. Bill black with orange-red base. SONG/CALL: A weak trill, falling in pitch, *ji-ji-ji-ji-chi*, also a clear *piuu piuu piuu* and a rapid *chi-chi-chi-chi-chi-chi….*. HABITAT: Wadis with trees, not necessarily near water. RACES: *H. l. acteon* Cape Verde Islands, pale-headed, found in dry ravines, vineyards and around human habitation. Not illustrated.

5 COLLARED KINGFISHER (MANGROVE or WHITE-COLLARED KINGFISHER) *Halcyon chloris abyssinica* 23–25cm FIELD NOTES: Noisy, especially in mornings. Juvenile duller with dark scaling on white neck and breast. SONG/CALL: A harsh ringing note repeated 3–5 times. HABITAT: Mangroves. RACES: *H. c. kalbaensis* (fig 5b) Khawr Kalba (a mangrove lagoon between U.A.E. and Oman).

6 KINGFISHER (COMMON or RIVER KINGFISHER) *Alcedo atthis* 16–17cm FIELD NOTES: Often first sighted as a blue flash flying low along river uttering its high-pitched call. Female has orange-red base to lower mandible. SONG/CALL: A penetrating, high-pitched *tseee* or *tseee ti-ee ti-tee ti-tee*. When disturbed utters a harsh *shrit-it-it*. HABITAT: Rivers, streams, lakes etc. During winter also recorded on saline lagoons and estuaries.

7 MALACHITE KINGFISHER *Alcedo cristata* 13cm (Vagrant) FIELD NOTES: Usually perches prominently on waterside vegetation. Sometimes fans out lax head feathers. Juvenile duller, bill black. SONG/CALL: A short, shrill *kweek* or *seek*, often repeated. HABITAT: In native Africa: waterside vegetation of rivers, ponds, lakes, estuaries etc.

8 PIED KINGFISHER (LESSER PIED KINGFISHER) *Ceryle rudis* 25cm FIELD NOTES: Regularly hovers and dives in search of food. Often occurs in small parties. SONG/CALL: A repeated, noisy *kwik* or *kik*, also a high-pitched *TREEtiti TREEtiti*. HABITAT: Lakes, rivers, ponds etc. After breeding also on estuaries, saline lagoons and sheltered coastal areas.

9 CRESTED KINGFISHER (GREATER PIED KINGFISHER) *Megaceryle lugubris* 41–43cm FIELD NOTES: Unmistakable. Shy, solitary. Does not hover. SONG/CALL: A loud *ping*, deep croaks and raucous grating notes. When disturbed utters a loud *kek*. HABITAT: Fast-flowing rivers and streams in mountain forests. During the winter often moves to mouths of rivers.

10 BELTED KINGFISHER *Ceryle (Megaceryle) alcyon* 28–35cm (Vagrant) FIELD NOTES: Unmistakable. Usually feeds by diving from a perch but also hovers and dives in search of food. SONG/CALL: A far-carrying, rattling *kekity-kek-kek-kek-tk-ticky-kek*, also a harsh *caar*. HABITAT: In native N America: rivers, lakes, marshes, ponds and estuaries.

76 BEE-EATERS, ROLLERS AND DOLLARBIRD

1 BLUE-CHEEKED BEE-EATER *Merops persicus* 27–31cm FIELD NOTES: Highly gregarious. Juvenile duller, lacks elongated tail feathers. SONG/CALL: A rolling *diririp*, a mellow *tewtew* and when alarmed a sharp *dik-dik-dik*. HABITAT: Sandy areas and open cultivation with scattered trees, usually near water.

2 LITTLE GREEN BEE-EATER (GREEN BEE-EATER) *Merops orientalis cyanophrys* 22–25cm FIELD NOTES: Juvenile duller, lacks black gorget and elongated tail feathers. SONG/CALL: A quiet trilling *trrr trrr trrr trrr*, also a sharp *ti-ic* or *ti-ti-ti* given when alarmed. HABITAT: Arid country with scattered trees, cultivation with trees and bushes and riverbanks. RACES: M. *o. beludschicus* (fig 2b) Iran; M. *o. cleopatra* (fig 2c) Egypt.

3 RAINBOW BEE-EATER *Merops ornatus* 19–21cm (Vagrant) FIELD NOTES: Generally in pairs or small groups. Juvenile duller, lacks black gorget and elongated tail feathers. SONG/CALL: A rolling *prrrp prrrp*, *preee* or *drrrt*. When alarmed utters a *dip-dip* or *clip-lip-lip-lip*. HABITAT: In native Australia: various forms of open country.

4 BEE-EATER (EUROPEAN BEE-EATER) *Merops apiaster* 27–29cm FIELD NOTES: Sociable. Juvenile duller, lacks black gorget and elongated tail feathers. SONG/CALL: A liquid, often repeated, *prruip*, *pruik* or *kruup*. HABITAT: Open country, cultivated land, areas with scattered trees or bushes, also rivers with steep banks and locally on woodland edge.

5 WHITE-THROATED BEE-EATER *Merops albicollis* 19–21cm FIELD NOTES: Juvenile duller, elongated tail feathers either much shorter or lacking. SONG/CALL: A soft, high-pitched *prrrp prrrp prrrp….* HABITAT: Breeds on hills, plains and wadis with trees and bushes.

6 ROLLER (EUROPEAN ROLLER) *Coracias garrulus* 30–32cm FIELD NOTES: Distinctive diving, rolling display-flight. Juvenile duller, especially on head and breast. SONG/CALL: A short *rack*, a chattering *rack rack rackrak ak* and a screeching *aaaarrr* warning call. In display utters a loud rattling *ra-ra-ra-ra-raa-raa-aaaaaa aaaaar*. HABITAT: Open country with scattered trees, open woods, generally oak, also recorded in orchards, mixed farmland and dry thorn plains.

7 ABYSSINIAN ROLLER *Coracias abyssinica* 28–30cm FIELD NOTES: Habits similar to Roller. Juvenile duller, lacks elongated tail feathers. SONG/CALL: A loud *rack* given in flight and a screeched *aaaarh* when perched. During aerial display utters a strident *ra-ra-ra-ra-gaa-gaa-gaa-aaaaaar aaaaar*. HABITAT: Semi-desert and savanna with scattered trees.

8 INDIAN ROLLER *Coracias benghalensis* 30–34cm FIELD NOTES: In flight shows large pale patch on primaries. Juvenile duller. SONG/CALL: A harsh *chak* or *tschow*. During display-flight gives various cackling and screeching calls. HABITAT: Open country with bushes and trees, cultivated land and around human dwellings with large gardens or open areas.

9 LILAC-BREASTED ROLLER (LILAC-THROATED ROLLER) *Coracias caudate* 28–30cm (Vagrant) FIELD NOTES: Behaviour similar to Roller. Juvenile duller, lacks elongated tail feathers. SONG/CALL: A guttural *rak-rak-rak* given in flight and when perched. HABITAT: In native Africa: grasslands with scattered trees and bushes, light forest and riverside woods.

10 RUFOUS-CROWNED ROLLER *Coracias naevia* 35–40cm (Vagrant) FIELD NOTES: More sluggish than others of the genus. Juvenile duller. SONG/CALL: A muffled *ga*. HABITAT: In native Africa: open savanna woodland, rocky and shrubby hillsides and farmland with trees.

11 BROAD-BILLED ROLLER *Eurystomus glaucurus afer* 29–30cm (Vagrant) FIELD NOTES: Spends much time perched atop tall trees. Juvenile duller. SONG/CALL: A growling *giaow grrrd grrrd-grrrd g-r-g* and a rattling *g-r-r-r-r-r-r-r-d* or *kik-k-k-k-k-k-k-k-k-r-r-r-r-r*. In flight utters a falcon-like *crik-crik-crik-crik*. HABITAT: In native Africa: wooded savanna, forest edge and clearings.

12 DOLLARBIRD *Eurystomus orientalis* 25–28cm FIELD NOTES: In flight shows large pale blue patch at base of primaries. Juvenile has slaty underparts, bill dusky on upper mandible and yellow on lower mandible. SONG/CALL: A fast *krak-kak-kak-kak* and a hoarse *chak*. HABITAT: Forest edge and clearings and wooded riverbanks.

77 HOOPOE, PARAKEETS, HUMMINGBIRD, MOUSEBIRD, TROGON, HORNBILL, BARBET AND HONEYGUIDE

1 HOOPOE (EURASIAN HOOPOE) *Upupa epops* 26–28cm FIELD NOTES: Unmistakable, even in flight where gives the impression of a giant butterfly. SONG/CALL: A low *hoop-hoop-hoop*. HABITAT: Grassland and farmland with scattered trees, parkland, groves and orchards.

2 ALEXANDRINE PARAKEET *Psittacula eupatria* 53–58cm FIELD NOTES: Probably established in parts of the Middle East. Actions much as smaller Ring-necked Parakeet. SONG/CALL: A hoarse, screaming *kii-e-rick*. HABITAT: Plantations and gardens.

3 RING-NECKED PARAKEET (ROSE-RINGED PARAKEET) *Psittacula krameri* 37–43cm FIELD NOTES: Widely introduced, natural population occurs in N Baluchistan. Usually in small flocks, larger flocks at rich food sources or roosts. Flight fast and direct. SONG/CALL: A screeching *kee-a*. HABITAT: Open woodland, orchards, parks and gardens.

4 LORD DERBY'S PARAKEET (DERBYAN PARAKEET) *Psittacula derbiana* 46–50cm FIELD NOTES: Gregarious. Often seen in strong, fast flight above montane forests. Juvenile duller with green head. SONG/CALL: A high-pitched shrill whistle, also recorded is a long, raucous, metallic cry. HABITAT: Coniferous and mixed montane forests.

5 SLATY-HEADED PARAKEET *Psittacula himalayana* 39–41cm FIELD NOTES: Usually in small flocks. Flight swift, direct and very agile, especially when flying among trees. Juvenile has a green head with brownish tinge on cheek. SONG/CALL: A high-pitched *scree-scree* and a drawn-out *wee...eenee*. HABITAT: Woodland and cultivated areas with large trees.

6 GREY-HEADED PARAKEET *Psittacula finschii* 36–40cm FIELD NOTES: Often considered a race of Slaty-headed Parakeet, actions and habits similar. SONG/CALL: As Slaty-headed Parakeet? HABITAT: Open, mixed deciduous forests and cultivated land.

7 MONK PARAKEET (QUAKER or GREY-BREASTED PARAKEET) *Myiopsitta monachus* 28–29cm FIELD NOTES: Introduced in various parts of the W Palearctic. Gregarious and noisy. Flight swift, with rapid wingbeats. SONG/CALL: A loud, staccato shrieking and a high-pitched chattering. HABITAT: Farmland, parks and large gardens.

8 RUFOUS HUMMINGBIRD *Selasphorus rufus* 10cm (Vagrant) FIELD NOTES: Unmistakable. Wings make a heavy *zz-zzz-zz-zzz* noise when hovering. SONG/CALL: A sharp, high *bzee*. HABITAT: In native America: woodland edge, streamsides and meadows.

9 BLUE-NAPED MOUSEBIRD *Urocolius macrourus* 33–35cm (Vagrant) FIELD NOTES: Gregarious, first sighting is often of a flock flying from tree to tree. Works way among tree branches like a rodent. SONG/CALL: A plaintive *peeee peeeeeeeeee* and a shorter *pyee pyee pyee* or *pew t-lew pew t-lew*. HABITAT: Semi-desert with bushes and trees.

10 WARD'S TROGON *Harpactes wardi* 35–38cm FIELD NOTES: Rare. Usually sits very still, often hidden, with occasional fluttering flights to catch winged insects. SONG/CALL: A mellow *kew-kew-kew-kew*. HABITAT: Evergreen montane forests.

11 AFRICAN GREY HORNBILL *Tockus nasutus* 45–51cm FIELD NOTES: Unmistakeable. SONG/CALL: A mewing *piiiuuu*, a loud *kee-kee-kee* and during display a *coi-coi-coi-coi* that builds to a crescendo. HABITAT: Plains and hills with scattered trees, also acacia woodland.

12 GREAT BARBET (GIANT BARBET) *Megalaima virens* 32–35cm FIELD NOTES: Unmistakable. Usually alone or in small parties feeding in tall trees. Undulating flight. SONG/CALL: A mournful *piho piho piho*, a rapid *tuk tuk tuk* and a harsh *karr-r*. HABITAT: Deciduous and evergreen mountain forests.

13 YELLOW-RUMPED HONEYGUIDE *Indicator xanthonotus* 15cm FIELD NOTES: Often sits motionless on topmost branches of trees. SONG/CALL: A quiet *weet* a chipping *tzt* and a *chaenp-chaenp* given in flight. HABITAT: Mixed forests, wooded gorges and streams near Giant Honeybee colonies. RACES: *I. x. radcliffi* (fig 13b) W Himalayas.

78 WRYNECK, PICULET AND WOODPECKERS

1 WRYNECK (EURASIAN WRYNECK) *Jynx torquilla* 16–17cm FIELD NOTES: Usually shy. Forages mostly on the ground. Flight low and moderately undulating. SONG/CALL: A plaintive *quee-quee-quee-quee* and a hard *teck* when alarmed. HABITAT: Open woodland edges and clearings, orchards, parks and large gardens.

2 SPECKLED PICULET *Picumnus innominatus* 10cm FIELD NOTES: Presence revealed by persistent tapping while foraging. Agile in search for food, even hanging upside-down, also flies or hovers in pursuit of flushed prey. SONG/CALL: A high-pitched *ti-ti-ti-ti-ti* and a squeaky *sik-sik-sik*. HABITAT: Mixed sub-montane forest with areas of bamboo.

3 LEVAILLANT'S WOODPECKER (LEVAILLANT'S GREEN WOODPECKER) *Picus vaillantii* 30–32cm FIELD NOTES: Actions much as Green Woodpecker, which is often considered conspecific, although drums more often. SONG/CALL: Like Green Woodpecker but slightly quicker. HABITAT: Mainly oak, poplar, cedar and pine forests.

4 GREEN WOODPECKER (EUROPEAN GREEN WOODPECKER) *Picus viridis* 31–33cm FIELD NOTES: Spends a lot of time feeding on the ground. Flight undulating, showing prominent yellow rump. Rarely drums. SONG/CALL: A loud, laughing *klew-klew-klew-klew-klew*, also a *kyu- kyu- kyuk* given in flight. HABITAT: Forests edge, open woodland, copses, orchards, parks and large gardens. RACES: *P. v. sharpei* (fig 4b) Iberia and Pyrenees.

5 GREY-HEADED WOODPECKER (GREY-FACED or BLACK-NAPED WOODPECKER) *Picus canus* 25–26cm FIELD NOTES: Wary. Regularly feeds on the ground. In flight shows dull yellowish rump. Drums in rapid bursts. SONG/CALL: A slow, musical *peeu-peeu-peeu-peeu-peeu-peeu…* and when disturbed a *kyakyakyak….* HABITAT: Very varied, forests, open country copses, orchards, parks and gardens. RACES: *P. c. guerini* (fig 5b) NC China.

6 JAPANESE GREEN WOODPECKER *Picus awokera* 29–30cm FIELD NOTES: Feeds mainly in middle-level of trees and occasionally on the ground. In flight shows a yellowish rump. Drums in fairly long fast rolls. Southern birds slightly smaller and darker. SONG/CALL: A loud *peoo peoo* and a *ket ket*. HABITAT: Northern birds use open mixed forest, southern birds use evergreen forests.

7 SCALY-BELLIED WOODPECKER *Picus squamatus* 35cm FIELD NOTES: Feeds on trees and the ground. In undulating flight shows yellowish rump. Regularly drums during breeding season. SONG/CALL: A ringing, melodious *klee-guh kleeguh* or *kuik-kuik-kuik*, also a high-pitched *kik* or a drawn-out nasal *cheenk*. HABITAT: Mixed woodland, open country with copses, tamarisk scrub, orchards and groves.

8 OKINAWA WOODPECKER (PRYER'S WOODPECKER) *Sapheopipo noguchii* 31–35cm FIELD NOTES: Forages mostly low down on tree trunks, stumps, bamboo and fallen logs. In flight shows dull reddish rump. Drumming can be in short or long bursts. SONG/CALL: Clear whistling *kwe kwe kwe kwe*, also a *kyu-kyu* or *kyu-kyu-kup* and a single *whit* when alarmed. HABITAT: Mature subtropical forests.

9 YELLOW-BELLIED SAPSUCKER (COMMON SAPSUCKER) *Sphyrapicus varius* 19–21cm (Vagrant) FIELD NOTES: In moderate undulating flight shows white rump. Some females have crown completely black or with red only on forecrown. SONG/CALL: A mewing *cheerrrr* falling in pitch. HABITAT: In native America: woodlands, aspen groves and orchards.

10 BAY WOODPECKER (RED-EARED BAY WOODPECKER) *Blythipicus pyrrhotis* 27–30cm FIELD NOTES: Feeds low down on trunks, stumps and fallen logs. SONG/CALL: A loud laughing rattle that increases in tempo while dropping in pitch. When disturbed gives a chattering *churra-cha-churra-cha-churra*. HABITAT: Evergreen and mixed deciduous forest.

11 NORTHERN FLICKER (COMMON or YELLOW-SHAFTED FLICKER) *Colaptes auratus* 31–33cm (Vagrant) FIELD NOTES: In flight shows yellow underwing and white rump. SONG/CALL: A rapid *wik-wik-wik-wik…* and a squeaky *flick-a flick-a….* HABITAT: In native America: open woodland, forest edge, open country with scattered trees, parks and gardens.

79 WOODPECKERS

1 BLACK WOODPECKER *Dryocopus martius* 45–47cm FIELD NOTES: Forages on lower parts of trunks, at base of trees and on the ground. Flight slow and loose, slightly undulating. Drumming loud, recalls a machine gun. SONG/CALL: A loud *kwee kwee-kwee-kwee-kwee…*, also a clear *bleeeep* or *ke-yaa*. In flight gives a far-carrying *krry-krry-krry…* or softer *kruek-kruek-kruek….* HABITAT: Mature forests of most types, after breeding often in more open areas with scattered trees.

2 WHITE-BELLIED WOODPECKER *Dryocopus javensis* 40–48cm FIELD NOTES: Feeds on the ground as well as in trees, favours dead trees or stumps. Drumming loud and accelerating. SONG/CALL: A laughing *kek-kek-kek-kek-kek…* or *kiau-kiau-kaiu-kaiu…* also a loud, sharp *kiyow*, *kyah* or *keer*. HABITAT: Mixed forests and light secondary forest with tall trees.

3 GREAT SPOTTED WOODPECKER *Dendrocopus major* 22–23cm FIELD NOTES: Forages mainly in upper branches of trees, agile, often clinging tit-like to extricate prey, but will obtain food from a wide range of sources including bird nests and garden feeders. Drumming loud, rapid and far carrying. Juvenile has red crown. SONG/CALL: A high-pitched *kik* or soft *chik*. HABITAT: Many types of woodland and forest, copses, parkland and gardens. RACES: *D. m. stresemanni* (fig 3b) SE Tibet to C China; *D. m. numidus* (fig 3c) N Algeria and Tunisia.

4 SYRIAN WOODPECKER *Dendrocopus syriacus* 23cm FIELD NOTES: Behaviour similar to Great Spotted Woodpecker. Note lack of black bar at rear of ear-coverts and pinkish undertail. Juvenile has red crown. Drumming like Great Spotted Woodpecker but longer and fading at end. SONG/CALL: A soft *cheuk*, *gipp* or when disturbed *gip-gip-gip….* HABITAT: Broadleaved woodland, open country with scattered trees, orchards, vineyards, parks and gardens.

5 SIND WOODPECKER (SIND PIED WOODPECKER) *Dendrocopus assimilis* 20–22cm FIELD NOTES: Forages among branches of trees, often low down, on fallen trees and fence-posts etc. Drums in intermittent bursts. Has hybridised with Syrian Woodpecker. SONG/CALL: An explosive *ptik*, also a weak *chir-rir-rirrh-rirrh* and a *wicka toi-whit toi-whit toi-whit*. HABITAT: Riverine woodland, thorn scrub, oases and gardens.

6 HIMALAYAN WOODPECKER *Dendrocopus himalayensis* 23–25cm FIELD NOTES: Black line under and behind eye often lacking or indistinct. Mainly arboreal. Drums in short bursts. SONG/CALL: A sharp *kit* and a rapid, high *chissik-chissik* and a fast *tri tri tri….* HABITAT: Dense mountain forests.

7 WHITE-WINGED WOODPECKER *Dendrocopus leucopterus* 22–23cm FIELD NOTES: Little-known, actions probably much as Great Spotted Woodpecker. SONG/CALL: A *kewk* or *kig*, also rattling notes. HABITAT: Poplar forests by streams, desert scrub, orchards and gardens.

8 DARJEELING WOODPECKER *Dendrocopus darjellensis* 25cm FIELD NOTES: Forages from ground to tree canopy, sometimes in mixed-species flocks. Frequently drums in breeding season. Juvenile lacks ochre patch on side of neck. SONG/CALL: A low *puk puk* and a *tsik tsik tsik…* given when alarmed, also a rattling trill. HABITAT: High-altitude forests also open woodland, 2500–4000m.

9 CRIMSON-BREASTED WOODPECKER *Dendrocopus cathpharius* 17–19cm FIELD NOTES: Usually forages low down in trees and bushes, favours dead trees. SONG/CALL: A loud, repetitive *chip* or *tchick*, also a short, rapid, descending rattle. HABITAT: High-elevation evergreen and deciduous forest with oaks, chestnut and rhododendrons. RACES: *D. c. innixus* (fig 9b) C China.

80 WOODPECKERS

1 MIDDLE SPOTTED WOODPECKER *Dendrocopus medius* 20–22cm FIELD NOTES: Mainly arboreal. Sometimes joins mixed-species feeding flocks. Rarely drums, although gives loud taps at nest hole. SONG/CALL: A nasal *gueeah .. gueeah .. gueeah .. gueeah* also a short *teuk* and a rattling *kik keuk-keuk-keuk*. HABITAT: Mature broadleaved forests and woodlands, orchards and parks.

2 WHITE-BACKED WOODPECKER *Dendrocopus leucotos* 23–28cm FIELD NOTES: In flight shows white lower back and rump. Actions similar to Great Spotted Woodpecker, tends to favour dead wood, fallen timber and base of trees. Drumming loud, long and accelerating. SONG/CALL: A soft, sharp *kiuk*, *kok* or *gig*. When disturbed gives a series of *kyig gyig* notes. HABITAT: Mature broadleaved or mixed forests often near water or in swampy areas. RACES: *D. l. lilfordi* (Lilford's Woodpecker) (fig 2b) Pyrenees, Italy, Caucasus, Turkey and SE Europe; *D. l. owstoni* (Owston's Woodpecker) (fig 2c) N Ryukyu Islands.

3 RUFOUS-BELLIED WOODPECKER *Dendrocopus hyperythrus* 20–25cm FIELD NOTES: Mainly arboreal, after breeding sometimes joins mixed-species feeding flocks. Drums in short fading rolls. SONG/CALL: A reeling *chit-chit-chit-r-r-r-h* and a fast *ptikititititit* given in alarm. HABITAT: Conifers or mixed forests.

4 BROWN-FRONTED WOODPECKER *Dendrocopus auriceps* 19–20cm FIELD NOTES: Forages mainly in trees and bushes, often joins mixed-species feeding flocks. Drums for long periods in spring. SONG/CALL: A squeaky *chick* or *peek* also a *chitter-chitter-chitter-r-r-rh* or *cheek-cheek-cheek-rrrr*. HABITAT: Open temperate and pine forest, favours oaks, deodars and mixed stands.

5 LESSER SPOTTED WOODPECKER *Dendrocopus minor* 14–16cm FIELD NOTES: Forages in trees, favouring smaller branches, bushes and plant stalks especially reeds. Often joins mixed-species feeding flocks in non-breeding season. Drumming is high-pitched with a brief interval between bursts. SONG/CALL: A weak *kee kee kee…* or *piit piit piit piit piit…* also a sharp *pik* or *chik*. HABITAT: Open forests, often near water, forest edge, orchards, parks and gardens. RACES: *D. m. kamtschatkensis* (fig 5b) Urals east to Kamchatka; *D. m. buturlini* (fig 5c) S Europe (Iberia to Bulgaria and NW Greece).

6 GREY-CAPPED WOODPECKER *Dendrocopus canicapills* 14–16cm FIELD NOTES: Forages in tree crowns, bushes and saplings, favouring outer branches and twigs, agile, often hanging upside-down. Drumming muted. SONG/CALL: A soft *cheep*, *pic* or *tzit*, a *chip-chip* and a squeaky *ki-ki ki ki rrr…*. HABITAT: Most types of forests scrub and gardens. RACES: *D. c. doerriesi* (fig 6b) E Siberia, E Manchuria and Korea.

7 PYGMY WOODPECKER (JAPANESE PYGMY WOODPECKER) *Dendrocopus kizuki* 13–15cm FIELD NOTES: Forages among small branches and twigs, mainly in tree canopy, also visits bushes and strong plants. Regularly joins mixed-species feeding flocks. Drumming weak, short bursts in quick succession. SONG/CALL: A buzzing *kzz kzz* and a sharp *khit* or *khit-khit-khit*. HABITAT: Many types of forests, also parks and gardens.

8 ARABIAN WOODPECKER *Dendrocopus dorae* 18cm FIELD NOTES: Agile forager in canopy of acacia and other trees or on the ground. Drumming feeble and only occasional. SONG/CALL: An accelerating and descending *kek-kek-kek-ke-ke-kekekeke-ke-ke*, also a descending *keck-keck-keck-keck-keck* and a falcon-like *kik-kik-kik-kik*. HABITAT: Woodland, mainly acacia, also palm and fig groves often close to habitation.

9 THREE-TOED WOODPECKER (NORTHERN or EURASIAN THREE-TOED WOODPECKER) *Picoides tridactylus* 21–24cm FIELD NOTES: In flight shows prominent white back, this partly obscured by dark bars in races *P. t. alpinus* and *funebris*. Forages low down, tends to favour dead trees and stumps. Drum bursts are loud and slightly accelerating. SONG/CALL: A short, soft *kip* or *kyuk*, when alarmed gives a *kip-kip-kip-kip…*. HABITAT: Conifer and mixed forests often in boggy areas, in south of range in mountain forests. RACES: *P. t. crissoleucus* (fig 9b) Urals to Sea of Okhotsk; *P. t. funebris* (fig 9c) SW China to Tibet.

FURTHER READING

Ali, S. & Ripley, S.D. (1987) *Compact Handbook of the Birds of India and Pakistan*. Oxford University Press.

Beaman, M. (1994) *Palearctic Birds*. Harrier Publications.

Beaman, M. & Madge, S. (1998) *The Handbook of Bird Identification for Europe and the Western Palearctic*. Helm.

Brazil, M.A. (1991) *The Birds of Japan*. Christopher Helm.

Brown, L.H., Urban, E.K., Newman, K., Fry, C.H. & Keith, G.S. (eds) (1982–2004) *The Birds of Africa*. Vols. 1–7. Academic Press.

Cramp, S., Simmons, K.E.L. & Perrins, C.M. (eds) (1977–94) *The Birds of the Western Palearctic*. Vols. 1–9. Oxford University Press.

Dickinson, E.C. (ed.) (2003) *The Howard and Moore Complete Checklist of the Birds of the World*. Christopher Helm.

Fry, C.H., Fry, K. & Harris, A. (1992) *Kingfishers, Bee-eaters and Rollers*. Christopher Helm.

Grimmett, R., Inskipp, C. & Inskipp, T. (2001) *Pocket Guide to the Birds of the Indian Subcontinent*. Christopher Helm.

Hancock, J. & Elliott, H. (1978) *Herons of the World*. London Editions.

Hancock, J., Kushlan, J.A. & Kahl, M.P. (1992) *Storks, Ibises and Spoonbills of the World*. Academic Press.

Harrison, P. (1983 & updates) *Seabirds; an identification guide*. Christopher Helm.

Hayman, P., Marchant, A.J. & Prater, A.H. (1986) *Shorebirds: An Identification Guide to the Waders of the World*. Christopher Helm.

Hollom, P.A.D., Porter, R.F., Christensen, S. & Willis, I. (1988) *Birds of the Middle East and North Africa*. Poyser.

del Hoyo, J., Elliott, A. & Sargatal, J. (eds) (1992–2005) *Handbook of the Birds of the World*. Vols. 1–7. Lynx Edicions.

MacKinnon, J. & Phillipps, K. (2000) *A Field Guide to the Birds of China*. Oxford University Press.

Madge, S. & Burn, H. (1988) *Wildfowl: An Identification Guide to the Ducks, Geese and Swans of the World*. Christopher Helm.

Madge, S. & McGowan, P. (2002) *Pheasants, Partridges and Grouse. Including Buttonquails, Sandgrouse and Allies*. Christopher Helm.

Mullarney, K., Svensson, L., Zetterström, D. & Grant, P.J. (1999) *Collins Bird Guide*. HarperCollins.

Olsen, K.M. & Larsson, H. (2004) *Gulls of Europe, Asia and North America*. Christopher Helm.

Olsen, K.M. & Larsson, H. (1997) *Skuas and Jaegers: A guide to Skuas and Jaegers of the World*. Pica Press.

Olsen, K.M. & Larsson, H. (1995) *Terns of Europe and North America*. Christopher Helm.

Palmer, R.S. (ed.) (1962–88) *Handbook of North American Birds*. Vols. 1–5. Yale University Press.

Peterson, R.T. (1990) *A Field Guide to Western Birds*. Third Edition. Houghton Mifflin.

Peterson, R.T. (1980) *A Field Guide to the Birds*. Fourth Edition. Houghton Mifflin.

Porter, R.F., Christensen, S. & Schiermacker-Hansen, P. (1996) *Birds of the Middle East*. Christopher Helm.

Porter, R.F., Willis, I., Christensen, S. & Neilsen, B.P. (1981) *Flight Identification of European Raptors*. Third Edition. Poyser.

Sale, R. (2006) *A Complete Guide to Arctic Wildlife*. Christopher Helm.

Sibley, D. (2000) *The North American Bird Guide*. Christopher Helm.

Sonobe, K. (ed.) (1982) *A Field Guide to the Birds of Japan*. Wild Bird Society of Japan.

Stevenson, T. & Fanshawe, J. (2002) *Field Guide to the Birds of East Africa*. T & A D Poyser.

Terres, J.K. (1980) *The Audubon Society Encyclopedia of North American Birds*. Alfred A. Knopf.

Vinicombe, K., Harris, A. & Tucker, L. (1989) *Bird Identification*. MacMillan.

Voous, K.H. (1988) *Owls of the Northern Hemisphere*. Collins.

Winkler, H., Christie, D.A. & Nurney, D. (1995) *Woodpeckers: A Guide to the Woodpeckers, Piculets and Wrynecks of the World*. Pica Press.

Zimmerman, D. Turner, D.A. & Pearson, D.J. (1996) *Birds of Kenya and Northern Tanzania*. Christopher Helm.

SPECIES DISTRIBUTION MAPS

Key to maps

Summer distribution
Winter distribution
Resident distribution

Vagrants are not included in the distribution map section

Ostrich, Plate 1.1

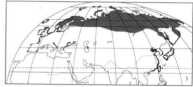
Red-throated Diver, Plate 2.1

Black-throated Diver, Plate 2.2

Pacific Diver, Plate 2.3

Great Northern Diver, Plate 2.4

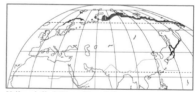
Yellow-billed Diver, Plate 2.5

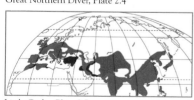
Little Grebe, Plate 2.7

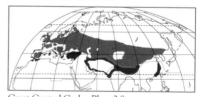
Great Crested Grebe, Plate 2.8

Red-necked Grebe, Plate 2.9

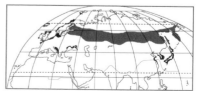
Slavonian Grebe, Plate 2.10

175

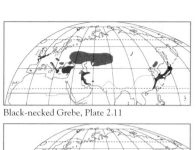

Black-necked Grebe, Plate 2.11

Black-footed Albatross, Plate 3.4

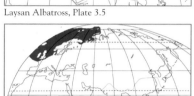

Laysan Albatross, Plate 3.5

Short-tailed Albatross, Plate 3.6

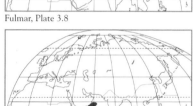

Fulmar, Plate 3.8

Bulwer's Petrel, Plate 3.10

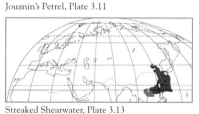

Jouanin's Petrel, Plate 3.11

Cory's Shearwater, Plate 3.12

Streaked Shearwater, Plate 3.13

Fea's Petrel, Plate 4.3

Zino's Petrel, Plate 4.4

Mottled Petrel, Plate 4.6

Providence Petrel, Plate 4.7

Bonin Petrel, Plate 4.10

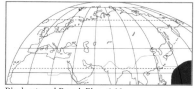

Black-winged Petrel, Plate 4.11

Stejneger's Petrel, Plate 4.14

Flesh-footed Shearwater, Plate 5.1

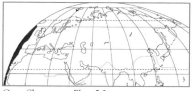

Great Shearwater, Plate 5.2

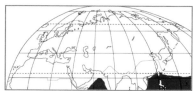

Wedge-tailed Shearwater, Plate 5.3

Sooty Shearwater, Plate 5.5

Short-tailed Shearwater, Plate 5.6

Manx Shearwater, Plate 5.8

Mediterranean Shearwater, Plate 5.9

North Atlantic Little Shearwater, Plate 5.11

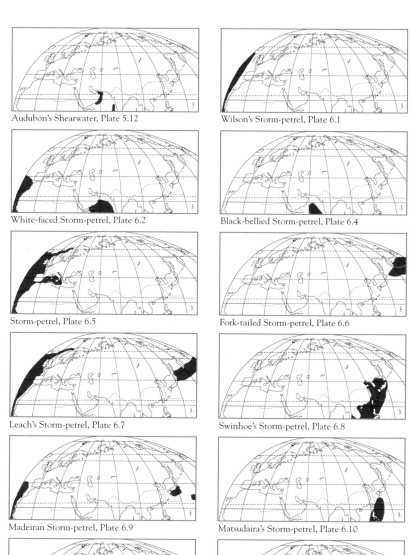

Audubon's Shearwater, Plate 5.12

Wilson's Storm-petrel, Plate 6.1

White-faced Storm-petrel, Plate 6.2

Black-bellied Storm-petrel, Plate 6.4

Storm-petrel, Plate 6.5

Fork-tailed Storm-petrel, Plate 6.6

Leach's Storm-petrel, Plate 6.7

Swinhoe's Storm-petrel, Plate 6.8

Madeiran Storm-petrel, Plate 6.9

Matsudaira's Storm-petrel, Plate 6.10

Tristram's Storm-petrel, Plate 6.11

Magnificent Frigatebird, Plate 7.2

Red-billed Tropicbird, Plate 7.5

Red-tailed Tropicbird, Plate 7.6

Brown Booby, Plate 7.8

Red-footed Booby, Plate 7.9

Masked Booby, Plate 7.10

Gannet, Plate 7.12

Cormorant, Plate 8.1

Japanese Cormorant, Plate 8.2

Pelagic Cormorant, Plate 8.3

Red-faced Cormorant, Plate 8.4

Shag, Plate 8.6

Socotra Cormorant, Plate 8.7

179

Pygmy Cormorant, Plate 8.8

Long-tailed Cormorant, Plate 8.9

Darter, Plate 8.10

Bittern, Plate 9.1

Little Bittern, Plate 9.4

Yellow Bittern, Plate 9.5

Schrenck's Bittern, Plate 9.6

Cinnamon Bittern, Plate 9.7

Malayan Night Heron, Plate 9.10

Japanese Night Heron, Plate 9.11

Night Heron, Plate 9.12

Green-backed Heron, Plate 9.13

Cattle Egret, Plate 10.1

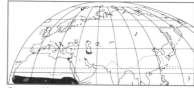

Squacco Heron, Plate 10.2

Indian Pond Heron, Plate 10.3

Chinese Pond Heron, Plate 10.4

Chinese Egret, Plate 10.6

Pacific Reef Egret, Plate 10.7

Western Reef Egret, Plate 10.8

Little Egret, Plate 10.9

Intermediate Egret, Plate 10.10

Great White Egret, Plate 10.11

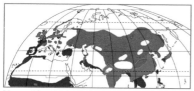

Heron, Plate 11.4

Purple Heron, Plate 11.7

Goliath Heron, Plate 11.8

Hamerkop, Plate 12.1

Abdim's Stork, Plate 12.5

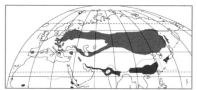

Black Stork, Plate 12.6

Oriental Stork, Plate 12.7

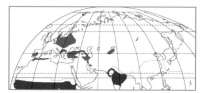

White Stork, Plate 12.8

Glossy Ibis, Plate 13.1

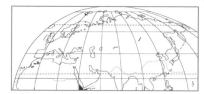

Bald Ibis, Plate 13.2

Crested Ibis, Plate 13.3

Sacred Ibis, Plate 13.4

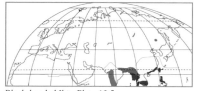

Black-headed Ibis, Plate 13.5

Spoonbill, Plate 13.6

182

Black-faced Spoonbill, Plate 13.7

Greater Flamingo, Plate 13.9

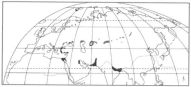

Dalmation Pelican, Plate 14.1

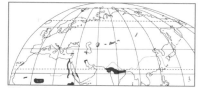

White Pelican, Plate 14.2

Pink-backed Pelican, Plate 14.3

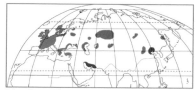

Mute Swan, Plate 14.4

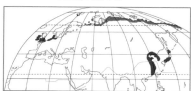

Bewick's Swan, Plate 14.5

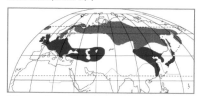

Whooper Swan, Plate 14.6

Egyptian Goose, Plate 15.4

Ruddy Shelduck, Plate 15.5

Crested Shelduck, Plate 15.6

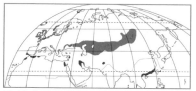

Shelduck, Plate 15.7

Canada Goose, Plate 15.10

Barnacle Goose, Plate 15.12

Brent Goose, Plate 15.13

Red-breasted Goose, Plate 15.14

Swan Goose, Plate 16.1

Bean Goose, Plate 16.2

Pink-footed Goose, Plate 16.3

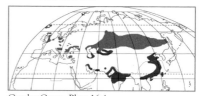

Greylag Goose, Plate 16.4

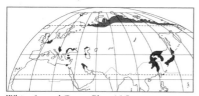

White-fronted Goose, Plate 16.5

Lesser White-fronted Goose, Plate 16.6

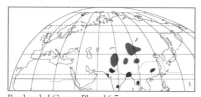

Bar-headed Goose, Plate 16.7

Emperor Goose, Plate 16.8

Snow Goose, Plate 16.10

Wigeon, Plate 17.1

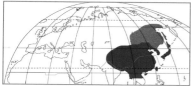

Falcated Duck, Plate 17.3

Gadwall, Plate 17.4

Baikal Teal, Plate 17.5

Teal, Plate 17.6

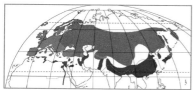

Mallard, Plate 17.9

Spot-billed Duck, Plate 18.1

Pintail, Plate 18.3

Garganey, Plate 18.5

Shoveler, Plate 18.8

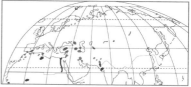

Marbled Duck, Plate 19.1

185

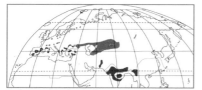

Red-crested Pochard, Plate 19.2

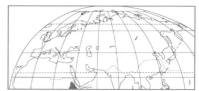

Southern Pochard, Plate 19.3

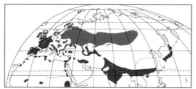

Pochard, Plate 19.5

Baer's Pochard, Plate 19.8

Ferruginous Duck, Plate 19.9

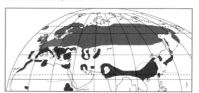

Tufted Duck, Plate 19.10

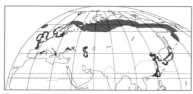

Scaup, Plate 19.11

Eider, Plate 20.1

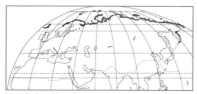

King Eider, Plate 20.2

Spectacled Eider, Plate 20.3

Steller's Eider, Plate 20.4

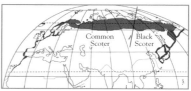

Common Scoter/Black Scoter, Plate 20

186

Velvet Scoter/White-winged Scoter, Plate 20

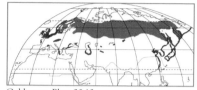

Goldeneye, Plate 20.12

Harlequin Duck, Plate 21.4

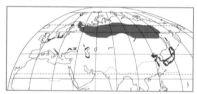

Smew, Plate 21.6

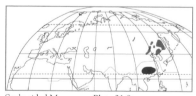

Scaly-sided Merganser, Plate 21.9

Ruddy Duck, Plate 21.11

Barrow's Goldeneye, Plate 20.11

Mandarin, Plate 21.3

Long-tailed Duck, Plate 21.5

Red-breasted Merganser, Plate 21.8

Goosander, Plate 21.10

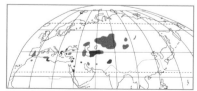

White-headed Duck, Plate 21.12

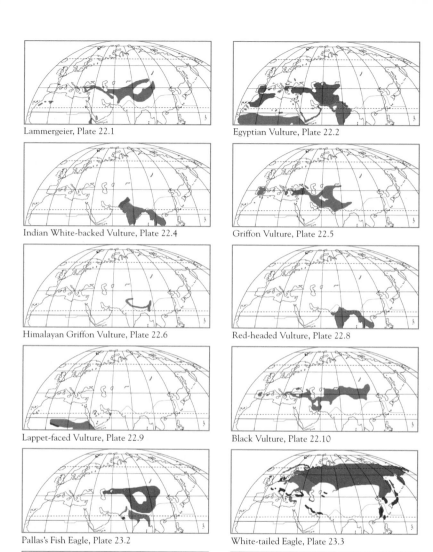

Lammergeier, Plate 22.1

Egyptian Vulture, Plate 22.2

Indian White-backed Vulture, Plate 22.4

Griffon Vulture, Plate 22.5

Himalayan Griffon Vulture, Plate 22.6

Red-headed Vulture, Plate 22.8

Lappet-faced Vulture, Plate 22.9

Black Vulture, Plate 22.10

Pallas's Fish Eagle, Plate 23.2

White-tailed Eagle, Plate 23.3

Steller's Sea Eagle, Plate 23.5

Bateleur, Plate 23.6

Mountain Hawk-Eagle, Plate 23.7

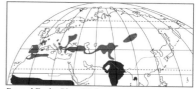

Booted Eagle, Plate 23.8

Bonelli's Eagle, Plate 23.9

Black Eagle, Plate 24.1

Lesser Spotted Eagle, Plate 24.2

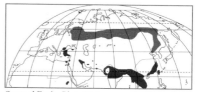

Spotted Eagle, Plate 24.3

Steppe Eagle, Plate 24.4

Tawny Eagle, Plate 24.5

Imperial Eagle, Plate 24.6

Spanish Imperial Eagle, Plate 24.7

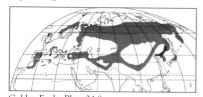

Golden Eagle, Plate 24.8

Verreaux's Eagle, Plate 24.9

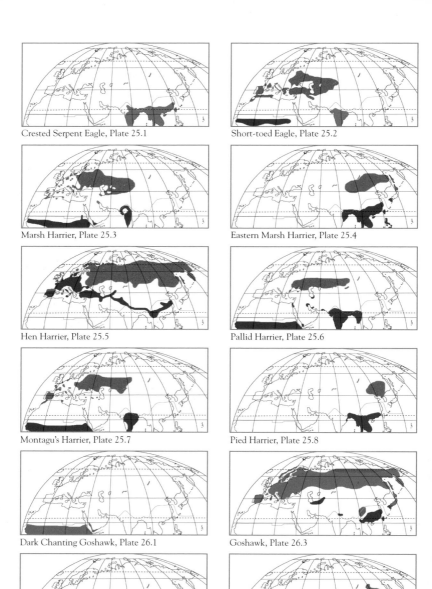

Crested Serpent Eagle, Plate 25.1

Short-toed Eagle, Plate 25.2

Marsh Harrier, Plate 25.3

Eastern Marsh Harrier, Plate 25.4

Hen Harrier, Plate 25.5

Pallid Harrier, Plate 25.6

Montagu's Harrier, Plate 25.7

Pied Harrier, Plate 25.8

Dark Chanting Goshawk, Plate 26.1

Goshawk, Plate 26.3

Besra, Plate 26.4

Japanese Sparrowhawk, Plate 26.5

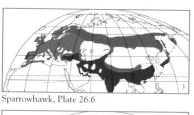

Sparrowhawk, Plate 26.6

Chinese Sparrowhawk, Plate 26.7

Shikra, Plate 26.8

Levant Sparrowhawk, Plate 26.9

White-eyed Buzzard, Plate 27.1

Grey-faced Buzzard, Plate 27.2

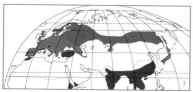

Buzzard, Plate 27.4

Long-legged Buzzard, Plate 27.5

Upland Buzzard, Plate 27.6

Rough-legged Buzzard, Plate 27.7

Honey Buzzard, Plate 27.8

Crested Honey Buzzard, Plate 27.9

191

Black-shouldered Kite, Plate 28.1

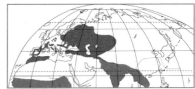

Black Kite, Plate 28.4

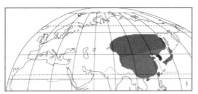

Black-eared Kite, Plate 28.4b

Yellow-billed Kite, Plate 28.4c

Red Kite, Plate 28.5

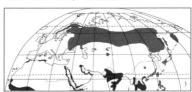

Osprey, Plate 28.7

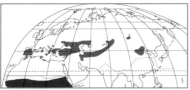

Lesser Kestrel, Plate 29.1

Kestrel, Plate 29.2

Red-necked Falcon, Plate 29.4

Red-footed Falcon, Plate 29.5

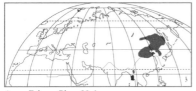

Amur Falcon, Plate 29.6

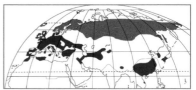

Merlin, Plate 29.7

Sooty Falcon, Plate 29.8

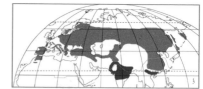

Hobby, Plate 30.1

Eleonora's Falcon, Plate 30.2

Lanner, Plate 30.3

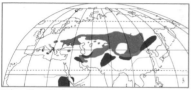

Saker, Plate 30.4

Lagger Falcon, Plate 30.5

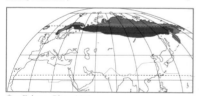

Gyr Falcon, Plate 30.6

Peregrine, Plate 30.7

Barbary Falcon, Plate 30.8

Blood Pheasant, Plate 31.1

Western Tragopan, Plate 31.2

Satyr Tragopan, Plate 31.3

193

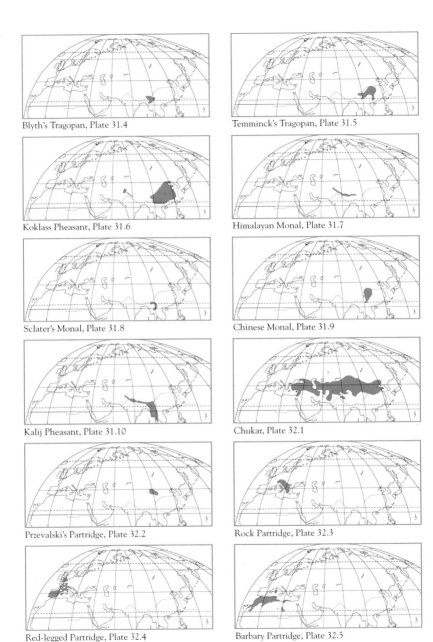

Blyth's Tragopan, Plate 31.4

Temminck's Tragopan, Plate 31.5

Koklass Pheasant, Plate 31.6

Himalayan Monal, Plate 31.7

Sclater's Monal, Plate 31.8

Chinese Monal, Plate 31.9

Kalij Pheasant, Plate 31.10

Chukar, Plate 32.1

Przevalski's Partridge, Plate 32.2

Rock Partridge, Plate 32.3

Red-legged Partridge, Plate 32.4

Barbary Partridge, Plate 32.5

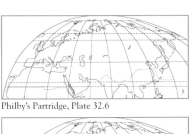

Philby's Partridge, Plate 32.6

Arabian Partridge, Plate 32.7

See-see Partridge, Plate 32.8

Sand Partridge, Plate 32.9

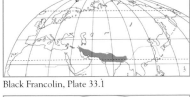

Black Francolin, Plate 33.1

Grey Francolin, Plate 33.2

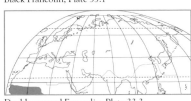

Double-spurred Francolin, Plate 33.3

Tibetan Partridge, Plate 33.4

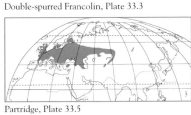

Partridge, Plate 33.5

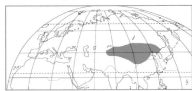

Daurian Partridge, Plate 33.6

Hill Partridge, Plate 33.7

Chinese Bamboo Partridge, Plate 33.8

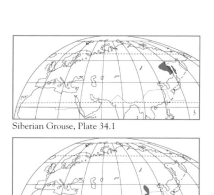

Siberian Grouse, Plate 34.1

Hazel Grouse, Plate 34.2

Severtsov's Grouse, Plate 34.3

Willow Grouse, Plate 34.4

Ptarmigan, Plate 34.5

Black Grouse, Plate 34.6

Caucasian Black Grouse, Plate 34.7

Black-billed Capercaillie, Plate 34.8

Capercaillie, Plate 34.9

Helmeted Guineafowl, Plate 35.1

Snow Partridge, Plate 35.3

Verreaux's Monal Partridge, Plate 35.4

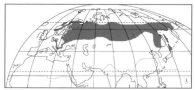

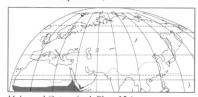
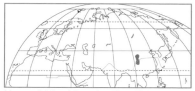

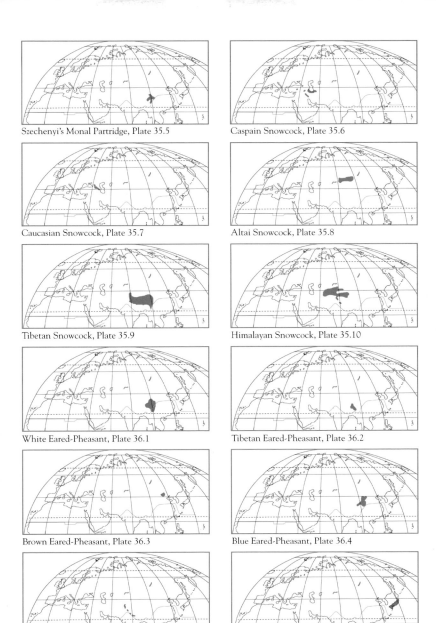

Szechenyi's Monal Partridge, Plate 35.5

Caspain Snowcock, Plate 35.6

Caucasian Snowcock, Plate 35.7

Altai Snowcock, Plate 35.8

Tibetan Snowcock, Plate 35.9

Himalayan Snowcock, Plate 35.10

White Eared-Pheasant, Plate 36.1

Tibetan Eared-Pheasant, Plate 36.2

Brown Eared-Pheasant, Plate 36.3

Blue Eared-Pheasant, Plate 36.4

Cheer Pheasant, Plate 36.5

Copper Pheasant, Plate 36.6

197

Reeve's Pheasant, Plate 36.7

Pheasant, Plate 36.8

Golden Pheasant, Plate 36.9

Lady Amherst's Pheasant, Plate 36.10

Quail, Plate 37.3

Japanese Quail, Plate 37.4

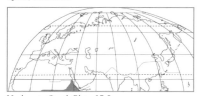

Harlequin Quail, Plate 37.5

Small Buttonquail, Plate 37.6

Yellow-legged Buttonquail, Plate 37.7

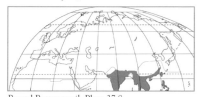

Barred Buttonquail, Plate 37.8

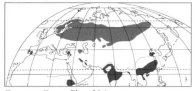

Common Crane, Plate 38.1

Black-necked Crane, Plate 38.2

Hooded Crane, Plate 38.3

Sandhill Crane, Plate 38.4

White-naped Crane, Plate 38.5

Japanese Crane, Plate 38.6

Siberian Crane, Plate 38.7

Demoiselle Crane, Plate 38.8

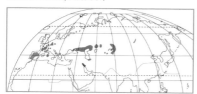

Little Bustard, Plate 39.1

Nubian Bustard, Plate 39.3

Houbara Bustard/McQueen's Bustard, Plate 39

Arabian Bustard, Plate 39.6

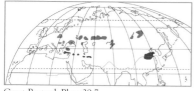

Great Bustard, Plate 39.7

Slaty-legged Crake, Plate 40.1

199

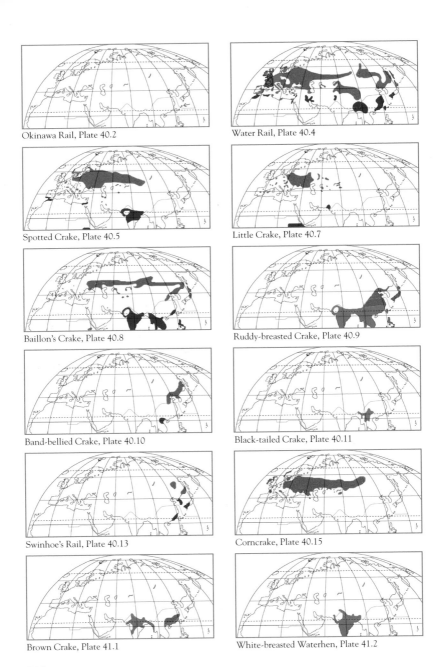

Okinawa Rail, Plate 40.2

Water Rail, Plate 40.4

Spotted Crake, Plate 40.5

Little Crake, Plate 40.7

Baillon's Crake, Plate 40.8

Ruddy-breasted Crake, Plate 40.9

Band-bellied Crake, Plate 40.10

Black-tailed Crake, Plate 40.11

Swinhoe's Rail, Plate 40.13

Corncrake, Plate 40.15

Brown Crake, Plate 41.1

White-breasted Waterhen, Plate 41.2

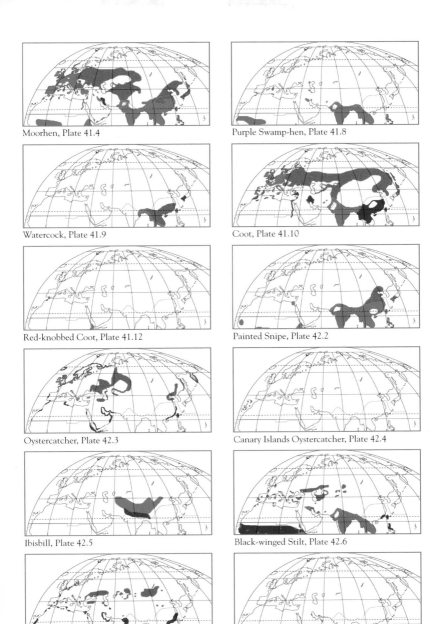

Moorhen, Plate 41.4

Purple Swamp-hen, Plate 41.8

Watercock, Plate 41.9

Coot, Plate 41.10

Red-knobbed Coot, Plate 41.12

Painted Snipe, Plate 42.2

Oystercatcher, Plate 42.3

Canary Islands Oystercatcher, Plate 42.4

Ibisbill, Plate 42.5

Black-winged Stilt, Plate 42.6

Avocet, Plate 42.7

Crab Plover, Plate 42.8

Collared Pratincole, Plate 43.1

Black-winged Pratincole, Plate 43.2

Oriental Pratincole, Plate 43.3

Cream-coloured Courser, Plate 43.5

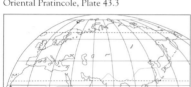
Egyptian Plover, Plate 43.6

Stone-curlew, Plate 43.7

Senegal Thick-knee, Plate 43.8

Spotted Thick-knee, Plate 43.9

Great Thick-knee, Plate 43.10

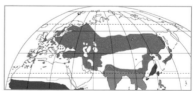
Little Ringed Plover, Plate 44.1

Ringed Plover, Plate 44.2

Long-billed Plover, Plate 44.4

Kittlitz's Plover, Plate 44.6

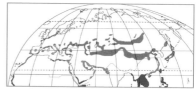

Kentish Plover, Plate 44.8

Lesser Sand Plover, Plate 44.10

Greater Sand Plover, Plate 44.11

Caspian Plover, Plate 44.12

Oriental Plover, Plate 44.13

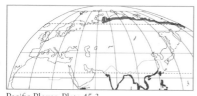

Dotterel, Plate 44.14

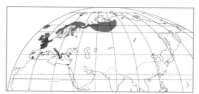

Golden Plover, Plate 45.2

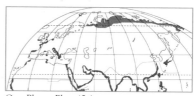

Pacific Plover, Plate 45.3

Grey Plover, Plate 45.4

Grey-headed Lapwing, Plate 45.5

Spur-winged Plover, Plate 45.6

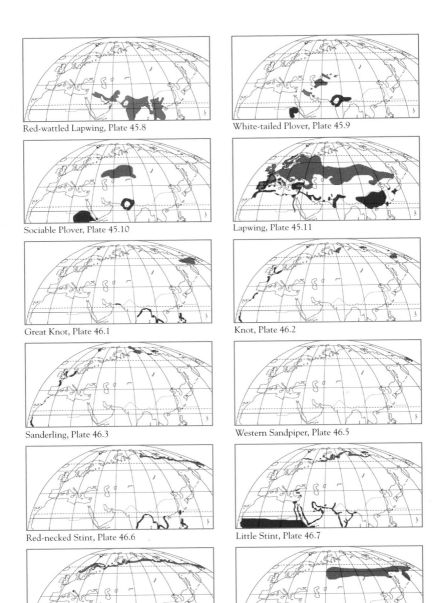

Red-wattled Lapwing, Plate 45.8

White-tailed Plover, Plate 45.9

Sociable Plover, Plate 45.10

Lapwing, Plate 45.11

Great Knot, Plate 46.1

Knot, Plate 46.2

Sanderling, Plate 46.3

Western Sandpiper, Plate 46.5

Red-necked Stint, Plate 46.6

Little Stint, Plate 46.7

Temminck's Stint, Plate 46.8

Long-toed Stint, Plate 46.9

Baird's Sandpiper, Plate 47.3

Pectoral Sandpiper, Plate 47.4

Sharp-tailed Sandpiper, Plate 47.5

Curlew Sandpiper, Plate 47.6

Dunlin, Plate 47.7

Rock Sandpiper, Plate 47.8

Purple Sandpiper, Plate 47.9

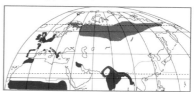

Jack Snipe, Plate 48.1

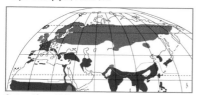

Snipe, Plate 48.2

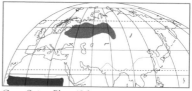

Great Snipe, Plate 48.3

Swinhoe's Snipe, Plate 48.4

Pin-tailed Snipe, Plate 48.5

Solitary Snipe, Plate 48.6

Latham's Snipe, Plate 48.7

Wood Snipe, Plate 48.8

Woodcock, Plate 48.9

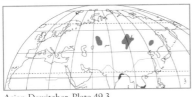

Amani Woodcock, Plate 48.10

Long-billed Dowitcher, Plate 49.2

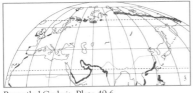

Asian Dowitcher, Plate 49.3

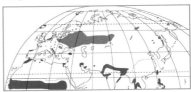

Black-tailed Godwit, Plate 49.4

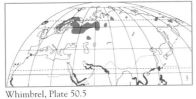

Bar-tailed Godwit, Plate 49.6

Little Curlew, Plate 50.2

Whimbrel, Plate 50.5

Slender-billed Curlew, Plate 50.6

Curlew, Plate 50.7

Far-eastern Curlew, Plate 50.8

Spotted Redshank, Plate 51.1

Redshank, Plate 51.2

Marsh Sandpiper, Plate 51.3

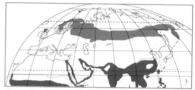
Greenshank, Plate 51.4

Spotted Greenshank, Plate 51.5

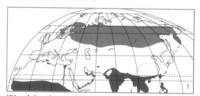
Wood Sandpiper, Plate 51.8

Green Sandpiper, Plate 51.10

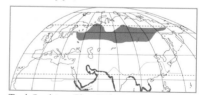
Terek Sandpiper, Plate 52.1

Common Sandpiper, Plate 52.2

Grey-tailed Tattler, Plate 52.4

207

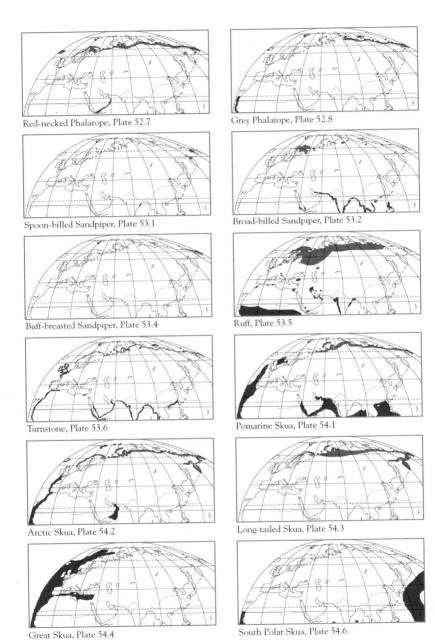

Red-necked Phalarope, Plate 52.7

Grey Phalarope, Plate 52.8

Spoon-billed Sandpiper, Plate 53.1

Broad-billed Sandpiper, Plate 53.2

Buff-breasted Sandpiper, Plate 53.4

Ruff, Plate 53.5

Turnstone, Plate 53.6

Pomarine Skua, Plate 54.1

Arctic Skua, Plate 54.2

Long-tailed Skua, Plate 54.3

Great Skua, Plate 54.4

South Polar Skua, Plate 54.6

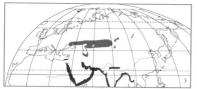

Great Black-headed Gull, Plate 55.1

Relict Gull, Plate 55.2

Mediterranean Gull, Plate 55.3

Little Gull, Plate 55.4

Sabine's Gull, Plate 55.5

Saunders's Gull, Plate 55.6

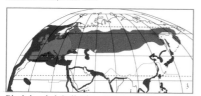

Black-headed Gull, Plate 55.8

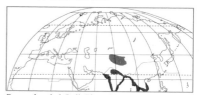

Brown-headed Gull, Plate 55.9

Sooty Gull, Plate 56.1

White-eyed Gull, Plate 56.2

Grey-headed Gull, Plate 56.5

Great Black-backed Gull, Plate 56.6

Slaty-backed Gull, Plate 56.7

Lesser Black-backed Gull, Plate 56.8

Herring Gull, Plate 57.1

Yellow-legged Gull, Plate 57.2

Armenian Gull, Plate 57.4

Iceland Gull, Plate 57.5

Glaucous-winged Gull, Plate 57.6

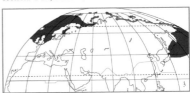
Glaucous Gull, Plate 57.7

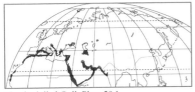
Slender-billed Gull, Plate 58.1

Black-tailed Gull, Plate 58.2

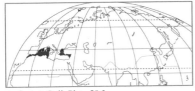
Audouin's Gull, Plate 58.3

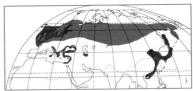
Common Gull, Plate 58.5

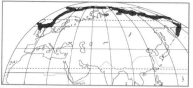

Ross's Gull, Plate 58.6

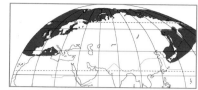

Kittiwake, Plate 58.7

Red-legged Kittiwake, Plate 58.8

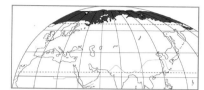

Ivory Gull, Plate 58.9

Black Tern, Plate 59.1

White-winged Tern, Plate 59.2

Whiskered Tern, Plate 59.3

White-cheeked Tern, Plate 59.4

Arctic Tern, Plate 59.5/Saunders's Tern, Plate 59.11

Common Tern, Plate 59.6

Roseate Tern, Plate 59.7

Little Tern, Plate 59.10

211

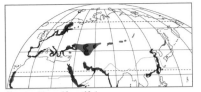

Caspian Tern, Plate 60.1

Royal Tern, Plate 60.2

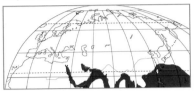

Crested Tern, Plate 60.4

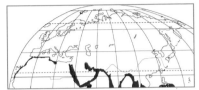

Lesser Crested Tern, Plate 60.5

Chinese Crested Tern, Plate 60.6

Black-naped Tern, Plate 60.7

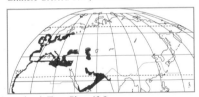

Sandwich Tern, Plate 60.8

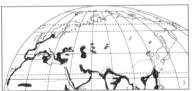

Gull-billed Tern, Plate 60.9

Grey-backed Tern, Plate 61.1

Aleutian Tern, Plate 61.2

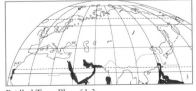

Bridled Tern, Plate 61.3

Black Noddy, Plate 61.6

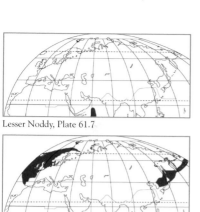

Lesser Noddy, Plate 61.7

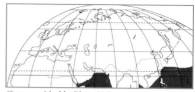

Common Noddy, Plate 61.8

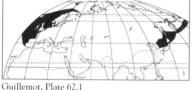

Guillemot, Plate 62.1

Brünnich's Guillemot, Plate 62.2

Razorbill, Plate 62.3

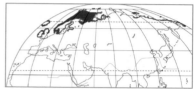

Black Guillemot, Plate 62.4

Pigeon Guillemot, Plate 62.5

Spectacled Guillemot, Plate 62.6

Marbled Murrelet, Plate 62.8

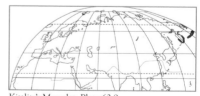

Kittlitz's Murrelet, Plate 62.9

Ancient Murrelet, Plate 62.10

Japanese Murrelet, Plate 62.11

Little Auk, Plate 63.1

Crested Auklet, Plate 63.3

Whiskered Auklet, Plate 63.4

Least Auklet, Plate 63.5

Parakeet Auklet, Plate 63.6

Rhinoceros Auklet, Plate 63.7

Puffin, Plate 63.8

Horned Puffin, Plate 63.9

Tufted Puffin, Plate 63.10

Lichtenstein's Sandgrouse, Plate 64.1

Crowned Sandgrouse, Plate 64.2

Spotted Sandgrouse, Plate 64.3

214

Chestnut-bellied Sandgrouse, Plate 64.4

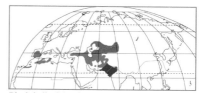

Black-bellied Sandgrouse, Plate 64.5

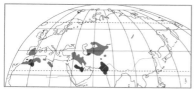

Pin-tailed Sandgrouse, Plate 64.6

Pallas's Sandgrouse, Plate 64.7

Tibetan Sandgrouse, Plate 64.8

Rock Dove, Plate 65.1

Hill Pigeon, Plate 65.2

Snow Pigeon, Plate 65.3

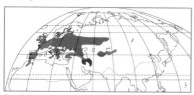

Stock Dove, Plate 65.4

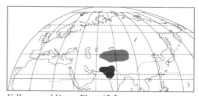

Yellow-eyed Dove, Plate 65.5

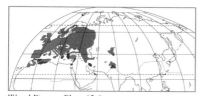

Wood Pigeon, Plate 65.6

Trocaz Pigeon, Plate 65.7

215

Bolle's Pigeon, Plate 65.8

Laurel Pigeon, Plate 65.9

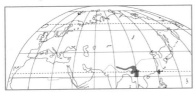

Ashy Wood Pigeon, Plate 65.10

Olive Pigeon, Plate 66.1

Speckled Wood Pigeon, Plate 66.2

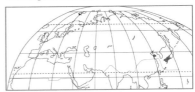

Japanese Wood Pigeon, Plate 66.3

Namaqua Dove, Plate 66.4

Black-billed Wood Dove, Plate 66.5

Emerald Dove, Plate 66.6

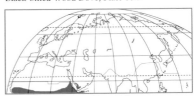

Bruce's Green Pigeon, Plate 66.8

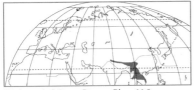

Wedge-tailed Green Pigeon, Plate 66.9

White-bellied Green Pigeon, Plate 66.10

Whistling Green Pigeon, Plate 66.11

Collared Dove, Plate 67.1

African Collared Dove, Plate 67.2

African Mourning Dove, Plate 67.3

Red-eyed Dove, Plate 67.4

Red Turtle Dove, Plate 67.5

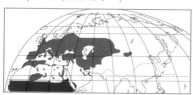

Turtle Dove, Plate 67.6

Oriental Turtle Dove, Plate 67.7

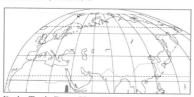

Dusky Turtle Dove, Plate 67.8

Laughing Dove, Plate 67.9

Spotted Dove, Plate 67.10

Jacobin Cuckoo, Plate 68.1

217

Chestnut-winged Cuckoo, Plate 68.2

Great Spotted Cuckoo, Plate 68.3

Large Hawk-Cuckoo, Plate 68.4

Hodgson's Hawk-Cuckoo, Plate 68.6

Didric Cuckoo, Plate 68.7

Klaas's Cuckoo, Plate 68.8

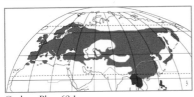
Cuckoo, Plate 69.1

Indian Cuckoo, Plate 69.2

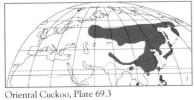
Oriental Cuckoo, Plate 69.3

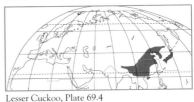
Lesser Cuckoo, Plate 69.4

Plaintive Cuckoo, Plate 69.5

Senegal Coucal, Plate 69.9

White-browed Coucal, Plate 69.10

Barn Owl, Plate 70.1

Snowy Owl, Plate 70.3

Eagle Owl, Plate 70.4

Spotted Eagle Owl, Plate 70.5

Blakiston's Fish Owl, Plate 70.6

Brown Fish Owl, Plate 70.7

Hawk Owl, Plate 70.8

Brown Hawk Owl, Plate 70.9

Tengmalm's Owl, Plate 70.10

Mountain Scops Owl, Plate 71.1

Collared Scops Owl/Indian Scops Owl/Japanese Scops Owl, Plate 71

219

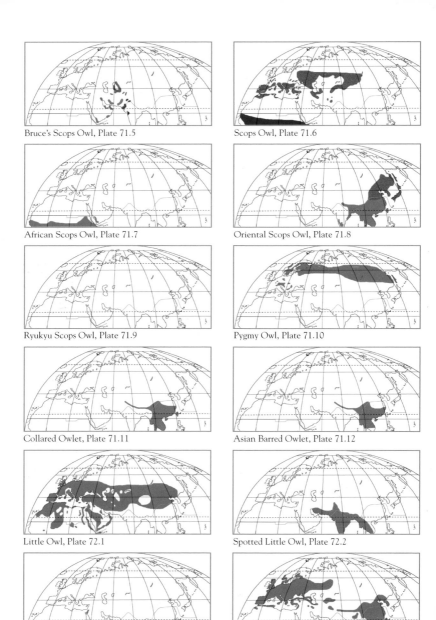

Bruce's Scops Owl, Plate 71.5

Scops Owl, Plate 71.6

African Scops Owl, Plate 71.7

Oriental Scops Owl, Plate 71.8

Ryukyu Scops Owl, Plate 71.9

Pygmy Owl, Plate 71.10

Collared Owlet, Plate 71.11

Asian Barred Owlet, Plate 71.12

Little Owl, Plate 72.1

Spotted Little Owl, Plate 72.2

Hume's Owl, Plate 72.3

Tawny Owl, Plate 72.4

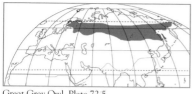

Great Grey Owl, Plate 72.5

Ural Owl, Plate 72.6

Brown Wood Owl, Plate 72.7

Marsh Owl, Plate 72.8

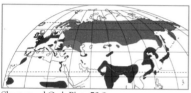

Short-eared Owl, Plate 72.9

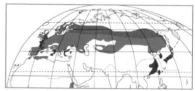

Long-eared Owl, Plate 72.10

Plain Nightjar, Plate 73.1

Mountain Nightjar, Plate 73.2

Nubian Nightjar, Plate 73.3

Vauries's Nightjar, Plate 73.4

Sykes's Nightjar, Plate 73.5

Indian Nightjar, Plate 73.6

Grey Nightjar, Plate 73.7

Nightjar, Plate 73.8

Red-necked Nightjar, Plate 73.9

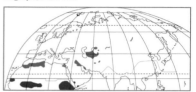

Egyptian Nightjar, Plate 73.10

Himalayan Swiftlet, Plate 74.1

White-throated Needletail, Plate 74.3

Plain Swift, Plate 74.4

Cape Verde Swift, Plate 74.5

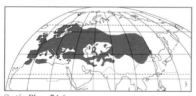

Swift, Plate 74.6

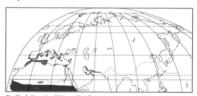

Pallid Swift, Plate 74.7

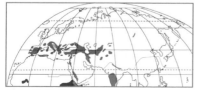

Alpine Swift, Plate 74.8

Fork-tailed Swift, Plate 74.9

White-rumped Swift, Plate 74.10

African Palm Swift, Plate 74.13

White-breasted Kingfisher, Plate 75.2

Grey-headed Kingfisher, Plate 75.4

Kingfisher, Plate 75.6

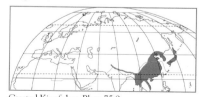

Crested Kingfisher, Plate 75.9

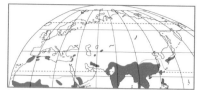

Little Swift, Plate 74.11

Ruddy Kingfisher, Plate 75.1

Black-capped Kingfisher, Plate 75.3

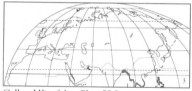

Collared Kingfisher, Plate 75.5

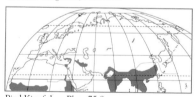

Pied Kingfisher, Plate 75.8

Blue-cheeked Bee-eater, Plate 76.1

223

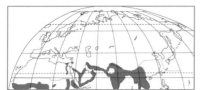

Little Green Bee-eater, Plate 76.2

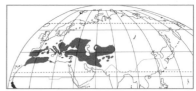

Bee-eater, Plate 76.4

White-throated Bee-eater, Plate 76.5

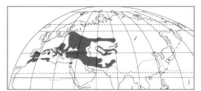

Roller, Plate 76.6

Abyssinian Roller, Plate 76.7

Indian Roller, Plate 76.8

Dollarbird, Plate 76.12

Hoopoe, Plate 77.1

Alexandrine Parakeet, Plate 77.2

Ring-necked Parakeet, Plate 77.3

Lord Derby's Parakeet, Plate 77.4

Slaty-headed Parakeet, Plate 77.5

Grey-headed Parakeet, Plate 77.6

Monk Parakeet, Plate 77.7

Ward's Trogon, Plate 77.10

African Grey Hornbill, Plate 77.11

Great Barbet, Plate 77.12

Yellow-rumped Honeyguide, Plate 77.13

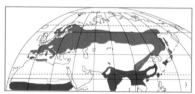
Wryneck, Plate 78.1

Speckled Piculet, Plate 78.2

Levaillant's Woodpecker, Plate 78.3

Green Woodpecker, Plate 78.4

Grey-headed Woodpecker, Plate 78.5

Japanese Green Woodpecker, Plate 78.6

225

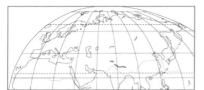

Scaly-bellied Woodpecker, Plate 78.7

Okinawa Woodpecker, Plate 78.8

Bay Woodpecker, Plate 78.10

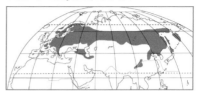

Black Woodpecker, Plate 79.1

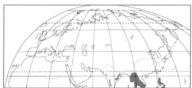

White-bellied Woodpecker, Plate 79.2

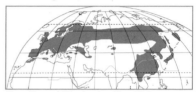

Great Spotted Woodpecker, Plate 79.3

Syrian Woodpecker, Plate 79.4

Sind Woodpecker, Plate 79.5

Himalayan Woodpecker, Plate 79.6

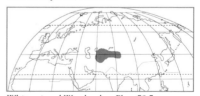

White-winged Woodpecker, Plate 79.7

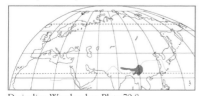

Darjeeling Woodpecker, Plate 79.8

Crimson-breasted Woodpecker, Plate 79.9

Middle Spotted Woodpecker, Plate 80.1

White-backed Woodpecker, Plate 80.2

Rufous-bellied Woodpecker, Plate 80.3

Brown-fronted Woodpecker, Plate 80.4

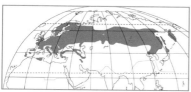

Lesser Spotted Woodpecker, Plate 80.5

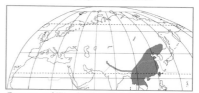

Grey-capped Woodpecker, Plate 80.6

Pygmy Woodpecker, Plate 80.7

Arabian Woodpecker, Plate 80.8

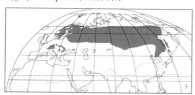

Three-toed Woodpecker, Plate 80.9

227

INDEX